A YOUNG GIRL READING
Jean-Honoré Fragonard
National Gallery of Art, Washington, D.C.
Gift of Mrs. Mellon Bruce
in memory of her father, Andrew W. Mellon

The Social Challenge to Business

THE SOCIAL CHALLENGE
TO BUSINESS

Robert W. Ackerman

Harvard University Press
Cambridge, Massachusetts
and London, England
1975

49031

Library of Congress Cataloging in Publication Data
Ackerman, Robert W   1938-
   The social challenge to business.

   Bibliography: p.
   Includes index.
   1. Industry—Social aspects—United States.
   2. Industrial management—United States. I. Title.
HD60.U5A3   658.4'08'0973   75-8921
ISBN 0-674-81190-9

                                        Rev.

To Meg

Preface

In the spring of 1971, I was invited to present a paper that was to summarize and interpret the growing literature on business responsibility to society for a conference at the Harvard Business School.[1] The topic was one I had shied away from despite its popularity at the time because it seemed to me so full of rhetoric and so void of sensitivity to the problems of managing the large corporation. Surveying the literature was instructive but tended to confirm this impression, and I fully intended to let the matter drop. Then one afternoon that summer a proposition came into focus that I had only dimly perceived before: the difficulty corporations were having in satisfying their social critics might lie precisely in the organizational innovations that had permitted them to cope effectively with diversification and competitive conditions. Ironically, the genius of American business might be flawed, not because of dubious intentions or its interest in profits, but because it could not implement responses to social change with sufficient speed or competence. Phrased in this way, the topic had a clear and practical relevance for the manager — and for business regulators and critics who so often express frustration at the time it takes for the large corporation to act.

Most of the research supporting this book was conducted from 1972 to 1974. Its scope may best be conceived by imagining a set of four concentric rings, each representing a field of data that has been progressively relied upon as one approaches the innermost ring.

In the outer ring are reports of studies done apart from the Harvard Business School which have some relevance to the implementation of social policy.[2] Unfortunately, the field is thus far rather sparse; little systematic research has been done that probes specifically into the organizational problems of effecting change of this sort in the large corporation.

Next are a grouping of research projects, including this one, conducted at the Harvard Business School under the general leadership of Raymond Bauer. Each has had a direct bearing on the questions raised here.[3] Altogether, five members of the faculty and eight doctoral students and research assistants have contributed to this program. In addition to an appreciation of their conclusions, I have had access to a rich store of descriptive material that has been gathered from field inquiry in a wide range of companies.

Progressing one step closer to the center, I have gained a modest first-hand understanding of a number of large corporations in addition to those investigated in depth. This understanding has been obtained through extended interviews with one or more executives involved in implementing social policy, supported by review of their company's strategic and structural profile.

Data from these last two sources cover more than forty corporations and have been important sources of illustration and confirmation for the concepts developed in this book. At this writing, nineteen case studies have been prepared by members of the Harvard Business School research team. They are available through the Intercollegiate Case Clearing House for use in the classroom, or, more generally, as examples of the corporate response to social demands. A listing of them is provided in the Appendix.

Primary reliance, however, was placed on extensive field research in two large corporations. The companies selected had sales of approximately $2 billion; both were divisionalized and diversified, though in each case, the component businesses had some product-market relationship to one another. In one, the organization structure was composed of ten product divisions. In the other, the structure combined product and geographically segmented divisions. Corporate management in both firms relied heavily on financial control systems to guide their relationships with these operating units. Finally, both companies consciously had attempted to respond early to certain issues of social concern. Although their posture on a range of social issues was investigated, in some instances at considerable length, the detailed reporting in Chapters VI-IX focuses on the areas in which they progressed the furthest in implementation. As it turned out, these related to ecology in one company and to equal employment in the other. Both issues shared the characteristic of being important national concerns on which public policy had been relatively well-defined. Consequently, the opportunity existed to monitor the response to relatively mature social demands (or at least demands closer to maturity than many others). More important, there was evidence to suggest that serious efforts were underway in these companies to incorporate these concerns in operating decisions. Hence I was able to report on two comprehensive and relatively complete social issue life cycles.

To diagnose corporate behavior in the depth required by the questions posed in this book, detailed field research was imperative. Published accounts of corporate activities, questionnaires, and discussions with the "corporate responsibility officer" could not, by themselves, do the trick. Rather, the questions suggested a need for data that (a) took the dimension of time into account, (b) described the participation of managers in at least four roles (corporate general management, corporate staff, division general management, and division functional managers) and numerous levels in the organization, and (c) traced the evolution of specific decision situations as well as the general history of the firm's social policy and formal efforts to impel its implementation. Quite clearly, the full cooperation of the participating corporations was a prerequisite for obtaining access to this sort of information. Moreover, a grasp of the social and political infrastructure in the organization was necessary to appreciate why a company functioned as it did.

The research plan involved three overlapping activities which for more than a year kept me busy shuttling back and forth between the two companies.

First, interviews were conducted with the top management groups, their immediate staffs, and a broad sampling of division managers to obtain an understanding of the corporation, its business strategy, its posture with respect to social issues, and significant events which had shaped policy formulation and implementation. This was combined with (a) documentation (reports, memoranda, and the like reflecting the history of the response to social issues, and (b) a comprehensive description of the organization structure and the planning, budgeting, and control system.

Second, attention was directed toward the specialists for environmental control and equal employment, particularly those on the corporate staff, who appeared to play an important role in social responsiveness. On several occasions, the researcher spent a week or more with the specialist sharing all his experiences. Such time was well spent, for it yielded a rich portrait of how the organization responded to problems and what relationships were critical to this adaptation. Moreover, the specialist served as both a repository of substantive knowledge and a listening post, through whom specific decision situations were identified for subsequent investigation and monitored as they took shape.

Third, considerable time was devoted to what might be termed process research. The attempt was made to understand as thoroughly as possible how specific decisions involving social issues were made. Attention was initially directed toward situations that emerged or were in progress during the course of the research. Documentation and correspondence were analyzed, participants in the decision process interviewed, and meetings attended. The research followed the drift of the deliberations. Later, as the evolutionary nature of the response process became clearer, the reach for documentation was extended several years into the past to pick up vital historical incidents. Combined with interviews of as many of those involved at the time as possible, this additional information permitted a reconstruction of what had happened.

Descriptive research of the type employed here has distinct advantages for the study of complex systematic phenomena, particularly in the early stages of exploration.[4] From the data it was possible to draw together case studies that served as a basis for the discussion of interim findings and as an aid in the development of the conceptual scheme for viewing corporate responsiveness. I have been fortunate to have had numerous opportunities to conduct classes and seminars using these materials with business, educator, and student groups, including the Advanced Management Program at the Harvard Business School, the General Management course at the General Electric Company, the National Academy of Management, and the National Association of Concerned Business Students. Such interaction has provided additional insights and confirmation as well as points of controversy.

Since completing the research and after six years on the faculty of the Harvard Business School, I have taken a leave of absence to join Preco, Inc., a medium-sized, multidivision pulp and paper company, as its Vice President of Finance and Administration. Sitting now on the other side of the desk and being confronted with many of the issues described in these pages, I have had numerous opportunities to test my understanding and convictions. I am finding the task of responding effectively to social demands to be no less difficult

than portrayed. Yet I am also finding the problems to be quite predictable and the suggested remedies, if not easily implemented, to
be strategically sound. Competent diagnosis, of course, is not the
whole of management — but it helps.

Lest some readers take offense at the shorthand use of the mascu-
line pronoun to describe managers, let it be clear at the outset that,
except when referring to specific individuals, the intended meaning
extends to both men and women.

Acknowledgments

My thanks are due to many colleagues and friends who have contributed to this effort. Raymond A. Bauer in particular has been of enormous help, both intellectually as a commentator and critic who frequently saw implications in the data that escaped me, and practically as a source of counsel on methodology and research sites. I have been privileged to work very closely with him these past three years. Neil C. Churchill and John K. Shank, also faculty participants in the research program, have provided valuable suggestions and encouragement. Although collecting all of the field data herein myself, I am very much indebted to the doctoral students and research assistants who conducted the research in other organizations; their work has broadened the base upon which my conclusions rest. They include Edwin A. Murray, Terry L. Cauthorn, Ranne P. Warner, Alden G. Lank, Frederick A. Cardin, David B. Kiser, Rikk Larsen, and Nancy Treverton.

I have also benefited from the advice and comments of colleagues with special interests in corporate social responsiveness, in particular Kenneth R. Andrews and George A. Steiner who reviewed drafts of the manuscript, and including Joseph L. Bower, Frederick K. Foulkes, George C. Lodge, John B. Matthews, S. Prakash Sethi, and John W. Rosenblum. Encouragement and counsel has come from numerous others, among them Norman A. Berg, Frederick T. Knickerbocker, Max R. Hall, Malcolm S. Salter, Charles H. Savage, Bruce R. Scott, C. Wickham Skinner, and Howard H. Stevenson. Aida DiPace Donald, Editor for the Social Sciences of the Harvard University Press, was most helpful in suggesting revisions in the manuscript. Notwithstanding the very real benefits received from these and others, full responsibility for the final product is, of course, entirely mine.

A special word of thanks is owed to those at the Harvard Business School who made eighteen months available for this undertaking: to C. Roland Christensen and Hugo E. R. Uyterhoeven, successive heads of the General Management Area, to Richard E. Walton, Director of the Division of Research, to Senior Associate Dean,

George F. F. Lombard, and of course to Dean Lawrence F. Fouraker. So, too, does my appreciation go to The Russell Sage Foundation which provided the financial support, and specifically to Eleanor Bernett Sheldon, now President of the Social Science and Research Council, who as a member of the Foundation staff recommended the approval of my proposal.

Clinical research requires a great deal of time, patience, and trust from the participating organization. I have been extremely fortunate in being able to work with two corporations in as frank and open a way as one can imagine. In return we agreed that all names and places would be disguised. Consequently, my thanks must extend to them in disguise also. "Bill West," "Carl Winters," "Philip Adler," and "Frank Wesley," in particular, occupied positions that stood athwart the response to social demands; not once did they duck an issue or shun a request for their time.

Nancy Hayes has been of invaluable assistance throughout this project. Her understanding of the material and knack for administration enabled me to progress further than would otherwise have been possible. She and Frances Charon also typed drafts of the manuscript with care and interest. Kathleen Ahern did a splendid job editing and helping with final revisions on the book.

But most of all I offer thanks to my wife, Meg, to whom this book is dedicated, and children, Ashley, Graham, and Todd, for their love and patience during the arduous three years it has been in progress. I am fortunate, indeed, to have a family capable of such understanding.

Contents

The Social Challenge to Business

I
Introduction

This book is about the corporate response to a dynamic social environment. Increasingly demanding public expectations may be forcing fundamental changes in the administration of large-scale economic enterprises in the United States. A quiet but profound transformation may be occurring inside the firm that is not readily apparent from a perusal of its financial statements or publicly discussed by its executives. This book explores the dimensions of social pressure, the organizational dilemmas it causes, the way corporations have reacted, and what can be done by those who manage big companies to respond more effectively to social change.

Corporate responsibility is a topic of current interest in the United States. The literature in the field has burgeoned as reporters, academicians, muckrackers, and businessmen try their hands at interpreting the role of the economic enterprise in society. The dialogue, if one can call it that, between business and its critics has made managers more aware of public concerns, and their awareness has no doubt had some constructive influence on their attitudes toward the purpose and conduct of the corporation. Unfortunately, there has also been a tendency among critics to make sweeping condemnations of business performance on complex environmental issues. Similarly, when pressed for a position on social demands, business leaders have all too often resorted to piety or righteous indignation. Neither condemnation nor righteousness has led to an effective diagnosis of the issues involved.

A Managerial Problem

I strongly believe that the problems posed by society's quest for socially responsive corporations are most usefully interpreted as managerial in nature rather than ethical or ideological. Consequently, unlike many recent observers of the relationship between business and society, I have stationed myself *inside* the corporation to study its response to social demands. The vantage point is from the inside looking out — not to offer criticism or praise, but rather to diagnose the reasons for corporate behavior. In particular, the

answers to two questions are of interest:
1. How have the managements of large corporations
    responded to social demands?
2. What effects have efforts to implement corporate
    policies in areas of social concern had on the ad-
    ministration of the firm?

This inquiry has been prompted by the convergence of two major
forces during the last decade. One is the rising social pressure just
mentioned. The other is a massive transition that was already taking
place in the structure of large corporations.

Following World War II, a great many companies embarked on
diversification programs which led them into businesses employing
different technologies and serving new markets. Diversification has
substantially altered the strategic profile of the *Fortune* 500. To
manage these new activities, corporations adopted a divisionalized
structure; they formed product divisions, each managed more or
less independently of the others. Through this means, a clear distinction has been drawn between the functions of the executive at
the corporate level and his functions at the division or operating
level. Executives holding the top offices concern themselves with
matters of financial and corporate-wide policy, while operating
executives are held accountable for formulating business strategies
to guide the divisions. Part of the division manager's responsibility,
under this arrangement, is to plan effective responses to competitive
technical and economic conditions in the environment which
impinge on his particular business. He is also responsible for the
profitability of the division, and his performance is regularly monitored by means of financial planning and control systems. Thus,
corporate executives in divisionalized firms, without detailed
involvement in or knowledge of operating decisions, rely more
heavily on result-oriented measures than do their counterparts in
single-business enterprises. Such measures have an important
bearing on the process through which resources are allocated among
divisions and middle managers are evaluated. Meeting short-term
financial targets is consequently a matter of considerable importance to managers many levels below the chief executive.

The other phenomenon — social pressure on the business community — is perhaps more obvious. It began anew during the 1960s,
after a thirty-year hiatus and after the postwar structural transfor-

mation in the large corporation had been essentially completed. Government, consumers, employees, and various interest groups have demanded changes in the conduct of business operations. The corporation has been called upon to control the environmental impact of its manufacturing processes, modify the racial or sexual composition of its work force, assume a greater responsibility for the safety and performance of its products, and exercise a greater concern for the health and well-being of its employees. In most cases, responses to these social concerns are likely to have some adverse impact on near-term economic performance, either directly because they cost money or indirectly because they take time and energy away from the traditional functions of running the business.

The convergence of divisionalization and social pressure holds two unfortunate consequences for the large corporation. First, the divisionalized structure, although proven effective in the management of the large, diversified enterprise, may inhibit flexible and creative responses to social demands. Second, efforts to incorporate social demands in the operations of the firm may have an adverse impact on its performance as a producer of goods and services. The dangers are significant. Unresponsiveness to public expectations is a clear invitation to increased government intervention in private sector affairs. By the same token an inability to generate profits sufficient to sustain investment may spell the end of an era in which exponential growth has been an overriding corporate goal.

Avoiding these dangers will require innovations in the way the large corporation is managed. The pattern of organization developed initially at duPont and General Motors in the early 1920s and widely emulated in the decades following World War II may yield to yet another form. It is perhaps too early to predict with high reliability the scope of the transition or the eventual outcome. Other factors, in particular multinationality, will have an important influence on the result. Nevertheless, certain manifestations of change are becoming visible, and the implications for management should be carefully understood.

Changes in the internal workings of the large corporation may also hold consequences for the broader society. In economic terms, the concentration of resources in a relatively small number of enterprises is impressive. *Fortune* reports that the top 500 industrials account for about 65 percent of the sales and three quarters of the profits and employment of all U.S. industrial corporations. They also account for a high proportion of the nation's capital spending, research and development expenditures, exports and overseas investments. Through ties with suppliers and a myriad of service businesses they command resources far beyond those shown on their financial statements or included in their payrolls. Moreover, there is a strong suggestion that the importance of the large corporation in the economy is increasing. Federal Trade Commission studies indicate that the share of manufacturing assets held by the largest 200 industrial firms increased from 48.3 percent in 1948 to 61.2 percent in 1968.

The corporation has traditionally been valued for its efficiency in the use of resources for the production of goods and services. This expectation has been accompanied by a desire for increasing employment, low cost output, and economic growth. In recent years many in society have come to expect responsiveness and even leadership from business in resolving a variety of perceived social ills as well. The corporation is expected to be efficient (and profitable) *and* socially responsive. This is quite a task. The research reported here gives a preliminary indication of the hurdles that managers must overcome in meeting this double challenge and the approaches being taken by some firms in dealing with them.

It is obvious from numerous accounts in the press of business malpractice, that rascals inhabit the executive suite as they do other stations of power and influence. Nevertheless, I am prepared to assume that most managers, and in particular those who provide leadership in the business community, would like to avoid doing what they believe to be irresponsible. This is not, of course, to say that their actions are necessarily accepted by others in this light. However, making this assumption now permits us to penetrate behind moral judgments in an effort to understand how social issues are dealt with in the large corporation. Some readers may dissent and remain firm in the conviction that the prime requirement for achieving corporate responsiveness is the ethical sensitization of top management. I hope to persuade such dissenters that even if ethical conversion were a prime requirement, it would not be sufficient in itself to provoke responsive behavior in the corporation. There is a substantial administrative task facing even the most converted executive.

Other readers may agree with George Lodge that "Business will be delaying the process [of social reform] and endangering itself if . . . it takes on the urgent task of change in the United States before the political order has produced a new and more useful ideology."[1] There may indeed be a need for reform in the political process that will provide a more comprehensive and useful framework for business involvement. However, dwelling on the immense philosophical questions underlying our economic system tends to mask the urgency of managing the corporation in the political milieu that currently exists. Consequently, I have elected to suspend comment on the broad topic of ideology in an effort to get on with a discussion of the concerns directly and immediately impinging on the corporation.

In doing so, I acknowledge the point developed at length by Neil Chamberlain that the quest for profit in the marketplace as it now exists is inevitable and further that the latitude and resources available to the corporation for social action are limited.[2] But I suspect that he has underestimated the scope and cumulative impact of social demands on the firm itself. By looking from the outside in, he has largely ignored the phenomenon to be explored in this book: the relationship of social responsiveness to the administration of the large corporation. Management's success or failure in developing the competence to adapt to a changing social environment may in the final analysis be significantly more important to both the firm and the public than its position on specific issues.

Changing Perspectives on Corporate Social Responsibility

Attitudes toward the role of business in society have changed dramatically in the last two decades. Today's business leaders have experienced sharp crosscurrents during their careers in the popular view of corporate social responsibility. Not surprisingly, many managers in policy-making positions have been influenced by the sentiments of colleagues and critics and touched themselves by the events giving rise to changes in perspective. This historical context is worthy of a brief review.[3] As Kenneth Andrews has persuasively argued, the choice of purpose in the firm is shaped in no small measure by the values and sensitivities of its senior management.[4]

The mood of the early postwar years was aptly captured by Raymond Bauer and Dan Fenn, who wrote that "In post-war America this discussion [about corporate responsibility] . . . was taking place against a most comforting philosophic background. Businessmen were happily telling themselves and anyone else who would listen that we in the United States had created a new kind of capitalism, a human capitalism which put the lie to both Lenin and Jay Gould . . . They were talking about building still loftier mansions for American business and so were expressing great interest in 'corporate citizenship' and 'business responsibility in action' and 'business statesmanship.' "[5]

During this period businessmen tended to view the problems of relating the corporation to society as bound up in matters of conscience and individual choice. Emphasis was placed on the ethical dilemmas of leadership. For instance, Clarence Randall, former chief executive of Inland Steel, commented: "The key . . . is the executive's personal sensitivity to ethical problems. Few men who are able and mature enough to carry significant responsibility in the business world transgress the general code of morality with the conscious intention of doing wrong. The difficulty is that the warning bell of their conscience does not ring as they make their decisions."[6]

It was difficult to disagree directly with such noble sentiments. Indeed, corporations were more active than ever before in the support of higher education, charitable institutions, and other good works. Nevertheless, there were in all likelihood a good many businessmen in agreement with Theodore Levitt who wrote in 1958, "The trouble is not that [business] is too narrowly profit oriented, but that it is not profit oriented enough."[7]

No compelling reason, other than conscience, existed for choosing among various social postures in those years. Criticism of business remained the province of academicians, labor leaders, and an occasional journalist, and they were more concerned with the potential dangers of unfettered corporate power than with effective protest.[8]

With the social dislocations of the 1960s, new views of corporate responsibility began to emerge. The environment was seen to offer both opportunities and risks. An appreciation in the country for civil rights, the "urban crisis," ecology, and so forth, appeared to present problems that would yield to the application of business skills in managing resources and projects. As a result, the corporation was asked to solve social problems for which it was not held directly responsible. The business community responded in a variety of ways. Over a hundred major corporations joined the National Alliance of Businessmen, a program designed to train and later secure employment for the so-called "hard-core unemployed." Others became associated with Keep America Beautiful, established subsidiaries in ghetto areas, supported minority enterprises, and entered the low-cost housing field.

Business also found itself beset with popular discontent on a scale that had heretofore been unknown. Perhaps beginning with the events surrounding Ralph Nader's book, *Unsafe at Any Speed,* the public began to take an increased interest in the social consequences of business decisions. Auto safety was only one of a number of publicity-grabbing topics that soon included protest against nuclear power plants, the production of antipersonnel weapons, discriminatory employment practices, and investment in South Africa. The General Motors annual meeting became a theater for acting out the hostility toward business.

John Gardner, Chairman of Common Cause, summed it up in a 1969 speech this way: "There are, as we all know, areas in which business can demonstrate its capacity to act responsibly. And when businessmen approach these areas, it's of critical importance that they understand the nature of the public dissatisfaction . . . They are facing something intangible but potentially explosive—the unanalyzed dissatisfaction of the bulk of the American people. That dissatisfaction is not a neat, paragraphed and numbered indictment. It is more like a huge charge of electricity ready to discharge itself."[9]

The attitude of many business leaders appeared to undergo a substantial revision during this period, though a generally accepted rationale for an expanded corporate role continued to be elusive. Some accepted it as a matter of self-defense or simply as an effort to allay their critics. Henry Ford phrased the matter more positively when he declared: "There is no longer anything to reconcile, if there ever was, between the social conscience and the profit motive . . . Improving the quality of society . . . is nothing more than another step in the evolutionary process of taking a more far-sighted view of return on investment."[10]

Undoubtedly, businessmen continued to differ in their convictions from what Andrews has termed "economic isolationists" to "social interventionists."[11] On balance, however, their expressed beliefs seemed generally to coincide with the report written in 1971 and approved by a wide majority of the Committee for Economic Development which stated in part:

> Today it is clear that the terms of the contract between society and business are, in fact, changing in substantial and important ways. Business is being asked to assume broader responsibilities to society . . . than ever before and to serve a wider range of human values. Business enterprises, in effect, are being asked to contribute more to the quality of American life than just supplying quantities of goods and services. Inasmuch as business exists to serve society, its future will depend on the quality of management's response to the changing expectations of the public.[12]

As the bluster of the late sixties and early seventies receded, however, the problem confronting the corporation again came up for reexamination. There was evidence to suggest that pressure on the corporation had relented. The college campuses had been quiet for several years, as had the urban ghettos. The novelty of expressing outrage at corporate malfeasance seemed to have waned and corporate legal staffs no longer reflected the air of panic that had been prevalent in the Dow Chemical and "Campaign GM" proxie contests of 1968 and 1970.

In the eyes of some observers, management had successfully exhausted, appeased, or in some way co-opted its critics. Moreover, as executives viewed their accomplishments with social action, many had reason to be disillusioned with earlier hopes for a rapid and decisive impact. The recessions of 1970 and 1974-75 proved the death knell for many special projects. Some managers may have recognized that to avow an interest in social action is one thing but to secure its implementation is quite another.

There was also considerable support in the middle 1970s, however, for the contention that pressure on the corporation might in fact increase in intensity in the future. The evidence was of three types.

First, the public respect for business and confidence in the corporation continued to deteriorate. For instance, Yankelovich[13] reported that favorable responses to the statement, "Business achieves a good balance between profits and service to the public," declined from 70 percent in 1968 to 32 percent in 1972 (after an uninterrupted rise since 1945). A variety of studies support this trend, though it should be remembered that business was not alone among institutions in the loss of public confidence. At the same time, the popular assessment of corporate resources was increasing; one survey[14] indicated that the mean estimate of after-tax profits as a percentage of sales rose from 21 percent in 1965 to 28 percent in 1971, while the actual figures decreased from 6.5 percent to 4.2 percent!

Second, social demands, which previously had been voiced in the press or on the streets, were gradually converted into regulations at local, state, and federal levels. Environmental protection legislation progressed particularly rapidly in this regard. Regulatory activity was also apparent in equal employment occupational health and safety, consumer protection, solid waste disposal, and product safety, to name only a few. Some 28 pieces of legislation affecting consumer rights alone were passed from 1966 through 1973.

Third, there was a growing sophistication among organizations interested in provoking corporate responsiveness. Environmentalist organizations very effectively used the courts to obstruct the construction of nuclear power plants and the harvesting of timber from government forests. After several years of denouncing (without result) the involvement of U.S. corporations in South Africa, church groups made it a point to learn the facts and apply pressure for specific action within the laws of that country, a tactic which met with some success.[15] Public interest groups were heartened both by the votes obtained for stockholder resolutions and by the willingness of managements to forestall proxy contests by agreeing to implement the desired reform voluntarily. The number of proxy contests continued to increase (from 20 in 1972 to 38 in 1973 to 71 in 1974) and, with institutional support, more resolutions were successful in obtaining the 3 percent vote necessary to remain on the ballot the second year (at least 7 in 1973 and 35 in 1974).

How will management attitudes toward corporate responsibility evolve? One cannot, of course, be certain, but it is probable that the scope of the public interest in private sector decisions will continue to increase. As resource constraints, both physical and financial, become more frequent and pronounced, and as individual desires for gratification expand, the boundaries of corporate responsibility will in all likelihood be commensurately enlarged. The sudden emergence of a severe recession in late 1974 has tended to intensify rather than diminish social pressure on the firm. With comparatively little relief from the burdens of previous demands, managers are expected to demonstrate a greater concern for the social impact of layoffs and plant closing than in previous periods of economic adversity.

As social demands come to have a greater impact on the operations of the business, managers will be well advised, if not forced, to include in the affairs of the company an explicit concern for social performance. The emphasis will inevitably fall on the **implementation of programs responsive to social needs rather than** on the philosophical rationale for corporate responsibility.

II
Social Demands from a Management Perspective

There are many areas in which corporations offer or are called upon to respond to social needs. In the past several years the top managements of a growing number of companies have voluntarily reported their performance in these areas.[1] For instance, Eastern Gas & Fuel Associates, a $350 million energy company, appended the results of a social audit to its 1972 annual report covering its three-year record in safety, minority employment, contributions, and employee benefits.* Such disclosures gain credibility if management is willing to report on activities that have been relatively unsuccessful as well as those in which progress has been substantial. For instance, during a period of turmoil for the United Mine Workers Union and heightened public awareness of the safety and ecology of coal mining, the Eastern Gas & Fuel audit showed an 81 percent increase in lost-time accidents per million employee hours from 1970 to 1972 for the Coke and Coal Division. In this instance, Eli Goldston, the company's president, readily acknowledged that performance in responding to social needs, e.g., for safe working conditions, should be based on achievement. In effect, he converted the social need into a management problem that could only be solved by implementing changes in the way the business was conducted.

Commentators are quick to point out that not all the social programs entered into by corporations are of comparable importance. Some relate to the strategic purposes of the business, as, for instance, mine safety for the Coke and Coal Division of Eastern Gas & Fuel Associates. Others are more akin to window-dressing. Contributing to the Metropolitan Opera may be a laudable gesture for the arts but only through the most circuitous reasoning can the

*For a full description of this document, the thinking behind its publication, and the stockholders' reaction, see Eastern Gas & Fuel Social Audit, (A), (B), (C), (D) case studies prepared at the Harvard Business School and available through the Intercollegiate Case Clearing House: Numbers 4-374-070, 4-374-071, 4-374-072, and 4-374-073.

donation be related to the sales of, let's say, milling machines. Some
are significant in terms of resources required, such as pollution
abatement; others exercise little call on funds or management time.
Some are mandated by law or contract, while others are more nearly
voluntary.

There is a need for a way of thinking about socially responsive
activities that will assist in the formulation and implementation of
policy in areas of major exposure or strategic significance. Thus far,
studies of business-society relationships have tended to focus on
social forces rather than on business decisions. Although some of
these studies have been useful,[2] they do not place the issues in the
context of the manager who must ultimately deal with them.

Social Responsiveness and Business Decisions

An important difference is evident between activities which have
an impact on the main-line operating functions of the business and
others which are essentially nonoperating matters. Efforts to curtail
pollution clearly entail expenditures in manufacturing facilities;
hiring and advancing minorities involve alterations in the employee
profile, and so forth. On the other hand, contributions to the arts or
higher education or investments in small businesses in the ghetto*
do not ordinarily disturb the ongoing affairs of the business.

There is also a distinction between those socially responsive activities which normally are the responsibility of managers at operating
levels in the company and those which typically are corporate-level
concerns. Employment practices, product safety, and response to
consumer complaints have customarily been included in the job
descriptions of managers in charge of operating functions. Civic
involvement and community relations are also, at least partially, in
the province of individuals at division levels and below. On the other
hand, the decisions to withdraw from a country or a business due to
social pressures — from South Africa for example, or from the
manufacture of antipersonnel weapons — are normally ones that

---

*It could be argued that starting a business in the ghetto may drain management
resources from other uses or, if the ghetto business is a supplier, it could affect
other units through its cost and delivery performance. However, such investments
are typically insignificant relative to the over-all size of the enterprise and managed
as special projects.

must be made and executed at the corporate level.* So also is the decision to diversify into a field of social interest, mass transit and low-cost housing being two obvious illustrations. Similarly, matters of governance, such as the addition of public directors, are clearly also activities that must be implemented at the top.

The results of sorting social activities according to these two distinctions may be illustrated by the matrix in Table II-1. The

Table II-1

Operational Impact / Level of Implementation	Activities Directly Affecting Operations	Activities Having no Significant Effect on Operations
Corporate	. Entry or withdrawal from businesses	. Contributions . "Special interest" investments . Disclosure . Governance, Board of Directors . Civic Involvement
Division	. Ecology (pollution, solid waste) . Equal employment . Occupational health and safety . Product safety and use . Advertising and selling practices . Employment practices (compensation and conditions)	. Community relations . Civic involvement

*This need not always be the case. A new manager assigned to a plant that had been manufacturing a product under government contract found to be offensive by antiwar groups purposefully filled the plant to capacity with other commitments. When the contract expired he informed the government that he could not bid on the next one. During this time, the board of directors and corporate management had been resolute in their opposition to the antiwar group's demands for withdrawal from the business.

primary focus of this book is on the implementation of policy which has an impact on main line operations *and* which must be ultimately integrated into management practices at operating levels. The reasons for this are threefold. First, as later evidence will indicate, these activities involve substantial amounts of money and management effort. To be sure, the entry or withdrawal from a business may have significant financial implications but such decisions occur infrequently and then often under very special circumstances. Second, to the extent that social issues have an effect on business strategy at the operating level, they most likely will be felt through pressure on activities that contribute to the production and sale of goods and services. Third, policies in this category turn out to be the ones which produce the organizational challenge for the large corporation.

The initiation of programs responsive to social demands of the type identified above calls for changes in facilities, work force composition, marketing practices, product design, and so forth. An indication of the relationship between external pressures and operaing functions is illustrated in Table II-2. However, to get at the effect of attempts to implement policy in areas of social concern, one must go further than simply identifying the operating profile desired. It is not enough to support a policy of equal employment by specifying a targeted number of minorities and women at various levels in the organization. One must also identify and then influence the decision processes which result in minorities and women being hired and promoted, including recruiting and placement, training and executive development, and performance evaluations.

In essence, a further relationship must be drawn between the social demand and the decision process to be invoked in responding to it. Hence pollution abatement has an effect on manufacturing operations which can be analyzed in terms of technical requirements and cost. Responsiveness will only be obtained, however, through a consideration of these factors in the context of the resource allocation process through which funds are divided among divisions and projects. The importance of this relationship has been recognized by some corporate critics. For instance, in *Unsafe at Any Speed* Nader claimed that the instability of the rear-end suspension on the Corvair was known to the design engineers prior to the introduction of the car. However, he maintained that their concerns were

Table II-2

Business operating functions	Social issues	Management decision processes
Product development	Product safety and use Ecological impact (e.g., biodegradability, exhaust emissions)	Product feasibility, design and introduction
Manufacturing	Occupational health and safety Ecological impact (e.g., air and water pollution)	Manufacturing process design Capital investment allocation
Personnel administration	Equal employment opportunity Employment practices	Employee selection, placement, evaluation and reward
Sales and marketing	Selling and advertising practices Consumer rights	Marketing program definition Consumer relations policies

overruled in the eventual decision to proceed with the product by the "cost cutters and stylists" who sought the more marketable qualities of looks and a smooth ride.[3] The president of General Motors, though an engineer and a member of the engineering policy group, indicated that he was not aware of the design questions but instead relied on his organization to make judgments of this kind.

In summary, then, it is necessary to analyze socially responsive activities in an organizational context. It should be clear that if a corporate-wide policy is to be implemented at operating levels, the decision process which governs the firm's behavior in the area of concern will have to be modified to take the policy into account.

Profiles of Social Demands and their Operational Impact

The sophistication of environmental forecasting has increased dramatically in recent years. Corporate planners have expanded the scope of the information considered relevant to include social and political as well as competitive and technological trends. They have also sought to capture second-and third-order consequences of trends which may not appear to have a direct bearing on their firms.

For example, since 1967 the Public Issues Committee of the Board of the General Electric Company has labored to develop a systematic methodology for environmental forecasting.[4] To sharpen the analysis, the study group reporting to this committee compiled a list of 97 threats or demands having a potential impact on various functions or aspects of the corporation. They ranged from the dismemberment of large diversified firms to the provision of day-care centers to consumer boycotts and class action suits. Further lists of 14 principal social trends and 15 constituencies or pressure groups were also assembled. By assessing the degree of "convergence" between the social trends and the "intensity" and "diffusion" of support among constituencies, the study group was able to obtain a rough indication of the likelihood of each demand coming to fruition. Demands which appeared to be in line with social trends and to have some muscle behind them were then subjected to further screening to ascertain their relative significance to GE and to differentiate between those having an impact on the corporate office and those falling on the company's forty-odd strategic business units.

Unfortunately, environmental scanning of this sort is not easily translated into concrete guidance for operating managers in the far reaches of a large corporation. Operating managers have immediate concerns associated with designing, producing, and marketing products at a profit. Drawing the connection in a systematic fashion between broad social trends and specific business decisions is often too complex an undertaking for either the planner or the operating manager, even assuming the latter is interested in the attempt. Yet social forces, as the brief survey below suggests, are having a profound impact on traditional business functions; manufacturing, personnel administration, product development and marketing. Three broad and largely self-evident conclusions are offered at the outset.

The impact on the corporation of individual demands in terms of cost and operational change, and therefore management time and skills, is consequential, though not of a magnitude that threatens the survival of an otherwise healthy business.

This impact varies widely among industries; by the same token, an industry will find some to be of more significance to it than others.

The social concerns have a time dimension; some are immediate while others are as yet vague suggestions of future demands.

Manufacturing

Production managers and process engineers have been beset by demands that they adopt a more inclusive definition of environmental impact in the design and operation of production processes. The problem is manifested in two ways, one of which relates to degradation of the environment and the other to the health and safety of the work place itself. Each bears a brief elaboration.

Ecologists have provoked dramatic controversies resulting in a five-year delay in the trans-Alaskan pipeline,* the abandonment of the cross-Florida barge canal, and the severe retrenchment in the start-up of nuclear power plants.[5] Less noticeable but cumulatively more significant (and costly) are the results of thousands of meetings held each year between company and government officials to negotiate schedules for achieving compliance with fast-changing and ever-expanding federal, state, and local environmental protection regulations.

The weight of these regulations, most notably the 1970 Clean Air Act Amendment and the 1972 Water Pollution Control Act, and the persistent pressure from environmental groups are felt in both financial and operational terms. McGraw-Hill surveys reveal a steady increase in the expenditures of manufacturing firms for pollution control equipment, from $1.4 billion in 1969 to $2.6 billion in 1972, with estimates of $4.1 billion and $4.7 billion for 1973 and 1976.[6] The proportion of capital expenditures devoted to this purpose is also increasing and represents something on the order of 10

---

*The pipeline was finally approved but only after the nation's access to imported oil was threatened in the wake of renewed hostilities in the Middle East.

percent of the total. A Conference Board survey reported on another dimension of the financial burden: the ratio of operating costs to capital outlays for pollution control equipment in companies reporting expenditures for both purposes was 48.7 percent in 1970.[7] Thus, both the capital budget and the annual profit plan are affected.

Considerable pains have been taken by the Environmental Protection Agency (EPA) to indicate that the economic dislocation likely to ensue from a more stringent view of ecological damage is relatively minor. A government-funded report (issued prior to passage of the 1972 Water Pollution Control Act) estimated that 200 to 300 of the 12,000 plants involving 1 percent to 4 percent of the employment in the 14 industries studied could be shut down by 1977 because of pollution control regulations.[8] The report also predicted that the effect on prices and demand would be modest; for instance, aluminum smelting and refining, one of the most affected industries, was expected to require a 5 percent to 8 percent price increase by 1976 and experience a 4 percent to 6 percent decline in sales relative to what it would have been in the absence of the regulation. According to EPA, plant closings directly attributable to the regulations were running lower than estimated,[9] though in the booming economy of 1972-73, that result was hardly surprising since the marginal facility is generally the one most susceptible to shutdown and most dependent on strong demand and rising prices. On the other hand, as EPA formulated the industry-by-industry guidelines supporting the water bill, the financial impact appeared certain to exceed earlier estimates.[10]

Although environmental control requirements may not have catastrophic consequences for the economy as a whole, the impact on the production function in a number of industries is nonetheless substantial. A case in point is the steel industry. Spokesmen for that industry point out that from 1965 to 1972, capital spending exceeded internally generated cash flow by $1.9 billion. These expenditures contributed to the need for an increase in long-term debt of $2.4 billion, which caused the ratio of debt to total capitalization to rise from 19.3 percent to 25.5 percent.[11] They also maintain that to build low-cost capacity to compete with foreign firms in the U.S. market *and* meet pollution control standards will produce further deterioration in its financial condition. Various studies of this industry conducted by independent agencies confirm the importance of "environmental considerations." For instance a 1975 study by Arthur D. Little placed its total annual capital needs through 1983 at $5.5 billion ($1.4 billion of it for pollution control purposes) or more than three times the industry's average internal funds generation from 1968 through 1972.[12]

The real crunch for managers, however, is observed in the circumstances of specific incidents. For instance, Bethlehem Steel in June 1973 announced that it was reducing by 25 percent the capacity of its old Johnstown, Pennsylvania, works by replacing four open hearths with two electric furnaces. Company officials cited pollution control expenditures of $100 million to maintain the existing facility as a major contributing factor in the decision. Of the $87 million to be spent under the new plan, $35 million was allocated for the electric furnaces (which accept a "cold charge" of 100 percent scrap, thus eliminating the need for the heavily polluting coking process) and $42 million for the other plant environmental control purposes.[13] It can hardly be argued that this incident alone constituted a severe threat to Bethlehem, which had sales of $4 billion and net income of $206 million in 1973. But for the managers concerned with capital spending and more specifically with the mill in question, ecology had a significant influence on the outcome of the investment decision process.

Only partially reflecting in the cost estimates are a variety of technical uncertainties and operational changes that prove troublesome to facility-oriented managers. In some cases regulations cannot be met with available control technology. For instance, the steel industry has not as yet developed a practical means of abating air pollution in the coking process. Nor have electric utilities been successful in devising a method of reducing sulfur oxide emissions that is both technically viable and economically feasible. Since regulations and compliance schedules generally impose deadlines, pressure is often exerted for early experimentation with new equipment which is time-consuming, disruptive, and expensive. Yet unwillingness to experiment may delay the start-up of new facilities or threaten shutdowns with the attendant loss of jobs and badly needed capacity.

Broader changes in raw materials, processes, and products may also be dictated by ecological pressures. Thus, the expense of treating the noxious cooking liquor residues in paper mills employing a sulfite pulping process (once the dominant process in the industry) has contributed to the adoption of the kraft process in new mills. In another case, a glass company withdrew from a profitable specialty market because the cost of eliminating the particular emissions created by the composition of the glass was prohibitive. The economic impact of environmental protection is often being incorporated in the cost of production through such second-order effects.

No sooner had the last round of environmental control legislation begun to take effect than production managers were confronted with a major complicating factor in the form of an energy shortage. In some instances, environmental concerns were overridden. The Alaskan pipeline was finally approved, and New York City eased rules forbidding the burning of high sulfur fuel, thus permitting Consolidated Edison to convert several of its power generating plants back to coal. Plant location decisions, already influenced by ecological requirements, became sensitive to energy constraints as well. The relationship between the energy shortage and environmental protection is not altogether clear. For instance, there is some suggestion that before receiving variances from regulatory agencies to burn higher sulfer fuel, corporations are being placed under *increased* pressure to install pollution abatement equipment.

Working conditions, a second source of concern for the production function, has received increased attention since the passage of the Occupational Safety and Health Act (OSHA) in 1970. Unions have recently become more aggressive in pressing for safer working conditions. Moreover, in a recent Shell Oil strike (occasioned by the company's refusal to include various health and safety provisions in the contract), the union received unaccustomed support from ecology groups.[14] Immediate emphasis is being given to eliminating dangerous conditions which in 1972 contributed to the 14,000 on-the-job deaths in the United States. However, more significant implications may be felt in reducing the impairment to health from sustained exposure to noise, heat, cotton dust, silica, asbestos, carbon monoxide, and a host of other process-related conditions. Less tangible at present but in the long run a matter of great importance are "quality of life" factors relating to job content and the work place.

The financial impact of these concerns is difficult to assess, in part because of the uncertainties surrounding the scope of future regulation, which continue to expand into new areas, and the strictness of enforcement, which is steadily increasing.* Nonetheless, a McGraw-Hill survey indicated that business spent $2.5 billion in 1972 and plans to increase that to $3.2 billion in 1973 on OSHA-related projects.[15] Not surprisingly, the burden again falls unevenly with iron and steel, textiles, mining and communications bearing relatively heavy obligations.†

The operating ramifications of demands for safer working conditions may be substantial. For instance, according to the Bituminous Coal Operators Association, frequent inspections and other "nonproductive elements" prescribed in the 1969 Coal Mine Health and Safety Act has contributed (along with strikes) to the 22 percent drop in output per day in deep mines from 1968 to 1972.[16] In metalworking operations, the requirement that a worker keep his hands out of the die area of a press may necessitate automated transfer devices. Textile mills may face dramatically increased loom costs if noise levels are to be brought down to the 90 decibels specified in the regulations. Some means will have to be found for reducing the danger to the 1.1 million workers in iron and mineral processing, sandblasting, and abrasives-handling who come in potentially hazardous contact with silica. In many instances, economical and feasible remedies cannot be found without a basic redesign of the manufacturing process or the product.

Personnel Administration

Decisions in the corporation having a bearing on the composition and treatment of the work force have been affected by a variety of social concerns. Most immediate are demands for equal employment, first occasioned by discriminatory practices against blacks and later extended to Chicanos, native Americans, and women. The emphasis for minorities has passed from entry-level hiring activities to facilitating advancement into managerial and professional ranks. Equal pay, the removal of job barriers, and career opportunities are also needs expressed by women in business.

---

*OSHA expected to conduct 80,000 inspections in fiscal 1973 up from roughly 30,000 the year before.

†McGraw-Hill is quick to point out that this survey (the first of its kind) may overstate the expenditures in that some companies may tend to include pollution control investments as well.

There is little doubt that the problem of discrimination is serious. A cursory look at the information supplied to the Equal Employment Opportunity Commission (EEOC) reveals that in virtually all large corporations huge deficiencies exist in the proportion of high-level jobs occupied by minorities and women. While there is little argument that much needs to be done, disagreement exists over the progress already made[17] and the means adopted to correct inequalities.[18] A report prepared for the Labor Department describes a deep-seated pessimism among black managers about upward mobility;[19] It is merely one of a growing number of studies suggesting that the difficulties of resolving the problem penetrates far more deeply into the organizational fabric of the corporation than employment and relative income figures suggest.

A number of equal employment advocates have been particularly active and in some cases have scored what appear to be impressive victories. With the passage of the Civil Rights Act in 1964, which established EEOC, the government has increased its voice in employment matters. The Office of Federal Contract Compliance (OFCC), acting through other government agencies, has conducted thousands of compliance reviews each year. If satisfaction is not obtained for infractions of the authorizing executive order, OFCC has the power to withhold or cancel government contracts. In March 1972, EEOC was given authority to initiate suits in federal courts against employers, in addition to responding through conciliation or legal action to employee complaints which in that year numbered over 52,000.* With these new powers, EEOC announced plans to file 10 to 15 new suits every two weeks[20] and began by issuing sweeping charges of discrimination against four of the nation's largest corporations — General Motors, General Electric, Ford, and Sears, Roebuck, and their related unions.

Private action groups have also proved to be effective advocates in employment matters. Using the threat of a boycott, People United to Save Humanity (PUSH) negotiated a convenant with the Jos. Schlitz Brewing Company whereby the company agreed, among other commitments covering relationships with black-owned busi-

---

*Generally, EEOC finds "reasonable cause" to believe bias exists in two thirds of the charges it investigates, though in less than half is it able to achieve a successful conciliation.

nesses, to make serious efforts to attain as quickly as possible a minimum of 15 percent minority employees in all job classifications. To attain this goal the company concurred that blacks and other minorities should account for at least 30 percent of the new hires. General Foods signed a similar convenant calling for actions estimated by PUSH to cost $65 million.[21] Caucuses organized by women and blacks have sprung up in numerous companies to act as bargaining agents for their constituencies. With the threat of legal action or outside intervention, even reluctant managements have concluded that it is prudent to take their grievances seriously.

The cost of eliminating inequality or the financial implications of discriminatory practices (be they positive or negative) has not been ascertained,[22] but the penalties associated with legal action can be substantial. In the largest settlement to date, AT&T was ordered to make lump-sum payments of some $15 million to 15,000 minority and women employees and give immediate raises aggregating $23 million to another 36,000. Further, the company was to provide better jobs for roughly 100,000 employees over a fifteen-month period. In another case, Wheaton Glass was assessed $900,000 under the Equal Pay Act for discriminatory practices against women. The list of major settlements specifying financial awards and employee compensation in hourly and management ranks is certain to grow as awareness of the law and the sophistication of the aggrieved or their representatives increases.

From an operating viewpoint, efforts to meet demands for equality have had far-reaching ramifications for personnel administration. Job testing has been sharply curtailed because of potential cultural biases, preferential hiring has been encouraged, qualification standards altered, job titles and the boundary line between exempt and nonexempt positions changed, and special training programs developed. The impact extends, of course, beyond the personnel function to all managers in supervisory positions who play a part in determining the careers of those reporting to them. In the case of AT&T, one clear implication of the court ruling is that fewer opportunities for advancement will be available for white males than they previously anticipated. The basis on which promotions are made in that company will be subjected to intense scrutiny and will no doubt provoke controversy and at times animosity.

Personnel administration is also affected by concerns about occupational safety and health. In fact, there is a lively debate in some companies as to whether responsibility for working conditions should lie primarily with engineering or personnel. Inevitably, elements of both functions are involved. While the engineers may figure prominently in process and facility redesign, personnel specialists are accountable for the job specifications and work rules that govern employment practices.

Personnel managers generally concede, however, that equal employment and working conditions are merely the tip of the iceberg. Less visible at the moment, but potentially of larger import, are concerns among managers and hourly employees alike about performance evaluations, career paths, and benefits. The tendency has been often reported that employees expect more sensitivity to individual needs and greater participation in decisions involving their work than before.[23] "Alienation," "blue (and white) collar blues" and "the Lordstown syndrome"* have become catch words for a discontent thought by many to loom over the future of corporation-employee relationships.

Product Development

Consumerism is a much overworked term that has come to encompass a plethora of complaints about corporate behavior. One commentator wrote:

> Consumer activists share a surprisingly narrow view of what the consumer movement wants: safe, reliable products and services that are performed as advertised and that are repaired or remedied promptly when they fail. In addition, the activists say, consumers want more detailed information about goods and services to enable intelligent comparison before a purchase is made.[24]

In such a way is "narrow" defined.

---

*Named after the 1972 strike at the new General Motors plant in Lordstown by assembly line workers. Among the causes of the strike reported at the time was the feeling among the workers, including many young Vietnam veterans, that the restriction of job content and the speed of the assembly line created dehumanizing conditions. Subsequent studies in the company by independent researchers, however, have suggested that the strike may have been prompted less by alienation than by more traditional disputes over contract terms and administration. See "Blue Collar Blues?," *Business Week,* April 29, 1974, p. 90.

Part of what is grouped under the rubric of consumerism relates to product planning and design and part to the activities associated with marketing goods and services. Of course, there is considerable overlap in the functions affected, and many activist groups have an interest in both types of issues. Nonetheless the distinction is helpful in that it facilitates the identification of where in the organization the critical decisions and responsibilities for implementation are located.

Product safety scored an impressive comeback as a political issue in the 1960s after a period of quiescence during and following World War II.[25] The thalidomide disaster and the Corvair exposé were instrumental in reawakening public interest. The growing technological content, performance expectations, and potency of many products appear to have increased the risk and hazard of malfunction. Recent examples from among those causing an estimated 110,000 disabling injuries and 30,000 deaths each year[26] have included radiation emitted from color television sets, potentially harmful monosodium glutamate, side-effects from powerful drugs, and unsafe toys.

Public demands in this area have become more complicated and serious for the corporation because the degree of liability attributed to the manufacturer for the use of its products has increased. Walter Schirmer[27] points to a "deterioration" in the manufacturer's legal position caused by an erosion in the concept of privity and the tendency to hold the manufacturer liable for injury regardless of negligence on its part. The financial burden on the corporation has been weighted by the willingness of the courts to expand the jury's responsibility for assessing questions of "fact" concerning product performance and to bloat the magnitude of settlements, a phenomenon that has no doubt led to more numerous claims.

Aside from individual or class action suits, corporations have come under the scrutiny of various public interest advocates and government agencies, the latter including the Consumer Product Safety Commission and the Office of Consumer Affairs. The outcome of this surveillance has frequently been performance or design standards covering product composition (flame-resistant mattresses) and added features (auto safety belts). Product recalls, public warnings, and customer refunds frequently entailing considerable expense and loss of sales, have become commonplace.

In some cases, industry groups have petitioned government agencies to tighten regulations; for instance, some months after botulism was found in cans of Bon Vivant soup, resulting in one well-publicized death the National Canners Association asked the Federal Drug Administration to adopt stricter regulations for the industry.

The impact on the product development and quality assurance functions promises to be substantial. The designer is expected to understand the circumstances in which a product will be used, anticipate the effects of aging and changing conditions on its performance, and incorporate these factors in product specifications. Like the process engineer and personnel specialist, he is expected to meet performance and cost criteria while being cognizant of recognized or potential social demands.

The product development function is also influenced by ecological considerations. The most prominent example of this has been the controversy over automobile exhaust emissions occasioned by the time limits established in the 1970 Clean Air Act Amendments. The U.S. auto industry steadfastly maintained that the standards could not be met with existing technology by 1975-76 as originally prescribed in the 1970 amendments to the Clean Air Act. The merits of this position have been debated at length by the industry and its critics and delays in the implementation schedule obtained as a result. Suffice it to say here that the design of the automobile can no longer be guided wholly by marketing considerations of cost, style, and comfort.

The solid-waste issue is another concern impinging on product development. Consumption of packaging materials amounts to some 55 million tons a year in the United States and is growing at a rate of about 5 percent. To this must be added mountains of junked automobiles, refrigerators, and other refuse. The disposal problem is manifested in unsightly litter, shrinking land fill capacity, air pollution from incineration, material shortages, and energy and other resources consumed in producing the discarded material. The ultimate solution, generally thought to be recycling systems, is at present far from being a reality.[28] Public interest in the problem has prompted consideration of partial measures, including subsidies or preferential treatment for recycled materials, bans or taxes on nonreturnable containers, and prohibitions against certain kinds of packaging. From the corporate perspective, the waste disposal issue has led to the development of a greater interest in utilizing recycled materials in the manufacturing process, and the redesign of products to minimize the eventual disposal difficulty.[29] In most instances, product characteristics are altered in the process.

Selling and Marketing Practices

Many of the complaints registered by consumerists relate not to the product itself, but to the fashion in which it is marketed and serviced. A simple way of categorizing these complaints is to relate them to the typical sequence of consumer experiences in the purchase of goods and services. First, prior to making a purchase, he may encounter and be influenced by advertising and packaging. Second, at the time of the transaction he comes in contact with the selling practices of the vendor. Then, having made the purchase, he may seek service or performance against warranties stipulated in the sales agreement. Corporate behavior at each step has been the subject of public criticism and governmental survelliance and regulation.

Since its creation in 1914, the Federal Trade Commission has gradually expanded, through subsequent legislation and administrative interpretation, the scope of the blanket prohibition in the Federal Trade Commission Act that "unfair methods of competition are hereby declared unlawful." Deceptive advertising and packaging have been at the top of the FTC's list of abuses. Considering the growth of mass media (especially television) and self-service retailing during the intervening years, this emphasis is hardly surprising. In tracing the evolution of the FTC, Gaylord Jentz[30] noted that 897,609 advertisements were reviewed by the Commission in 1966 of which 43,107 were set aside for further examination. Consent orders signed by offending companies refer to such malpractices as deceptive use of research studies, unsubstantiated claims, inadequate disclosure, and deceptive television demonstrations.

In the face of consumer complaints and an obvious concern about the credibility of advertising in general, industry groups have also taken a hand in the policing job. One organization, the National Advertising Division of the Better Business Bureaus, with its separate "court of appeals," The National Advertising Review Board, has gained some measure of respect since it was established in late 1971.[31]

Selling practices have long been sources of consumer complaint. Typified by the proverbial snake oil salesman, the culprits have often been fly-by-night operators who foisted their wares on a gullible public. An extreme case was that of the Holland Furnace Company whose salesmen visited homeowners sometimes in the guise of "safety inspectors." Not wanting to be "accessories to murder" they offered to have the family furnace replaced, one salesman performing his duties so adroitly that an elderly woman purchased nine furnaces in six years at a cost of $18,000![32] Less pernicious, though recently the subject of legal sanction, have been various high-pressure sales tactics employed by companies relying on door-to-door or telephone solicitation. A different and more consequential charge has been leveled at the drug industry for its use of detailmen to acquaint doctors with products developments. Critics maintain that the cost and practice of detailing increase the price of drugs and tend to inhibit the prescription of less expensive generic formulations.

Public frustration with the large corporation has perhaps been most vocally expressed through the accounts of irate consumers who are miffed by unresponsiveness to their requests for service or redress. "Your man in Detroit" has proved to be a less than effective pacifier for the Chrysler Corporation in its efforts to mollify indignant car owners.[33] As in the case of product safety, part of the corporation's current difficulty stems from extensions in the warranty, expressly given or merely implied, for the quality of its products. Encouraged by tangible court rulings and the publicity accorded consumer activists, the public has become more assertive in pressing its complaints.

Conclusion

A common reflection among managers today is that their jobs have become more complex and in some respects uncomfortable as a result of the welter of public expectations that have arisen or intensified in the past decade. As the brief survey above illustrates, each of the functional managers involved in the development, production, and sale of goods and services shares in this burden. Of course, the cost and difficulty of responding to a particular concern varies widely among industries. In some instances the response may be trivial (advertising and packaging for an electronics company);

in others it strikes at the heart of the business (pollution abatement for a copper company). For functional managers in the latter circumstance especially, responsiveness calls for new skills and knowledge and the willingness to incorporate new concerns in the discharge of traditional responsibilities. Social responsiveness is time-consuming, involves risk and uncertainty, and is frequently expensive to execute.

Social responsiveness is also a general management problem. Although the primary burden for understanding and administering the response to a particular issue may fall on a single function, implementation is rarely limited to that function. The personnel manager may be held accountable for identifying female applicants for sales jobs; he cannot integrate the sales force. Similarly, the development engineer may labor to eliminate product defects, but he cannot do so in isolation from those who will later have to make and sell the redesigned product. The general manager is responsible for both the conduct of individual functions and the integration across them. The complexity of managing social responsiveness from his viewpoint is reflected in the number of interfunctional relationships that must be coordinated.

The relationship between some of the more prominent social concerns and the operating functions of a business is summarized in Figure II-1. The breadth of the impact from an administrative viewpoint provides some indication of the increased scope of the general manager's responsibility in today's environment.

Figure II-1
Functional Responsibilities for Social Responsiveness

Social Demands \ Operating Functions	Personnel Administration	Manufacturing	Engineering	Product Development	Marketing
Pollution Control		╱	▨		
Occupational Health and Safety	▨	╱	▨		
Equal Employment	▨	╱	╱	╱	╱
Product Safety and Pollution		╱	╱	▨	╱
Solid Waste		╱	╱	▨	╱
Advertising and Selling Practices				╱	▨

▨ = Functions having primary skills for responsiveness to social demands.

╱ = Other functions directly effected or influenced by social responsiveness.

III
Social Change
and Corporate Choice

The large corporation interacts with a dynamic environment in which the social demands placed upon it are evolving over time. Organizational dislocation may be more a function of changing conditions than of the sheer weight of social demands. Further, it is the response to changes in the environment that creates for managers the necessity for choice. Before the nature of the choice can be discussed, however, it will be helpful to have a simple way of thinking about the implications of social change for the decision processes in the corporation.

The Social Issue Life Cycle

Most social issues follow patterns that, in retrospect, appear to be quite predictable. There was typically a time in which the issue was unthought of or unthinkable. In fact, social and economic sanctions are frequently applied to those who foster issues of some consequence that have no public support. However, should interest develop and be sustained, the issue passes through a period of increasing awareness, expectations, demands for action and ultimately enforcement. At the end of this period, probably measured in decades, it may cease to be a matter of active public concern. New standards of behavior may then have become so ingrained in the normal conduct of affairs that to behave otherwise would bring the social and economic sanctions formerly reserved for the contrary behavior. Thus, like the product life cycle, there is an analogous social issue life cycle.[1]

The right to collective bargaining in the United States is an apt example. To have demanded, let alone countenanced, an independent union in the steel industry in 1890 would have been viewed as folly, if not openly subversive to the American way of life. Over the next forty-seven years, however, a great deal happened to change that attitude. The workers in the steel industry were no longer easily intimidated immigrants, the depression raised massive unemployment concerns, the rhetoric of the New Deal nurtured the awareness of social inequities, and the passage of legislation favorable to labor made unionism socially acceptable and legally enforceable. In a sense, when Myron C. Taylor (then chairman of U.S. Steel) met privately with John L. Lewis (then president of the Committee for Industrial Organization) in the Mayflower Hotel on March 1, 1937, and agreed to recognize the Steel Workers Organizing Committee, he accepted collective bargaining as a logical consequence of social change in the country.[2] Within nine years all of the major steel companies were unionized, and by the 1970s, the union-management relationship, while not always amicable, had become an integral part of doing business in that industry.

Managers, of course, do not have the luxury of managing the response to changing social demands in retrospect. On closer examination, issues of social concern present mammoth uncertainties to those who are forced to deal with them during the time in which they are vying for public acceptance. The uncertainties are of three types: the first has to do with the urgency and durability of the issue. While the quest for equity and justice may be eternal, the current array of activists and the causes they champion are subject to change. Some will become enduring facets of business operations (like the child labor laws), others will fall by the wayside (like prohibition). Predicting the implications of social trends for a business may be no easier than assessing the impact of nascent technologies.

Second, acceptable standards of behavior are often difficult to determine and they too change with time. What was greeted with praise yesterday may be tolerated today and considered reprehensible tomorrow. Thus, one firm has a mural of one of its plants in the corporate foyer. Until 1972 smoke belched proudly from the smoke stacks. The smoke has now been painted out. In many cases, attempts are made to codify standards in law or regulation. The difficulty arises because these formal statements are ambiguous or changing, may differ among jurisdictions, and, most significantly, occur toward the end rather than the beginning of the cycle. Moreover, the equity and thoroughness of enforcement may be highly variable while the standards are new or uncertain, and very possibly for some time thereafter, as enforcement agencies struggle with funding and organizational problems of their own.

Third, the means of responding to evolving social issues are generally unknown when the demands first arise. Technologies may have to be developed, new sources of employees identified, and so forth. The money and energy that should be expended seeking solutions is naturally dependent to some degree on the credibility of the threat, the eventual standards to be met and the time frame within which response is necessary.

The Zone of Discretion

The basic argument here is that social issues pass through a period in which very substantial uncertainties exist in those factors of importance to the corporation in determining its response. But uncertainty gives rise to discretion. During this period, managers have a wide variety of options available for approaching the problem. Ultimately, those options will be narrowed or even eliminated as a new standard of behavior becomes generally accepted and thoroughly enforced through regulatory or other means. This "zone of discretion," though of varying duration, is evident for each social issue. Its presence affords the corporation the choice of how soon and in what way to respond to emerging social issues. The evolution of interest in air and water pollution control and in equal opportunity serves to illustrate the significance of this phenomenon; both are also germane to the descriptions of corporate responsiveness in later chapters.

Air and Water Pollution Controls

As is true with many current social issues, air and water pollution has been a matter of concern for many years. Writing in 1949, William Kapp[3] summarized an impressive literature on the damage to property and human health caused by industrial emissions. He notes that as early as 1913 the Mellon Institute of Industrial Research estimated that smoke nuisance cost the people of Pittsburgh roughly $10 million per year. However, aside from a few conservationists, ecology had no constituency in those days. "Smoke means jobs" so the saying went. Despite a 1948 air pollution disaster in Donora, Pennsylvania, which claimed 20 lives, and increasing evidence of a smog problem in Los Angeles in the early 1950s, emission controls, to the extent they existed at all, were matters for local ordinances.

The ecology movement has garnered a large and powerful constituency since the early 1960s. Prompted by such accounts as Rachel Carson's *Silent Spring,* public awareness of the social costs of environmental degradation increased and was gradually converted into legislation at the federal level aimed at controlling air and water pollution. Tracing the development of this regulation provides some indication of the evolving nature of the demands placed on the corporation.

In 1956 the Water Pollution Control Act provided the first federal enforcement procedures for processing complaints against industrial polluters. The procedure was so complex and timeconsuming, however, that only one case appeared in court as a result of it in the fourteen years that the act was operative. Furthermore, not until the 1965 Water Quality Act was there an attempt to set systematic national standards. That act required the states to specify water quality in terms of the desired usage (from drinking water to navigation only) for each interstate and coastal waterway and implementation plans for attaining it. More time passed before the first state plans were approved by the newly created Federal Water Pollution Control Administration (FWPCA) in July 1967, and as of February 1972 four states had still not complied with the act. Regulations on specific emission levels for water contamination were not broached until a 1970 law, and then coverage was directed primarily toward oil spills.

The regulators were confronted with two further problems in the water pollution area; obtaining information on emissions and wielding credible sanctions. The Environmental Protection Agency, (EPA), the successor to FWPCA, attempted to solve both in 1971 by resurrecting the 1899 River and Harbor Act. Although successful in eliciting emissions data and initiating some suits under this old law, EPA soon ran into legal difficulties of its own which forced the agency to rely for several months on "voluntary" compliance efforts on the part of industrial polluters.*

Finally, the 1972 Water Pollution Control Act established the framework for a comprehensive network of standards and compliance procedures. The act prescribes that every company dis-

---

*Two cases went against EPA in lower courts. One held that an "environmental impact" study had to be prepared by either EPA or the Corps of Engineers for each permit application (a monumental undertaking), and the second that suits could not be filed for failure to comply with the 1899 Act when the enforcing agency, the Corps of Engineers, had made no provision for issuing permits.

charging waste into an interstate waterway must obtain a permit
from a state agency which will set emission limits under EPA guidelines for various industries and processes. Then by July 1, 1977,
companies must employ the "best practicable control technology"
and by July 1, 1983, they must have the "best available technology."
A goal, though not enforceable under the act, is the complete
elimination of water discharge by 1985. Interpretation of the law, of
course, remains uncertain. "Best practical" has been taken to mean
the most effective technology in use at the time a permit is granted
considering the age and nature of the facility. "Best available" has
been interpreted to be, at a minimum, the most advanced technology in any plant in the industry, and perhaps more stringent still
if process changes or technology employed elsewhere would yield
superior results. Thus the standard in itself is dynamic; each time
the corporation requests a permit renewal (permits are usually
issued for five years) or constructs a new facility, it can expect to
meet stiffer terms.

The history of air pollution control for industrial sources follows a
roughly analogous pattern. In this instance the 1963 Clean Air Act,
coming in the wake of the London "killer smog," provided procedures for the redress of complaints similar to those under the 1956
water control legislation. In 1967 further legislation specified air
quality control regions and required the states to set standards and
implementation programs subject to federal approval. Then the
1970 Amendments to the Clean Air Act required EPA to set
national ambient air standards and strengthened the government's
enforcement capabilities. In April of the following year, EPA
promulgated standards for six common classes of pollutants, and in
1972 EPA issued source performance standards for several industries based on the capabilities of the best adequately demonstrated
emission reduction systems. The states were to propose regulations
which insured that these levels would be met by June 30, 1975. As in
the case of water pollution control, the states were also to operate
the construction and operating permit system through which
compliance schedules are negotiated.

Though tersely stated, this review of the legislative history of
pollution control illustrates three characteristics that are relevant
for the manager concerned with constructing or operating production facilities.

Time: a decade or more passed between the first federal legislation, itself a lagging indicator of public concern, and the date a reasonably comprehensive set of performance standards were to be operative.

Standards and enforcement: During this time uncertainty existed about the likely configuration of future standards and sanctions, although it appeared to be a fair bet that they would grow progressively more stringent.

Technology: the emissions standards were ultimately related to state-of-the-art control technology which necessitated continuing, though uncertain, development and operating costs.

The constraints suggested by factors such as these determine the boundaries of corporate choice.

Equal employment

The revival of civil rights as a national concern in the 1950s was manifested initially by the quest among blacks and liberal whites for integrated schools and public accommodations, and the elimination of voting restrictions. Gradually, attention turned as well to the more complex areas of discrimination in housing and employment. The ghetto riots of the mid-1960s provided dramatic evidence of the deep-seated antagonisms existing in the black community toward white-dominated institutions. Innumerable studies, including the widely circulated Report of the National Advisory Commission on Civil Disorders (The Kerner Commission), documented evidence of systematic discrimination and called for pervasive, corrective action. Pressure for reform was exerted on the corporation from many sources, not the least of which were minority employees seeking redress for alleged inequity. The government action sketched below is merely illustrative of the development of these demands.

The principle underlying equal opportunity has long been recognized; it is unlawful for an employer to discriminate in matters related to employment because of race, color, religion, sex, or national origin. Words to this effect were contained in Executive Order 10925 signed by President Kennedy in 1961 prohibiting discrimination by government contractors. The effect of this order was minimal, however, because exceptions for bona fide occupational qualifications were broadly construed, the employer was held responsible for little or no affirmative action to redress existing imbalances, and there was no enforcement machinery. Over the next decade, employer latitude in each instance was substantially reduced through subsequent legislation and court interpretation.

Title VII of the 1964 Civil Rights Act extended nondiscrimination provisions to all employers and established the Equal Employment Opportunity Commission (EEOC) with a limited mandate to conciliate employee grievances, take the employer to court if necessary, and formulate and issue guidelines for the enactment of Title VII. In 1965 the Office of Federal Contract Compliance (OFCC) was established in the Department of Labor by Executive Order 11246 which amended the earlier order so as to require government contractors to take affirmative action. Moreover, OFCC was given authority to inspect company records and, in the event of noncompliance, to cancel, suspend, or terminate government contracts. As OFCC delegated its compliance review duties to other government agencies, the number of on-site inspections began to increase, though few contracts were actually terminated.

In 1970 the requirement that each location with over 50 employees have formal affirmative action programs was imposed, again by Executive Order, and in December 1971, the order was amended to include the underutilization of women as well as minorities. Guidelines were also specified for use in determining whether underutilization existed, and affirmative action had come to encompass the establishment of goals and timetables to correct identifiable deficiencies. The goals were to be "significant, measurable, and attainable." Care was taken to state that goals were not firm quotas which had to be met, but rather were "targets reasonably attainable by means of employing every good faith effort to make all aspects of the entire affirmative action program work."

Meanwhile, the courts were steadily narrowing the exceptions for special occupational qualifications, particularly those which

resulted in sex-specific jobs. In another instance, the Labor
Department moved against a long-standing seniority system at a
Bethlehem Steel facility because it fostered discrimination. Finally,
in 1973, EEOC was granted authority to initiate suits in federal
courts. While there were differences of opinion about the avowed
intent of the Nixon administration to maintain the momentum
behind equal employment, the government organizations responsible for enforcement were remarkably successful in increasing their
budgets while other social agencies suffered cutbacks.[4]

Achieving equality of opportunity is in many respects a more
difficult problem than curbing pollution, for it involves attitudes
and prejudices as well as money and technical skills. Nonetheless,
though the issue may yield more grudgingly to pressure for reform,
the pattern of evolution bears a marked similarity. The manager is
again confronted by (a) a time span of a decade or more during
which the issue took hold; (b) a high degree of uncertainty regarding ultimate standards and enforcement; and (c) a task which
requires the continuing development of skills and the integration of
these skills into the decision processes in the corporation.

Corporate Choice

The environmental analysis developed in the preceding pages
permits the choices available to the large corporation to be stated
quite precisely. Fundamentally, the manager responsible for setting
policy in areas of public concern, often the chief executive, has to
decide what the corporation's position is to be relative to emerging
social demands. The available options may be stated in terms of the
degree of lead or lag in responsiveness with respect to social expectations. The choice may not be made explicitly, particularly where
there is a predilection to withhold response until discretion no
longer exists. Moreover, the decision may vary from issue to issue
within the same corporation, as subsequent chapters indicate.
Choice cannot be avoided, however; the dynamics of environmental
change force it on the manager whether or not he recognizes the
implications of his stance at the time.

Although choice as it has been specified here appears to be simple
in concept, a closer examination reveals that complex judgments
are required to unravel the implications of a decision to lead or lag
in response to social demands. For instance, by electing to respond

early, the manager accepts the burden of acting under conditions of greater uncertainty as to the eventual dimensions of the issue and the appropriate means for dealing with it than would be the case should he delay. In addition, he absorbs whatever cost may be involved at a time when they appear to be more nearly voluntary in the minds of investors and coworkers. In return, he protects to some extent the flexibility to set policy without undue outside interference. He may also have the hope of benefits that will ultimately outweigh any immediate penalties. Such assessments are not made and acted upon without corporate and personal risk.

At this point an important qualification must be broached: the limits to corporate discretion. Public policy or social pressure will in time impel response from corporate laggards. But what constrains the decision to lead?

It was at one time appropriate to contend that shareholders would object to expenditures that did not contribute in some fairly direct way to economic performance. However, since the classic Berle and Means study in 1932[5] the thesis has gained credence that stockholders exert little influence over the conduct of professional managers hired to direct large corporations. There are, of course, some important caveats to this argument which involve the growth of financial institutions in the equity markets,[6] the possibility of unsolicited tender offers, and the like. Nevertheless, there has been little indication of stockholder displeasure or even interest in corporate social policy.[7] Indeed, such advocacy as there has been has existed on the side of greater social involvement. Although perhaps not with the same confidence, most chief executives would probably agree with the chairman of Xerox when he stated: "If we ran this business Wall Street's way, we'd run it into the ground. . . We're in this business for a hell of a long time and we're not going to try to maximize earnings over the short run."[8]

A more cogent argument is that competition limits the extent of discretionary expenditures. Despite the dim view of marketplace vitality held by Galbraith and others,[9] one would normally expect competitive activity to be sufficient to exact a penalty from those who indulge in a significantly higher level of nonproductive expenditures than others in the same industry. With average pre-tax profit margins of 8 to 10 percent on sales among U.S. corporations, there is comparatively little room for charity. Looked at another way, executives express grave concern at the possibility of discriminatory treatment in the application of regulations. If all choose or are required to meet the same standards, it is probable, barring unaffected interindustry or foreign competition, that the costs of compliance can be passed on to the consumer in the form of higher prices.

Yet, within the relatively narrow bounds of corporate choice postulated here, the market does not appear to be sufficiently exacting to force conformity in social responsiveness. Although not abundant, there is enough evidence of distinctly different patterns of responsiveness to an important social issue among corporations in the same industry to support this contention. For instance, a study of pollution control in the paper industry revealed wide variations in the level of effluent treatment.[10] Moreover, there was a suggestion that the companies which exhibited the best ecological record were also the most profitable.[11] The results are particularly interesting because the paper industry has suffered from periodic overcapacity and low profits and is relatively unconcentrated. Other studies have shown comparable variations among steel companies[12] and public utilities[13] in pollution control, coal companies in mine safety,[14] and drug companies in a variety of social concerns.[15]

The influence of the market or the financial condition of a company cannot be disregarded as limitations to managerial discretion. Clearly, the dominant company in a stable oligopoly is more likely to have time and money available for minority training programs and consumer affairs than the weak company in a declining industry. Competitive considerations, however, are only one among a number of elements influencing corporate choice, and in many instances may not be a particularly significant one at that.

Conclusion

Social responsiveness entails the management of discretion. The corporation has the opportunity of setting policy to govern its relationship to emerging social expectations. Choice, though fleeting and bounded, is obligatory. Between the formulation of policy and changes in performance, however, is the organization, the mediating element that must be applied to the implementation of corporate choice. This dimension must now be explored further.

The purpose of the next chapter is to develop the organizational implications of social responsiveness in the divisionalized corporation. As we shall see, the administrative characteristics of these firms suggest a number of dilemmas that complicate the implementation of socially responsive policies.

IV
Organization Barriers to Social Responsiveness

In the fall of 1970, the newly created Environmental Protection Agency (EPA) made headlines across the country by its actions against a Union Carbide plant in Marietta, Ohio. The following vignette, describing these events, is not intended to single out that company for criticism. It is important to recall that in those months of rapid transition in both public attitudes and government regulations many companies were in similar predicaments. Union Carbide happened to be an inviting target for EPA's first assault on a large industrial polluter. The case is in a sense a period piece; it is unlikely that the company would handle the situation in the same way at the present time. But this transitional quality is precisely why the case is useful as a backdrop against which to identify the management dilemmas for large corporations in responding to social demands.

UNION CARBIDE'S MARIETTA PLANT[1]

THE SOCIAL DEMAND

In December 1970, William Ruckelshaus, who the previous month had been appointed head of the new Environmental Protection Agency (EPA), rejected a Union Carbide proposal for sulfur dioxide emission abatement at its ferro-alloy plant in Marietta, Ohio, and ordered an immediate 40 percent reduction in emissions and a 70 percent reduction by April 1972. The EPA timetable was similar to one recommended by the National Air Pollution Control Administration (NAPCA) in April 1970 to which the company had responded with the counter offer rejected by EPA.

The Marietta plant, built in 1951, had first been pinpointed as a major polluter by NAPCA in a 1967 abatement conference held in Vienna, West Virginia, directly across the Ohio River. According to published commentaries, NAPCA officials from 1967 to 1969 were unable to obtain complete data on emissions from local company management and, at one point, federal inspectors were barred from the plant. A second abatement conference was called in October 1969 which Carbide officials did not attend. EPA entered the picture amidst a public outcry in Vienna.

In January 1971, Carbide announced that it could meet the immediate 40 percent reduction requirement by switching to low-sulfur coal. To achieve the remaining 30 percent reduction, the company would invest $8 million in scrubbers to be operational in 1974. Until the scrubbers were installed, coal costs which then represented $4.5 million, or about 20 percent of annual production expenses, would increase 50 percent. From April 1972 until the scrubbers were ready, the company said that a portion of the plant would have to be shut down, resulting in a layoff of 125 workers (out of 625). Later it agreed to "explore" ways of avoiding the layoff.

THE CORPORATE SETTING

In 1970, Union Carbide had sales of $3 billion and after-tax profits of $157 million. Since 1965, sales had increased 30 percent, profits had decreased 34 percent, and return on equity had dropped from 16 percent to 9 percent. Declining margins were attributed largely to overcapacity and price erosion in several of the company's major product areas. 1970 revenue and contribution by product group were as follows:

	Revenue	Contribution
	%	%
Chemicals and plastics	40	16
Gas, metals, carbons and material systems	38	52
Consumer and related products	22	32

The company had four domestic product groups, sixteen operating divisions, and many plants, including eight in the West Virginia-Ohio area. Included on the corporate staff since August 1970 was a director of environmental affairs who reported to an administrative vice president. Capital expenditures in 1970 were $394 million, of which pollution control projects in the United States and Puerto Rico accounted for approximately $20 million.

The Problem in Management Terms

The Union Carbide case may appear to be unusual, but in fact it is not. Comparable, though less dramatic, situations involving the same or different issues in other corporations could be cited at length. Common to this and other episodes like it are three factors which create organizational problems for individual managers as well as the corporation as a whole. The first was touched on in the previous chapter: the corporation is confronted by a rapidly changing and uncertain social and regulatory climate. When the Marietta plant was constructed, Union Carbide had reason to think the investment was serving a current (and at the time popular) social need by creating jobs in a depressed area. Nearly two decades later, an effective attack on the plant was mounted by citizens in another state on grounds that had until recently not been taken seriously: the political climate was unpredictable and threatening. From the plant manager's perspective, an unpleasant harassment had turned into a matter of survival.

The second factor is that difficult judgments are required to determine how best to respond to a problem as it unfolds. To make matters worse, since the issue is often a new one for the managers involved, relevant data are probably hard to come by, even assuming the right questions are asked. Financial and technical implications may be extremely difficult to assess. The Marietta plant was a relatively old and probably high-cost operation. Loading it with pollution control equipment and more expensive fuel must certainly have raised questions about its capacity to remain competitive in the ferro-alloy markets. On a larger scale, Union Carbide had been suffering for a decade from overcapacity and declining margins in its chemical businesses. The prospect of making nonproductive investments and incurring additional operating expenses could hardly have been greeted with enthusiasm. On the other hand and in retrospect, the heavy-handed settlement meted out by EPA and the spate of unfavorable publicity was a stiff price to pay for delaying until public pressure forced a response. The balance between serving economic and social goals is not an easy one to strike, despite the talk of long-term profitability depending on the satisfaction of both.

The third consideration is that these judgments are not made by a single individual but are spread among numerous organization levels, each with its own perspective on the problem and stakes in the outcome. As the saying goes, "Where you stand depends on where you sit." The plant manager and the president of Union Carbide were both involved in the events culminating in the Marietta incident. By virtue of differing tasks and responsibilities, their concerns about environmental protection were likely to be different. Between them were several additional layers of general management and associated staff functions. The difficulty of communicating policy and eliciting consistent judgments in such a setup is immense.

Responding effectively to new social demands is certain to prove challenging for any large-scale organization. Insensitivity to rapidly changing conditions is a frequently noted phenomenon among both private and public institutions. The reasons are not difficult to find. Responsiveness entails interjecting new considerations into the decision processes. There is, however, a strong tendency for organizations to be guided by generally accepted policies (or standard operating procedures) which have been successful in solving apparently similar problems in the past.[2] This tendency is not irrational; it has the virtues of promoting efficiency in analysis and consistency in response. Nonetheless, such virtues are also the symptoms of a malaise that obstructs innovative responses to changing conditions. Had the 1967 abatement conference in Vienna been recognized by Union Carbide as significant, the events three years later might well have turned out quite differently.

For the divisionalized corporation, social responsiveness poses particularly acute problems. Ironically, these corporations have in general pursued a strategy and developed administrative practices which have enabled them on balance to achieve above-average performance measured in terms of growth and profitability. The dilemmas, which are rooted in the organization, are important to understand, for they raise some basic questions about the management of our largest and progressively dominant economic institutions.

The Design of the Divisionalized Organization

A series of events at duPont and General Motors in the early 1920s, largely unappreciated at the time even by the participants, heralded a significant transformation in the organization structure observed today in most large U.S. corporations. DuPont, suffering from the loss of its market for gunpowder, turned to diversification, first as a means of employing excess capacity and later as an avenue for growth. The tasks of managing new businesses were added to a functional organization with strong central direction in which department heads for sales, purchasing, development, production, and engineering reported through the chairman of the executive committee to the president. The company soon was experiencing losses, particularly in its diversified ventures.

General Motors was also having difficulties, though for very different reasons. William Durant had pieced together a vast enterprise in the automobile business but never had much interest in coordinating or controlling its many parts. Quite the reverse of duPont, General Motors operated with autonomous divisions but little concept of a general office. The sharp recession of 1920 proved to be Durant's undoing; overspending for plant and equipment and an accumulating inventory in the face of a collapse in the automobile market led to a financial crisis.

Despite differing histories and operating problems, the response in both companies was the adoption of a similar divisionalized organization structure. Alfred Chandler, in his book *Strategy and Structure,* described the development of this innovation and its subsequent proliferation in other large corporations.[3] Stripped to its barest essentials, the new structure meant (a) the formation of divisions, each encompassing a discrete segment of the corporation's activities, usually based on product line though occasionally also on geographical area; (b) the redefinition of the role of the central office; (c) the development of systems for communicating with and maintaining control over the divisions; and (d) the formalization of procedures for evaluating and rewarding executives.

A simplified view of the divisionalized organization is provided in Figure IV-1. In some companies one or two levels of general management may be inserted between the president's office and the division manager, and in others there may be some interdependencies among divisions involving product flow, shared facilities, or pooled functions. The tenor of the relationships between headquarters and the divisions may also differ, especially with regard to the amount of delegated authority. Yet the pattern of organizational change is unmistakable. The four characteristics of the divisionalized structure noted in the previous paragraph are of importance to this research and bear a few words of elaboration.

Management at the Division Level

The middle-level general manager is granted substantial autonomy in the direction of his business. He is held accountable for responding to environmental and competitive threats and opportunities and is expected to direct and coordinate the operating functions involved in the development, production, and sale of goods and services. He typically plays the key role in formulating a strategy for his division's business and securing resources from the corporation in support of that strategy.[4]

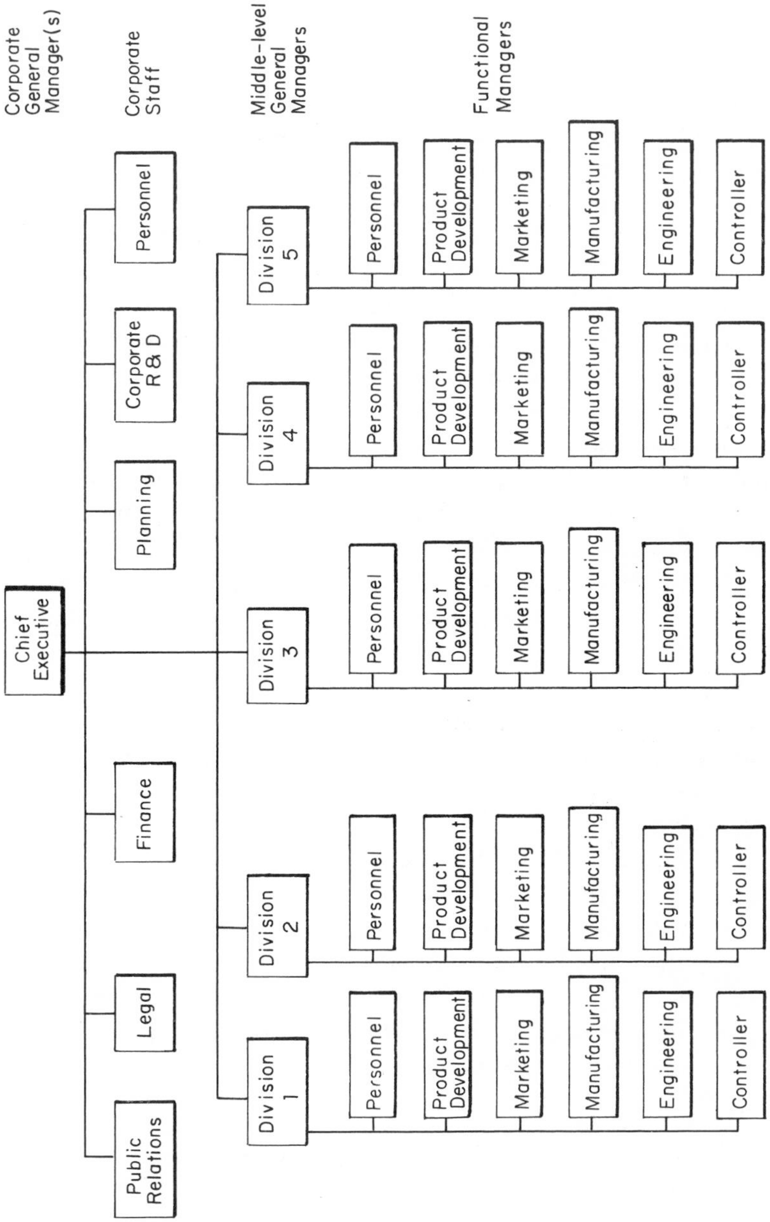
Corporate General Manager(s)
Corporate Staff
Middle-level General Managers
Functional Managers
Chief Executive
Public Relations
Legal
Finance
Planning
Corporate R & D
Personnel
Division 1
Division 2
Division 3
Division 4
Division 5
Personnel
Product Development
Marketing
Manufacturing
Engineering
Controller
Personnel
Product Development
Marketing
Manufacturing
Engineering
Controller
Personnel
Product Development
Marketing
Manufacturing
Engineering
Controller
Personnel
Product Development
Marketing
Manufacturing
Engineering
Controller
Personnel
Product Development
Marketing
Manufacturing
Engineering
Controller

Management at the Corporate Level

General managers at the corporate level[5] have little direct involvement in the operating affairs of the divisions. This does not mean that they are unaware of what is going on in the business or are unable to influence strategic decisions at division levels. However, the diversity of technologies, products, and markets in most large corporations creates an order of complexity that is not easily managed by one individual with staff support or a management committee.[6] Consequently, there is a reasonably clear separation of tasks between corporate and division managers. The former are concerned with the entry and withdrawal from businesses, the allocation of resources among divisions, the establishment of performance targets, and the maintenance of policies and processes within which division managers operate. They are also responsible for responding to external factors affecting the corporation as a whole; its relationship with stockholders, financial institutions, government, and the like.

Also at the corporate level are staff managers who typically perform two types of services. Some, such as the treasurer and legal and public relations personnel, support the chief executive in external affairs. Others, such as the controller and functional specialists in personnel, marketing, and research, elicit information, provide assistance, and seek to police the execution of corporate policy in the operating divisions. Depending largely on the degree of autonomy accorded middle-level general managers, the corporate staff may have more or less influence. For instance, the scope of activities performed by the staff has been found to vary widely between the "free form" conglomerates that rose to prominence in the late 1960s and the older, diversified corporations.[7] The minimal headquarters involvement in division affairs among the conglomerates extended the duPont-General Motors innovation to an extreme from which most now seem to be retreating.

Financial Planning and Control Systems

Coincident with the delegation of product-market responsibilities to division managers was the institution of financial budgeting and control systems and some years later the development of longer-range planning. Alfred Sloan, the architect of the General Motors reorganization, commented on the role of financial controls.

It was on the financial side that the last necessary key to decentralization with coordinated control was found. That key, in principle, was the concept that, if we had the means to review and judge the effectiveness of operations, we could safely leave the prosecution of those operations to the men in charge of them. The means as it turned out was a method of financial control which converted the broad principle of return on investment into one of the important working instruments for measuring the operations of the divisions.[8]

Financial budgeting and control systems have become essential to the management of the divisionalized corporation. The operating divisions are accounted for as profit centers, a device that in some instances may be extended to individual plants or product lines within the division as well. The control system provides information that is relatively easy to understand and can be presented in comparable terms for all units year after year. Accounting reports are not immune to misinterpretation but they relieve the reviewer of the need to sift through and comprehend operating data from diverse businesses. Ironically, but perhaps inevitably, as large corporations become more complex, the gauges used to control them become simpler. Moreover, financial controls provide the type of information corporate-level managers need to guide the allocation of resources and construct corporate profit and cash flow forecasts.

Most important, financial controls are result-oriented. They monitor the actual and expected outcomes and not the process used to secure them. This characteristic tends to reinforce the delegation of responsibility to operating levels. It becomes possible for a president to negotiate "bottom line" commitments with his division managers and then rely on them to meet their targets. In the case of poor performance against plan, the president or his staff may intervene. However, managing by exception implies that those divisions which are performing satisfactorily can expect little corporate interference. Thus, financial controls tend to promote an interesting bargain; the division manager commits to results in return for the expectation of autonomy. He does not, of course, make the commitment alone. Before doing so, he extracts from his subordinates concurrence that they will assume responsibility for their part of the plan.

Management Appraisal and Reward Process

With a reasonably clear delineation of responsibilities and an objective means of monitoring results, the next logical step in designing the divisionalized structure was to relate executive appraisals to the performance reflected in the financial control system. With varying degrees of formality this process has become a characteristic of the divisionalized corporation.[9] A manager's "track record"—that is, his demonstrated ability to deliver on financial commitments, is an important credential when he requests funds for a major project or is considered for a promotion. Moreover, in recent years, incentive compensation plans through which bonuses or stock options are directly related to success in meeting targets have become commonplace.

Of course, there is much that remains subjective in decisions affecting a manager's career: luck, personality, background and judgment, to name a few. It would also be naive to think that his motivation for working is limited to a desire for the rewards he may obtain by meeting budgets (or the fear of punishment should he fail to do so).

Yet ambition is served by achievement, and for upwardly motivated managers the processes that shape careers are consequently powerful tools for securing desired behavior. If the rewards are high and the measurements frequent, as they tend to be in the large corporation, middle-level general managers and their subordinates are encouraged to pay close attention to the near-term profitability of their units, be it a whole division or a single plant. The further tendency for managers to experience relatively short tenures in each assignment reinforces their efforts to meet the current budget, even though it may mean sacrifices in potential future benefits from the unit.

The Spread of the Decentralized Organization

The organization form sketched above was implemented by only a few corporations in the 1920s. The Depression then forced a contraction in industrial organizations in the next decade and postponed the adoption of what seemed to be a more expensive and perhaps risky structure. The war years afforded little time for experimentation with organization design. Consequently, it was not until the decades following World War II that the divisionalized structure gained widespread use.

Recent studies show that by the late 1960s the divisionalized structure had replaced the functional organization as the dominant organization form in the United States. Richard Rumelt, building on earlier research by Chandler,[10] Bruce Scott,[11] and Leonard Wrigley,[12] found that the estimated proportion of divisionalized firms represented in the *Fortune* 500 industrials had grown enormously from 1950 to 1969, as shown in Table IV-1. In addition, he found that divisionalized firms were, on the average, more profitable and enjoyed more rapid growth than those having other structures. He also confirmed the fact that large corporations had become progressively more diversified during the two decades covered by his study and, quite naturally, the more diversified the enterprise, the more likely it was to be organized by product divisions.

The attractiveness of the divisionalized organization form has been even broader than is suggested by the studies noted above. First, it is rapidly gaining acceptance in Europe as large corporations there extend the diversity of their activities and are subjected to greater competition in the marketplace.[14] Scott argues more generally that "the divisional structure appears to be the most effective way to manage the strategy of diversification under highly competitive conditions."[15] Second, large nondiversified corporations have also adopted the trappings of the divisionalized structure. For

Table IV-1[13]

Organizational structure	Estimated percentage of companies		
	1949	1959	1969
Functional	62.7	36.3	11.2
Functional with subsidiaries	13.4	12.6	9.4
Product division	19.8	47.6	75.5
Geographic division	.4	2.1	1.5
Holding company	3.7	1.4	2.4
TOTAL	100.0	100.0	100.0

instance, divisions have been established in vertically integrated paper companies to manage the various stages in the product flow (timberlands, pulp and paper-making, and finished products), each treated as a profit center with one division selling some or all of its output to the next in the conversion cycle. Although strategic business decisions such as when and where to build a $200 million pulp mill may continue to be made at the corporate level, these large, single-industry firms have attempted to secure the organizational benefits perceived to exist in the divisionalized structure.[16]

Management Dilemmas

Ironically, the strengths of the divisionalized structure which have permitted diversified corporations to manage competitive conditions effectively are the sources of difficulty in the response to social demands. The dilemmas suggested by the coincidence of social demands and this organization structure are three in number:

(1) Social demands subvert corporate-division relationships.

(2) Financial control systems are ineffective in explaining and evaluating social responsiveness.

(3) The process for evaluating and rewarding managers is not designed to recognize performance in areas of social concern.

It is important to recall, as these dilemmas are elaborated, that they occur as social phenomena pass through the *zone of discretion* for corporate choice.

Corporate Division Relationships

Managers in the operating divisions clearly bear a heavy responsibility for accommodating social demands in such a way that they do not weaken the division's competitive posture. For the general manager overseeing the ferro-alloys business at Union Carbide, controlling pollution not only meant higher costs, but engineering and factory management time taken from other projects. Had the issue been a new technology for metals-processing introduced by a competitor or unexpected overcapacity in the industry, he would have been held accountable for figuring out what to do and then petitioning the corporation for the necessary resources or arguing that his budgeted profit was no longer supportable.

The responsibility for accommodating social demands, however, often does not remain neatly with the operating manager. There is a strong tendency for corporate executives by choice or necessity to intervene. Although the triggers provoking top management intervention are varied, they tend to stem from two generic roots.

First, social demands typically have implications for the entire corporation, or at least numerous parts of it, and not just for a single operating division. For instance, solid-waste disposal is a general concern for the diversified packaging company which manufactures metal, plastic, and paper containers. A position taken on recycling by the plastics unit might prove detrimental to the corporation as a whole. Similarly, Union Carbide had eight plants in the vicinity of Marietta, Ohio, not all from the same division, but each with its own environmental impact. Employment matters, too, are very clearly of corporate-wide significance. The chief executive may also deliberately intervene because he has concluded that the corporation should attempt to lead social expectations on some issue. Hence, it may become apparent to him that responsiveness to the issue calls for an inclusive and systematically enforced policy.

Second, through ignorance or insight, social critics interpret the chief executive's position to mean that he is in fact the person to execute decisions in conformity with their wishes. They do not recognize the careful distinction drawn between corporate and division responsibilities. Richard Simpson, chairman of the Consumer Product Safety Commission put it this way: "If a company violates our statute, we will not concern ourselves with its middle-level executives; we will put the chief executive in jail. Once we do put a top executive behind bars, I am sure that we will have a much tighter degree of compliance from other companies."[17] Some demands are included in the proxy statement or presented orally at the annual stockholders' meeting over which the chief executive presides. Others are voiced in the press or at business or social gatherings or by his children home from college on vacation; or consumer and environmental groups, out of frustration with the treatment accorded them by operating managers, may petition the chief executive directly.

The first dilemma arises, then, because responsibilities are ambiguous. If the chief executive attempts to reduce this uncer-

tainty by relying on the customary ground rules governing his relationships with the operating divisions, thereby minimizing the
incidence of intervention, it is probable that social responsiveness
will lag. At the least, there will be no coordinated response. The
division managers have made commitments to short-term financial
targets and are likely to take a dim view of spending their time and
money on activities which for the moment appear to be discretionary. Of course, the harder the chief executive drives his division
managers in budget negotiations to accept "tough but achievable"
goals, and the harsher the view he takes of their not being met, the
stronger his subordinates' impulse will be to sacrifice social responsiveness.

On the other hand, if the chief executive takes a strong hand in
implementation beyond merely issuing a policy statement, he may
indeed secure greater responsiveness but at the expense of increased
organizational ambiguities. By assuming some of the responsibility
for accommodating social issues, he may diminish the extent to
which he can hold the divisions accountable for achieving agreed-
upon financial results. For instance, centralizing judgments on
pollution control expenditures means for the division managers a
partial loss of control over the investments made in their units. Since
added expenses, and very possibly operating schedules and yields
are involved, the question will sooner or later arise, from whose
budget are these penalties to be paid? It may seem equitable to let
those who make the judgments bear the burden of proving that the
money was well spent. But then who is to determine how if at all, the
expense is to be recovered in the marketplace? A marketing decision
may be required having to do with pricing or product policy which
should logically be made by division management. A web of mixed
responsibilities may be woven between corporate and division
managers concerning matters that had previously been delegated. If
repeated in response to several social issues — for example, an advertising review office, centralized minority hiring at exempt levels,
and so forth — the cumulative effect would be a withdrawal from the
current design of the divisionalized organization. For general
managers at both corporate and division levels, that would in all
likelihood be an unwelcome outcome.

Ineffective Financial Controls
Resolving the first dilemma would be simplified considerably if it

were possible to integrate the financial implications of socially responsive policies with the budgeting and control system. Unfortunately, this has not been feasible, at least so far.

The difficulty lies in systematically measuring social costs and benefits. To be sure, a portion of the costs can be accounted for rather easily. Capital spending for pollution control equipment or expenditures for special minority training or work safety programs can be readily isolated and dealt with through special appropriations. But even in these simple examples, determining the effect on operating costs—yields, productivity, and the like—is far more complicated. The measurement problems are enormous if one considers such actions as withdrawing allegedly deceptive advertising campaigns or adding safety features on the product line. In these instances the second-order effects on market position become a relevant cost (or benefit) as well. With great effort and liberal interpretation one might compile an ad hoc estimate of "true costs" in special situations, but even that is a long way from systematic and reliable reporting.

Determining costs is an easy matter compared to assessing the benefits of social responsiveness to the firm. The statement is often heard that long-term profitability, if not the survival of the corporation as we know it, ultimately depends on its ability to relate successfully to its many constituencies. Leaving aside the question of benefits to society, there is presumably some advantage accruing to the corporation for its efforts. To make judgments tied to long-range profitability, the manager should know what such advantages are. Conceptually, the measurement problem is exceedingly complex; practicably, it is probably impossible, and even if it were possible, would be prohibitively expensive.

What is the value to the corporation of, for instance, reducing noxious emissions into the atmosphere below the levels required by current law? There may be some fairly direct benefits in a rosier public image, a better bargaining position with government regulators seeking compliance at other plants, pride among managers that "we're one of the good guys," an attractive posture for recruiting on campus, a jump on meeting future regulations at today's prices; if good fortune abounds, perhaps even a process innovation that will increase yields. The list could be extended indefinitely. But what are these benefits worth? From the accountant's point of view, they have the unfortunate characteristics of being largely intangible, unassignable to the costs or organizational units creating them and occurring over an undeterminable future time period.

This is not to imply that social measurement of any sort is impossible. Bauer and Fenn have traced the promising, though limited, beginnings of social auditing. After examining the state of the art, however, they contend that efforts at measurement may best be devoted to a process audit which reflects what was done rather than a performance audit which attempts to demonstrate how well it was done. They comment that "the notion that somehow social performance will be integrated with financial performance envisions that a baby which has not yet started to crawl will someday run."[18]

In one sense the financial reporting system is irrelevant while a social demand is evolving. The division profit-and-loss statement has no easily discernible relationship to the extent of discriminatory employment practices, deceptive packaging, and so forth. Nor can it serve as an early warning device to spot future difficulties or reflect progress in managing those encountered in the past.

In a second sense, the financial reporting system may actually inhibit social responsiveness. By focusing on economic performance, even with appropriate safeguards to protect against sacrificing long-term benefits, such a system directs energy and resources to achieving results measured in financial terms. It is the only game in town, so to speak, at least the only one with an official scorecard. To illustrate how absorbing it can be, a regional general manager in one company had been granted a $5,000 allotment for community action. In the press of meeting a stiff budget, neither he nor his staff had taken time to spend it until a particularly vexing minority relations problem called it to their attention.

If attention is to be secured for addressing social demands, some credible means of measuring progress appears necessary. It is certainly possible to devise systematic reporting for some issues, and numerous companies have done so. Moreover a plethora of reports are prescribed by regulatory agencies. For instance, there are

> —work force analyses, isolating the proportion of
>   women and minorities in various job categories;
> —accident reports;
> —noise-level surveys;
> —air and water emission level reports;

—end-user product safety surveys; and

—customer complaint surveys.

Two problems are immediately encountered with reports of this nature. First, while suggestive, they afford only a limited assessment of the corporation's position. That is, employee demographics cannot adequately measure equality of career opportunity. They are helpful but not conclusive or incontrovertible. Second, and more important, reporting of this type is ordinarily no match for the sophistication of the accounting system, which has been fine-tuned through repeated use in securing resources, negotiating performance targets, and evaluating results.

Herein lies the second dilemma. Relentless pressure for growth exerted on the organization through the financial reporting system diminishes the prospects for aggressive responses to social pressures at operating levels. If responsiveness is desired without creating this pressure, corporate managers might well find that they are in the position of making the judgments on implementation themselves. Such an outcome is equivalent to the chief executive telling his operating managers: "You are to make as much profit as you can, and we'll take care of the social consequences." In theory, this position is not as absurd as it might seem at first. It rests on the premise that what cannot be measured in financial terms should not be delegated. Going one step further, it suggests that the sensibilities necessary to make complicated and largely subjective judgments on discretionary expenditures cannot be adequately communicated, and hence should be made only under the direct supervision of top management. In practice, however, it is unlikely that centralized control over the details of implementing responses to social demands would be viewed as either feasible or desirable.

Executive Evaluation and Rewards

The third dilemma is in large part a consequence of the first two. The evaluation of managers and the distribution of rewards is a vital part of managing any organization. In the large corporation the task is both large and complex because of the numbers involved. For instance, a company with ten divisions and sales of $1.5 billion may have 75,000 employees of whom 4,500 are in exempt positions. Of this latter group, 750 may be classified as managers. Clearly the job of guiding that many careers cannot be done effectively by a single individual or department. Consequently, to provide a degree of predictability and equity for the employee, a process of some kind evolves, some of it codified (as with incentive bonus plans) but much of it embedded in the folklore of the company.

In the divisionalized firm, designing and maintaining this process is a critical corporate-level responsibility.[19] Through it the chief executive is able to influence indirectly the allocation of resources within the operating divisions and to encourage or discourage various kinds of behavior. Thus, if the risk-takers are conspicuously reprimanded when they fail, and if budget attainers are consistently rewarded, managers soon recognize that the best alternative (for them) in a decision situation is the one which contributes most certainly to meeting plan. They calibrate their careers with the decisions they make.

I have said earlier that the evaluation and reward process for middle-level managers has been simplified considerably in the divisionalized firm by (a) reasonably clear delineations of responsibility and (b) a dominant, well-understood, and relatively unambiguous measure of performance. Now, however, both these conditions have been challenged by social demands. With this background, the third dilemma becomes apparent.

Only recently has performance measurement been recognized explicitly as a factor influencing corporate responsiveness to social issues.[20] If managers feel that the process governing their careers does not include rewards for this sort of activity, they are unlikely to give it much attention (unless of course they are personally inclined to take the risk of doing so). There are numerous accounts of unresponsiveness that can be explained in large part by this phenomenon.[21] However, to say the process should be revised is far easier than determining what the revision should be or how it should be administered.

Determining and communicating performance expectations is complicated by the difficulties in measurement described earlier. In a changing and uncertain environment, standards that are both indicative of performance and amenable to systematic reporting are not easily established. The chief executive's simple exhortation to his division managers to "operate within the law" is not particularly helpful if the intent is to encourage them to anticipate future and as yet ill-defined social demands. The chief executive's reasoning is similar when he talks of anticipating competitive conditions, but in this instance, there are reasonably objective and generally understood standards to guide his evaluation.

Therefore, to the extent the chief executive is concerned about creatively accommodating social demands but cannot (or will not) articulate objective and measurable performance 'expectations, he will, perforce, have to rely on his own judgment of how effectively his subordinates are managing social responsiveness. To a far greater extent than with other matters he will have to assess the process for obtaining results and not simply the results themselves. Herein lie two further barriers to responsiveness in the divisionalized firm.

First top management will have to penetrate further into the hurly-burly of decisions at operating levels than it has had to do in the past. The lack of clarity in assignment of responsibilities complicates both the analysis and the evaluation. Given the time and cost of obtaining and sifting through the data necessary to make dispassionate judgments, the tendency may exist to limit the exercise to instances of conspicuous failure, which would be neither systematic nor equitable. The manager unfortunate enough to be caught in a predicament of this sort might well feel unfairly treated relative to a colleague suspected of having an equally dismal but uncontested and unresearched record. Thus, to obtain a reasonable picture of how the Marietta plant incident occurred, one would have to understand the involvement of managers at perhaps half-a-dozen levels in the organization.

Second, such an approach to evaluation and rewards will be relatively more subjective than is striven for in the large corporation. The personal inclinations of the evaluator are almost certain to play a part in judging the response of others to social issues. If the chief executive is firmly committed to the advancement of minorities, he may distribute rewards to those who hold or adopt his view and punishments to those who do not. One would expect this to occur in small or even large functionalized organizations which tend to exhibit closer interpersonal relationships between the chief executive and key line managers and less formal bases for management evaluation. But the presumed efficiency of the divisionalized organization has rested in part on its official amorality,[22] evaluation is

related to results measured in terms which have no ethical intent.*
The encroachment of values upon performance measurement may
be good or bad (depending on how one views the values in question);
in any event, it would represent a reversal of direction for the
divisionalized firm.

Conclusion

The reader may feel at this point that divisionalized firms have
been dealt with too harshly and without recognition of the very
substantial differences among them. For instance, it is abundantly
clear that the remaining large single-industry corporations, and certainly many smaller ones, having functional or highly interrelated
organization structures also have problems adapting to social
demands. Responsiveness may be more or less difficult to achieve in
these firms (though the problems encountered in doing so may be
different). Similarly, there are obvious and substantial variations in
diversification and operating unit autonomy among divisionalized
firms. Top management involvement in strategic operating decisions in corporations with a dominant product-market thrust such
as IBM or Xerox is clearly more intense than in equally large firms
with a greater industrial base such as Westinghouse or General
Electric. Attitudes toward social issues may, of course, also vary
enormously among executive groups.

The intent of this inquiry, however, is not to test the proposition
that diversified firms are more or less adaptable than others to social
change. Rather it is to diagnose the sources of resistance found in an
organization form that has rapidly come to dominate the management of the large economic enterprise in the United States. If the
diagnosis is accurate, the divisionalized structure, and more importantly the management processes that accompany it, have certain
characteristics that tend to inhibit social responsiveness. The barriers are generic. They are not insurmountable, nor are they set at
the same height in all firms. In the next chapter the pattern observed
for overcoming them is explored.

---

*It should be emphasized that amorality is not intended to mean that individuals
are necessarily amoral. In fact, if the manager is evaluated solely on the economic
results achieved by his business, he can express and act on his own values without
fear of internal reprisal.

V
The Process of
Corporate Responsiveness

The response to a social issue changes dramatically in the corporation with time. Adaptation is forced by increasing top management expectations and a progressively more exacting environment; old accommodations are found wanting in the face of escalating demands, and new ones are developed to take their place. As the organization struggles to adapt, learning takes place. Corporate responsiveness is evolutionary and not ad hoc as it might seem from accounts in the popular press. The evolution may not even be appreciated by managers caught up in the events of the moment for it is neither mechanistic nor placid. It pulses with their experiences and is at times laced with conflict and crises. The drama is acted out under stressful and ambiguous conditions that produce personal as well as organizational strain.

In observing these machinations at close range over a period of time, I have consistently discerned a pattern in the behavior of corporations that have enjoyed some success in meeting social demands. The pattern was not the result of forethought on the firm's part; rather it emerged sometimes hesitantly, sometimes abruptly, over a number of years and often in response to trauma or frustration. I also began to see that, in the course of defining and implementing social policy, managers of numerous corporations encountered similar difficulties related to the organizational barriers described earlier and were led to contemplate broadly similar remedies.

These findings have significance for two reasons. First, they suggest that the response to social demands may be more susceptible to analysis than has heretofore been recognized. Thus far corporate behavior in this area has typically been treated at one of two extremes: as conspicuous, unrelated actions or as generalized attributions supported by aggregate economic or social indicators. Moreover, there has been a tendency to describe *what* the firm has done and not on *how* it arrives at the decisions that result in these outcomes. The latter emphasis is more likely to be useful for manager and researcher alike, for focusing on how the large corporation works permits what it does to be interpreted and not simply recounted. Second, if a recurring pattern can be identified and analyzed, it can also be consciously managed. If the critical decisions and the order of their appearance can be predicted with reasonable accuracy beforehand, managers may be more successful in coping with environmental uncertainties. By devoting attention to improving the management of the process, corporate responsiveness may be obtained with greater speed and effectiveness and with fewer unpleasant organizational side effects.

Phases and Transitions

As the corporation has been characterized in earlier chapters, three generic questions await management attention as it contemplates the response to social demands.

> *Policy:* What position should the corporation adopt with regard to a social demand? Specifically, should it attempt to lead social expectations?

> *Learning*: What has to be understood about the social demand, the alternatives available for responding to it, and the economic and organizational implications of implementation?

> *Commitment*: How is the organization to be applied to implementation in the face of dilemmas in locating responsibility, controlling and measuring performance, and evaluating managers?

In the course of responding to social demands, answers of one kind or another are found to each of these questions. The problems underlying them are not all readily visible — or at least not perceived as urgent — at the outset. They tend to arise sequentially over a period of years as the social issue and management's attitude toward it matures. In fact, the response process passes through three distinct phases, each devoted in large measure to a single question, ordered in the sequence presented above. The phases are marked by comparative stability in the approach taken to meet the social demand. To be sure, traces of more than one phase may be visible simultaneously (for instance, policy continues to require definition long after the basic choice of positioning has been made), and some divisions may exhibit more advanced behavior than others. The distinctions are sufficiently sharp, however, that at any point a corporation may be placed in a single phase* or in transition to a later phase.

The transitions are a second, and in some respects more important, part of the process. The complexity of the implementation job is underscored by the tendency on the part of managers to accept the first two phases in turn as the last. However, under pressure, both exhibit flaws which suggest further problems in adaptation. As a result, a time of instability ensues during which new accommodations are worked out that enable implementation to move forward. Typically, one or a series of incidents bring matters to a head. In at least some organizations such incidents provoke a crisis and, like all crises, each has its unique antecedents and consequences. Yet there is a pattern in the way these episodes are handled which differentiate them from others that may have appeared in substance to be similar. The transition from the second to the third phase is particularly significant and difficult, for it is during this period that the organizational barriers to responsiveness are frontally assaulted.

There is, then, an adaptive process which describes how policy on a social issue is defined and implemented. It evolves through phases as the issue passes through its zone of discretion as Figure V-1 suggests.

The social response process is described in general terms in the remainder of this chapter. It has been developed on the basis of observations by members of a research team at the Harvard Business School in over twenty-five corporations and supported by discussions with representatives from several dozen other firms.** The next four chapters then enrich this rather sparse account by documenting the experiences of two firms that have been successful in implementing social policy.

---

*The distinctions among phases are likely to be more sharply drawn in firms that are leading social expectations than in those which lag, a tendency that has interesting implications to be discussed in Chapter X.

**A summary of the research program and the methodology underlying these findings is included in the preface.

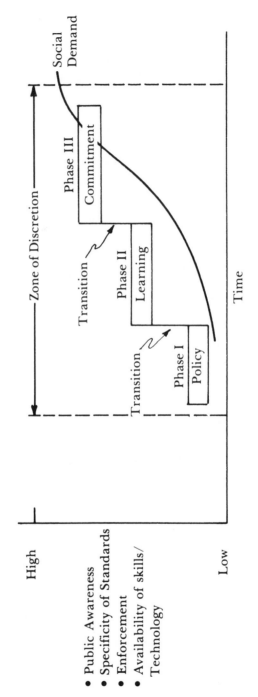

Figure V-1
Patterns of Corporate Responsiveness

Phase I

In the history of a corporation's response to a social issue, a period could normally be identified that marked the issue's emergence as a top management concern. During this time the chief executive made the critical judgment that the firm's posture on the issue deserved his personal attention. Without his willingness to be assertive, the probability of early action on a corporate-wide basis appeared to be practically nil.

How a chief executive made this judgment varied enormously from case to case. In broad terms, he probably became convinced that the issue was important to society and ultimately to the company and he may have been sympathetic to its intent. The stimuli prompting this conclusion tended to differ from those influencing decisions that affected the conduct of operating divisions.

In the first place, the chief executive's personal assessment of the environment often loomed large in a decision to devote time and resources to exploring involvement. He may have been appalled by decay in the inner city surrounding the corporate headquarters or alarmed by mounting support for ecology. In one case the chief executive of a large food processor was shaken by criticism that had been leveled at his company by the press and at annual meetings concerning nutrition and food additives. Such reactions were seldom accidental or impersonal. They could often be traced to some earlier experience that aroused his interest and enabled him to interpret and give meaning to an evolving issue. In some instances, a sensitivity to urban problems appeared to grow out of the chief executive's long-standing participation in civic affairs. In others, an appreciation for the public resentment caused by pollution could be traced to earlier experiences in factory management.

Second, analysis of the potential impact of the social demand on the operating divisions was generally skimpy at best. The chief executive may have asked his staff to draw up a position paper or research studies prepared by outside agencies. However, seldom was the corporation's vulnerability specifically and systematically analyzed. The paucity of staff work should hardly be surprising. Indeed, at this stage in the evolution of the social issue, very little could be stated with confidence. The eventual standards and the dimensions of the call on corporate resources were largely conjectural. Though it may seem archaic today, equal employment in

1962 as a practical matter meant entry level jobs for minorities, not vice presidencies for both minorities and women.

Thus, the chief executive accepted the responsibility for formulating social policy without benefit of the detailed feasibility studies which generally accompany major changes in product-market policy. Under these circumstances, he quite naturally related to the environmental conditions as he encountered them from a corporate perspective, conditions which overlapped, yet were distinctly different from those relevant to his division managers and their staffs. In particular, how the chief executive conceived of the company's obligations to society and his affinity for the particular issue at hand were critical determinants in the emergence of a corporate policy.

Although policy was formed at the top, the chief executive was rarely alone in expressing an interest in the issue. He could usually count on finding support (as well as apathy or opposition) in the organization. In some instances, these pre-existing attitudes and activities had a direct bearing on the timing and content of the policy. Thus the chief executive in one of the later case studies felt the need to provide visible support to his staff by commiting his thoughts to writing. He had little choice but to deal with the issue in its historical organizational context.

A cursory review of the corporation's posture may also reveal wide variations in philosophy and practice among the operating divisions. For instance, Dow Chemical has major producing groups in Michigan and the Southwest. For a variety of reasons, including the limited absorption capacity of the Tittabawassee River on which its facilities are situated, the Michigan-based division has historically been an industry leader in controlling pollution. Until recently, however, far less attention was given to the matter in the Southwest facilities. In another case, the chief executive of a diversified corporation set out to reassess the company's position on a number of social issues. He found that the Defense Systems Division had taken a more aggressive role in minority hiring, purchasing from minority vendors, community affairs, and the like, than the other industrial products divisions. Managers in the company attributed the disparity in part to business-related factors (government contractors are required to be more sensitive to such issues) and in part to individual and group interests (the systems people were younger, more experimentally inclined, and interested in public issues).

The subject may also have been broached in the past, but beaten down because it failed to gain top-level support or was raised before the intensity of public expectations rendered it credible. For example, in the mid 1950s a second-echelon manager in the corporate personnel office of a large firm was among several who became interested in eliminating barriers to the employment of blacks in jobs that by custom had been closed to them. With the tacit support of the vice president of personnel, he composed a policy statement to that effect which was duly approved by the management committee (composed of division and senior staff managers) and signed by the president. When practices remained unchanged after a year, he wrote a comprehensive report for the committee on how the policy might be implemented. The report was returned with the comment, which remained clear in his mind seventeen years later, "I know this will break your heart, but I'm not passing your report on. You might get branded as a troublemaker." Two years later he revised the document and resubmitted it; this time it was returned without comment. Then, in another three years a new president, within weeks of assuming office, was among the original signatories to Plans for Progress, a voluntary government program to promote jobs for minorities. In a heated debate with the management committee beforehand, the president was finally provoked to say, as one manager recalled it, "*I'm* going to sign and *you're* going to live with it."

In my observation, policy did not emerge full-blown with the chief executive's first serious look at the issue. Rather, it grew over time as the result of an amalgamation of corporate-level activities, at times complemented and sustained by continued progress in operating units that were already sensitive to the issue. Frequently the chief executive or one of his immediate staff instigated or volunteered for panels and commissions that inevitably accompany the maturation of a social demand. The topic began to receive mention in speeches made by senior managers at the Rotary Club and was included in the company's newspaper. In a more substantive way, the corporation sometimes contributed manpower and money to research projects sponsored by universities and industry associations that delved into pollution control technology, for instance, or recycling, or the impact of advertising on children. In scores of firms participation was approved in government-initiated programs such as the National Alliance of Businessmen.

Such activities created relatively few organizational difficulties.

Managers may have been assigned to outside agencies or set up with their own office and with funds allocated from the corporate kitty, but they were typically supervised apart from the operating units. For the most part they were volunteers who had a personal interest in the matters at hand. Reaction in the field usually ranged from mild approval to disinterest or, as one middle manager, put it: "If I ever get to be where he [the chief executive] is, I guess I'd do the same thing."

Such expressions of corporate interest had an important cumulative impact. To the independent observer, the chief executive had expressed the intention of his company to act aggressively, though he may not have said just how. For example, because of the initial fanfare associated with its Bedford-Stuyvesant connection cable plant and the venture's apparent success, IBM added to the expectations outsiders and minority employees held for equal opportunity throughout the company. Although perhaps not intended, corporate pronouncements constituted an implied commitment that begged for affirmation in practice. They also created the risk, borne first by the chief executive, that the company would be found wanting in the fulfillment of those expectations. In a real sense, these early statements contributed to the pressure encountered later at operating levels. A vivid illustration of this phenomenon occurred during the protest at Polaroid over the firm's business in South Africa in 1970; the egalitarian values expressed by Polaroid's chairman and president, Dr. Edwin O. Land, were compared unfavorably by the protestors to reality as they understood it.

To the operating manager, corporate involvement tended to produce an awareness that the social issue was to be treated with care. Naturally, skepticism about the chief executive's resolve was also noticeable in some quarters. Managers could be found asking one another, "Did he mean what he said about equal employment"—or was it done because, as one public affairs officer commented, "I told him he had to"? Equivocation was readily detected in an offhand remark or a casual ordering of priorities. On the other hand, if consistently expressed over a period of time, the chief executive's interests gradually came to constitute a corporate position even though it was often not codified as such. Thus, policy was fashioned primarily from corporate-level perceptions and, as it evolved, the implied commitment to future results increased.

At some time during these formative years, the chief executive's attention, which was generally drawn initially to the social demand "out there," turned to the performance of the operating divisions. In the case of one food services firm, top management became curious about the implications of several social demands for its widespread distribution network. To its surprise, pollution and solid wastes turned out to be important trouble spots. In another instance a chief executive became concerned that the intent of his speeches on equal employment was not reflected in the conduct of the business. His attention was drawn by several episodes in the company that filtered up to his office. In these and other instances, the policy was gradually extended to encompass internal as well as external affairs.

A variety of approaches was attempted to secure the cooperation of operating managers. A policy statement was sometimes disseminated and followed by hard-line speeches about the importance of considering the social demand in business decisions. On one occasion a chief executive questioned whether product safety had been considered in the proposal for a new line, a question that had not been asked before and for which the operating managers had no ready answers. However, almost invariably, responsibility for implementing the corporate policy was lodged explicitly with operating managers as part of their normal assignment.

The chief executive's appeal for more vigorous response to the social demand was largely unsuccessful. Those divisions that had historically been sensitive to it continued their efforts, but the remainder seldom budged. The reasons for inaction fell into four categories, generally all of them visible to some degree.

1. Public expectations, although mounting, were not viewed in the organization as an immediate concern. There were no credible government enforcement powers and, if pressure groups existed, their demands were at the time perceived as outrageous. There was no pressing reason, from the operating manager's vantage point, to accord the social policy a higher priority. In essence, the profits he could expect from his unit were unlikely to be adversely affected in the short run by ignoring the social demand.

2. The corporation's social policy was sufficiently general as not to constitute much more than an evidence of concern. There were no specific standards or even precedents that could be used as benchmarks. There was also little systematic reporting that would uncover trouble spots (assuming one knew the right information to collect). As a result, corporate level managers had little to analyze, and operating managers had nothing tangible to perform against.

3. The division managers maintained that they did not have the skills or the staff to specify and implement their own course of action. Probably none of their subordinates had a background in the specialties required, and all were occupied with their normal assignments in any case. The immediate penalty for taking the corporate policy to heart was the cost of adding a new manager or displacing other work that was already spoken for in the business plan.

4. There was little incentive for attempting to interpret and implement the corporate policy. The only incentive was a negative one—stay out of trouble. But trouble often appeared to be more a matter of bad luck than systematic malpractice. Furthermore, the commitments negotiated with corporate management concerning financial performance remained in force. The rewards for meeting these commitments were reasonably well understood.

Therefore, the corporate social policy was weighed by the organization against the dangers of unresponsiveness as seen from a very different perspective and against other corporate expectations, and was on balance found wanting. The chief executive's response to this impasse heralded the coming of the second phase of the process.

Phase II

The transition to the second phase was marked by the addition of specialists to the corporate staff, generally at the behest of the chief executive. The problem was redefined as a technical one that could be attacked by isolating it and applying specialized skills and knowledge to its resolution. Justification for appointing a specialist from the chief executive's viewpoint was abundant. He typically felt someone was needed to (a) give emphasis and direction to the social policy; (b) interpret social demands and develop a corporate position on them; (c) add requisite skills to the organization; (d) coordinate the response of operating units; and (e) assist senior officers in the performance of their external duties.

The specialist's job was virtually certain to be ill-defined at the outset. In fact, the transition from Phase I to Phase II was devoted to assimilating and defining the specialist's function and, in the process, testing the mandate he had been given to disturb the status quo. His role in the organization was materially influenced by decisions made at the outset regarding the criteria for his selection, where he was to report, and what relationship he was to have with the chief executive. A moment's reflection on the alternatives available for each of these choices reveals the subtleties of designing a new function to facilitate response to uncertain demands.

An array of titles has been added to the corporate lexicon in the past decade: director, manager or vice president of consumer affairs, environmental protection, minority relations, urban or community affairs, public affairs, and so forth. The first incumbents were often hired specifically for the job and had considerable relevant experience through government or activist involvement. However, managers with this background had the difficult task of learning how to get along in an unfamiliar organization which, fairly or otherwise, often had them "typed" as proponents of the social issue who probably were fundamentally antibusiness. Conversely, they may have been selected from within the company and have had little detailed understanding of the social issue. Sometimes they were long-service employees nearing retirement, and in other cases younger managers anxious about the career implications of accepting the position. In any event, the appointment carried with it a variety of expectations and personal relationships that aided or impeded the acceptance of the new function.

The specialist may have been placed in an existing corporate staff group or set up in a separate office reporting independently to the chief executive or another of the senior officers. For example, pollution control was assigned to central engineering and minority affairs to corporate personnel in one company, while in another a new department was created to serve these needs. In the latter instance, the specialist was instructed to engage a number of issues, with the intention of making him a sort of multidisciplinary social watchdog. A new department tended to provide greater leverage for the chief executive and more visibility and emphasis for the issue. However, the increased emphasis available through this arrangement often contributed to conflict with the managers of established staff units, who felt their territory had been encroached upon. On the other hand, a decision to attach the specialist to an existing staff group raised the further question, which one? Distinctly different patterns of response to ecological demands are likely if the specialist is part of the engineering staff rather than assigned to public relations.

Finally, the chief executive had the responsibility for specifying the relationship between his office and the specialist. The options ranged from close personal adviser to seldom seen staff functionary. In the former case, the specialist often garnered considerable influence through the visible manifestations of this relationship, to the point that others in the organization felt he spoke the chief executive's mind on matters related to the social policy. It was probable, however, that the more the specialist was viewed as a top management stand-in, the more wary (if not hostile) his relationship was with the operating managers he was supposed to assist. At the other extreme, without tangible support from the chief executive, the specialist was dismissed by these same managers as a gadfly without portfolio.

No dominant pattern was found in the resolution of these issues, a conclusion generally confirmed in a variety of surveys conducted on such corporate staff positions in the past several years.[1] Where implementation of social policy was relatively successful, however, I found the chief executive favoring a balanced course. That is, firebrand activists and corporate "has-beens" were avoided in filling the position, and the specialist was provided with sufficient position and personal backing to force the organization to take notice, but not so much that resentment became unbearable. Managers with experience in line functions in the company and with recognized career aspirations seemed to be most effective in executing the specialist's role in the implementation of social policy. Nevertheless, seating this new manager effectively required considerable sensitivity to organizational acceptance and was likely to involve a period of questioning and adjustment.

The corporate response during this second phase bore the mark of the specialist. Whether assigned by the chief executive, solicited by operating managers, or initiated independently, activities for a time tended to flow through the specialist's office. In a real sense, he was an agent of change through whom the organization learned to adapt to the social demand. A number of activities were commonly observed. For example, the specialist was obliged to secure an understanding of the external forces behind the growing severity of the issue. He surveyed current legislative requirements and projected them into the future. He sought out regulators, activists, and independent experts to assess the items on their agendas and the likely form pressure would take. He began to inquire into alternative remedies and test their appropriateness for the firm. For instance, the environmental affairs director almost certainly examined various abatement technologies that held promise for controlling emissions on the production processes employed in the company. As he went about this analysis, the specialist assembled a network of contacts that were useful both in maintaining surveillance on the issue and fashioning responses to it.

The specialist also turned his attention inward in an effort to determine where the corporation might be vulnerable to attack. In effect, he embarked on a crude social audit, though it was not always labeled as such. The audit was sometimes conducted internally by nosing around the company or through a more elaborate request for documentation.[2] In theory, the question posed was straightforward: what is the status of the operating units on the social issue (or possibly several issues)? Experience with this first attempt however, particularly if it was a full-blown audit, was typically unsettling and only marginally useful. Part of the difficulty lay in the audit format itself. Unless the information requested was specifically keyed to reports that had been required previously (such as accident records for miners), the data were probably not readily available. Often they were buried in the files or not collected at all.

Moreover, efforts to measure the implementation of social policy were likely to raise organizational hackles. Interstaff conflict sometimes resulted if the specialist attempted to elicit information independently of normal reporting channels or requested more detailed information via the normal channels. In one firm the corporate personnel department was openly hostile to a public affairs department request issued to division personnel managers for employee demographics and policies. More significantly, the audit was almost always resisted by division level managers. Apart from the time and cost of gathering the data, these managers may have suspected that, without forewarning, the results would be used for evaluation purposes as well as information. The whole exercise smacked of staff harassment. Quite naturally, the divisions objected to reporting data that could be viewed critically at the corporate level. Bauer has recounted several instances in which resistance from this quarter has stopped the audit dead in the water.[3]

Thus, a major challenge that the specialist had to surmount early in his tenure was gaining access to his own organization. Support from the chief executive was a double-edged sword in this regard — it was vital yet burdensome. For a time implementation of the social policy appeared to hinge on the acceptance of the new function. In some cases the corporation's initiative was lost at this point either because top management resolve faded in the face of organizational opposition or the specialist decided, after several rebuffs, to assume a less aggressive posture. Continued forward motion appeared to be conditional on the combination of a specialist who was politically sensitive and able to relate quickly to division concerns and a chief executive who was prepared to insist on obtaining results.

As the specialist analyzed the information secured from the divisions, the rudiments of a measurement system began to emerge. Eventually, agreements were worked out specifying the types of primary records to be kept and the form in which results were to be presented. Content was continually adapted to changes in policy and regulation, which were evolving concurrently. One of the significant tasks performed by the specialist was the transformation of the basis of measurement from the ad hoc scrutiny of isolated malfunction to a systematic reporting scheme. In essence, he attempted to design a scorecard for the organization. Edwin Murray has referred to this as "administrative learning," which he distinguished from the "technical learning" required to obtain a grasp of the alternatives available for satisfying a social demand.[4]

The specialist also became embroiled in specific operating problems — negotiating compliance with government agencies, mediating employee grievances, and so forth. He was expected to participate in resolving such controversies, especially if they involved legal or regulatory action. Presumably he was equipped with the contacts and knowledge needed to help operating managers out of a jam. Recognizing the importance attached to the issue by the chief executive, these managers rested more comfortably having the corporate "expert" on the scene if there was a possibility that the matter might get out of hand. From time to time, curiosity or concern also prompted senior executives to dispatch the specialist without invitation. Although his intervention appeared to be necessary, it was at times painful; by rushing to fill a void in capability, he created ambiguities and friction in the organization that ultimately forced the reaction which spawned Phase III.

The specialist often won acclaim as a fire-fighter. However, as he attempted to secure more fundamental changes at operating levels in the conditions that contributed, for instance, to charges of discrimination or citations for pollution, he tended to encounter two disquieting reactions.

First, he was often simply ignored. The divisions frequently saw no need to include him in the decision process that shaped future conditions, such as the design of a major production facility in the case of environmental control. Or if the specialist proposed actions that appeared to be unavoidable or had no adverse effect on the division's budget, division management was inclined to stand aside and let him take the credit (or blame) for the results. Corporate-funded minority awareness programs and technical studies were typically accorded this treatment. The prognosis for effective utilization of the specialist's work without division involvement was not particularly good.

Second, he encountered opposition. As corrective measures, the specialist frequently recommended programs that would commit the divisions to increased near-term expenditures or fundamental changes in work force or operating procedures. Such recommendations were regularly set aside for "further study" or flatly rejected. The chief executive found himself in a difficult position if the specialist chose to contest the matter; he had to decide whether to support a general manager with profit responsibility (and probably a history of sound judgments) or a new and narrowly focused staff manager. Tradition favored the former and the specialist was often unwilling to test it.

When direct intervention proved ineffective, the specialist sometimes tried a second tack. He attempted to convert into a measurement device the information system used initially to report status. Thus, in one case a specialist sought to incorporate data on minorities and women in the human resources plan so that the plan could be used to set targets and evaluate performance. His reasoning was clear enough; if performance could be captured in the system, he might be successful in forcing the operating units to accept commitments for more aggressive action. However, the appeal to systems proved frustrating at this point. The scheme lacked credibility at operating levels; the reports themselves were attacked on technical grounds, and, more significantly, performance was considered incidental to the over-all rating for the unit. Furthermore, the specialist did not have the power to force negotiations and elicit meaningful commitments. Consequently, although he was successful in obtaining goals for the next year from division personnel managers, the data were never used. Meanwhile, top management's demands for financial results continued unabated by the existence of the social demand.

In summary, the social issue specialists battled the sources of inaction evident at the end of Phase I. In doing so, they added substantive understanding, systems, and a degree of professionalism that were heretofore lacking. They were, however, largely unsuccessful in prompting changes in the standard operating procedures that governed how division-level managers made decisions impinging on the social demand. An impasse had again been reached. The build-up of corporate staff competence created an unstable condition that was exacerbated by the organizational dilemmas confronting the divisionalized corporation.

Phase III

The third phase was characterized by yet another redefinition of the impediment to responsiveness. No longer could middle managers point to the lack of policy direction or the absence of skills to apply to implementation. While far from exhaustive, sufficient effort had been devoted to these areas to justify action at operating levels. Rather than a problem for specialists to segregate and resolve apart from the main-line activities of the divisions, responsiveness in the third phase was conceived as a general management concern that required integration into ongoing business decisions. The question was posed: How can commitment for implementation be secured at middle management levels?

Acting on this redefinition of the problem, chief executives were observed to contemplate further modifications in the way responsiveness was managed, now directed squarely at the organizational dilemmas raised in the previous chapter. A pattern emerged in which:

- —responsibility was firmly lodged with operating managers;
- —the information system, with all of its inadequacies, was accepted as a basis for performance measurement;
- —rewards and sanctions for responsiveness to the issue were related to performance and incorporated in some fashion into the process of management evaluation.

The problem need not have been solved in this way. For instance, it was conceivable that the impasse described earlier could have been surmounted by granting the specialist authority to design programs and to impel their execution under the chief executive's supervision. The existing mechanism for measuring division performance and evaluating middle-level managers might then have been left intact (with suitable allowance for whatever dislocations might be brought about by the specialist's initiatives). However, that alternative was consistently avoided. The chief executives of the firms studied ultimately chose to reaffirm division management's responsibility for all aspects of operations, even though it meant added complexities for the managers involved and increased ambiguity in the way their performance was assessed at the corporate level.

The transition from Phase II to Phase III tended to be traumatic. Although the chief executive may have announced his intentions beforehand, the new pattern of response typically emerged after one or more episodes which provided the impetus for change. The episodes centered on specific incidents, often far down in the organization, that were set off by social demands; a pollution complaint, an employee discrimination charge, and so on. The incidents did not necessarily involve significant expenditures, nor where they unusual except insofar as they came to the attention of top management. Trauma resulted not from the problem posed by the incident itself but from the organizational dynamics through which the problem was resolved.

The episodes were characterized by top management intervention. Corporate executives challenged the approach taken to an incident and evidenced a willingness to wrestle with the substantive issues themselves. For a time the normal corporate-division relationship was suspended as they delved into areas that were customarily delegated. The episodes were inherently chaotic (imagine seven levels of management, from the president to a first-line supervisor, located in four cities attempting to coordinate response to a delicate employee controversy), and were not always handled effectively. They proved to be unsettling for the operating managers involved, particularly because their judgment was held up for scrutiny and visibly challenged. Although corporate executives probably did not fully recognize the implications of their actions at the time, they communicated a number of messages through their intervention:

The importance of the social policy was graphically reinforced.

Implementing the policy was very clearly labeled as a division management responsibility that could not be dumped in the specialist's lap once crises arose.

In the course of intervening, corporate executives provided some important clues to the new operating procedures that were to be enforced in the divisions.

Corporate executives evidenced an intent to evaluate division managers and their subordinates in part by their handling of responses to the social issue.

The episodes introduced strain and instability which division management sought to ameliorate. Who, for instance, was in fact responsible for managing the incorporation of social policy in the activities of the business? Division managers now felt compelled to assume that burden. At least, they surmised, the likelihood of future corporate intervention would be diminished if they could present a convincing picture of constructive involvement. In a more positive vein, they also concluded that since the chief executive appeared determined to proceed with implementation, the prospects for doing so with minimum disruption to the operations of the business were brightest if division management were in charge.

Moreover, as the social demands matured, the time frame for mandatory response more nearly fitted with the divisions' planning horizon. Division managers were now often intent on acquiring the skills necessary to direct future activities from within their units. Although the corporate specialists continued to be keyed into major developments and were called upon in specific instances, their active participation in division affairs was generally sharply curtailed. Adding specialists to the division stafff presented relatively few difficulties. They were more readily available by this time (environmental control engineers were far more numerous in 1975 than in 1966), had a more specific function to perform, and reported to managers who were directly responsible for implementing their programs.

Resistance to measurement also tended to crumble. The corporate specialists' earlier attempt to construct a measurement system were now more likely to be condoned because they served division as well as corporate needs. Chief executives had a natural interest in monitoring the execution of the social policy. With responsibilities clarified, they were now in a position to insist on targeted levels of performance against which results could be evaluated. By the same token, division managers also tended to see the familiar budgeting and reporting format as preferable to the ad hoc surveillance that had existed previously. To the extent that expectations could be agreed upon and reflected in a report, uncertainties about evaluation were reduced. Moreover, such a scorecard permitted the division manager to elicit commitments from his subordinates and hold them accountable for achievement.

As the divisions worked through these realignments, the pattern of response to the social issue changed. The characteristics of this new pattern were likely to include the following elements:

A concern for the social demand was incorporated in business decisions at the division level with an eye to meeting corporate expectations for excellence; e.g., the new mill, as a matter of course, was designed to include the latest available control technology, though the law at the time might not yet require it.

Response became anticipatory; it was included in division business plans in the form of functional programs; e.g., management training, customer service programs, ombudsmen, the addition of staff capability, and anticipated resource needs such as funds for pollution control equipment.

Supplementary reporting systems and auditing practices tended to proliferate at division levels as managers attempted to acquire information that was specifically relevant to identifying problems and monitoring performance in their businesses.

The corporate role changed. The specialist concentrated less on initiating response and more on managing the reporting system and analyzing division programs. The chief executive became involved in division programs having corporate-wide policy implications (an employee council, for instance, may raise union questions) but otherwise tended to place emphasis on reviewing division plans and evaluating results.

Criteria used in performance evaluation at division levels began to incorporate responsiveness to the social demand. The formality with thich this was done varied widely, but the effects were similar; the division manager's subordinates became aware that the matter was of some personal significance.

In essence, the social demand had now been phrased in such a way that division managers handled it as they did changing competitive conditions. Response was triggered by the concerns of functional managers, who felt the weight of direct responsibility. Middle-level general managers negotiated expectations with corporate management and lent their personal influence to requests for resources or permission to institute special programs. The decision process fitted progressively closely into the established pattern of corporate-division relationships. The strengths of the divisionalized organization were ultimately applied to social responsiveness rather than being subverted by it.

Thus, operating managers assumed responsibility for producing results that met both economic and social objectives. At least for a while, they lived with parallel information systems and had to perform the mental calculus which calibrated with varying degrees of accuracy the relative importance of performance measured on multiple bases. The price paid for their involvement accrued through increased job complexity and possibly distaste for being required to deal with problems that were viewed as unpleasant or unrelated to professional aspirations.

Conclusion

The process of corporate responsiveness is summarized in Table V-1. The reader will have an opportunity to test its usefulness in the case studies contained in the next four chapters. As the response to a social issue becomes a matter of routine, a final rather mild transition to a fourth phase may ensue. It is probable that eventually the measurement system and the associated link to performance appraisal will be found superfluous and eventually discarded. The reason lies not in the fact that continued action on the issue is unnecessary, but rather that the process for responding to it has been so institutionalized that separate accounting has little usefulness. One should not assume from this prediction that middle managers will again find their task simplified, for it is also likely that they will encounter other issues which are then in formative stages but are moving through a similar sequence.

Table V-1

Conversion of social responsiveness from policy to action

	Phases of organizational involvement		
Organization level	Phase 1	Phase 2	Phase 3
Chief executive	Issue: Policy problem	Obtain knowledge	Obtain organizational commitment
	Action: Define and communicate corporate position	Add social issue specialists	Change performance expectations
	Outcome: Enriched purpose, increased awareness		
Social issue specialists		Issue: Technical problem	Provoke response from operating units
		Action: Design data system and interpret environment	Apply data system to performance measurement
		Outcome: Technical and administrative skills acquired	

continued

Table V-1 (cont.)
Conversion of social responsiveness from policy to action

Division management	Issue:	Management problem
	Action:	Commit resources and modify procedures
	Outcome:	Increased responsiveness

VI

The Response to Ecological Demands: Weston Industries

Weston Industries was a large manufacturing company with sales of approximately $2 billion. From a single industry base in the early 1950s the company had diversified by acquiring a number of businesses in related fields. By 1973 there were nine product divisions, divided into two product groups, and an international division. Altogether, Weston operated more than one hundred manufacturing facilities domestically and over two dozen overseas. Although Division #1, the "founding" unit, continued to account for 45 percent of sales, its growth and profitability had lagged behind the newer divisions as intense competitive pressures cut into its margins and market share.

The company had achieved annual increases in sales and earnings per share averaging about 10 percent and 6.5 percent respectively in the decade preceding the research. Emphasis had been placed on identifying and pursuing new opportunities for long-term growth during the early and middle 1960s. Heavy investments were made in physical facilities and research during this period, requiring large infusions of capital that were secured in part through a fourfold increase in long-term debt. In 1969 a change in focus became apparent to operating managers. Corporate management began to stress the conservation of resources and the attainment of near-term financial results. The divisions were told that capital expenditures for normal expansion were to be limited to internally generated cash flow. Fiscal stringency was introduced just as major investments in pollution control equipment became a concern for numerous divisions.

It was customary for top management to have long tenure with the company. In fact, promotion from within for all executive positions was a policy that only rarely was breached. Because of its relative size, Division #1 had served as a spawning ground for future managers in earlier years and to a lesser extent in 1973. A promising executive, once at the level of a plant or sales branch manager, could expect frequent transfers among functions and operating units and occasionally between these units and the corporate staff in the course of a career. Consequently, division managers were likely to have had a variety of job experiences including in some cases the management of other divisions.

Operating performance was guided by a comprehensive budget for the upcoming year and a broader plan for the ensuing four years. The targeted results in the budget were the subject of active negotiations during the fall months between corporate and division managers. Incentive compensation for the top executives was decided on an individual basis by the chairman and president. However, to cover the next 800 managers, a bonus pool was established for each division, its size related in part to corporate and in part to division performance against budget.

Development of the Corporate "Policy on Pollution"

In August 1966, Willard Britton, then president, signed the corporate "Policy on Pollution" reproduced in Exhibit VI-1 (see p. 86). The event was unusual in Weston. As one of his close advisers noted, "Britton dislikes policy statements. He has to feel very strongly about something before he will issue one. In fact, there have been only two others since he became president in 1961." One of the other policies, incidentally, related to equal employment. Britton had been among the original signatories to Plans for Progress and devoted considerable effort to promoting opportunities for minorities in both industry and the community.

The "Policy on Pollution" was issued toward the end of a period of organizational transition. A divisionalized structure had evolved during the late 1950s as the company diversified. Not until Britton became president, however, were concerted efforts made to disengage the corporate offices from the affairs of the original business and to press toward a uniform decentralization of operating responsibilities at division levels. A number of organizational and personnel changes occurred from 1962 to 1964 that placed general managers further down in the hierarchy; for instance, Division #1 was divided into four regions, each having a general manager. As a result, the corporate staff had become increasingly engaged in reviewing plans rather than initiating them.

The policy appeared to have its roots in a concern for community relations rather than ecology. A dictum of long standing in the company held that its reputation in the community had an important

EXHIBIT VI-1

WESTON MANUFACTURING COMPANY
INTRA-COMPANY CORRESPONDENCE

Attention of: Members of the Planning Committee
Subject: POLICY ON POLLUTION

Weston Manufacturing Company as a nationwide manufacturer of packaging and consumer products, recognizes the responsibility of maintaining facilities that are assets to the communities in which we are located.

In this regard, we attach the same importance to air and water pollution abatement that we attach to quality, safety, fire prevention, and operating efficiencies.

In constructing new facilities, we will, within the bounds of technical and economic feasability, provide the best pollution control equipment available to meet or exceed community criteria.

We will also review the performance of existing facilities to determine whether we are complying with pollution criteria, and will, where needed, and within the bounds of technical and economic feasibility, effect improvements to bring these operations to an acceptable level of performance in a reasonable time.

Weston Manufacturing Company will support and wherever desirable, help to establish, reasonable and effective criteria and the legislation required to enforce such criteria.

In general, Weston Manufacturing Company expects to provide its own pollution abatement measures, but since many of these problems are best solved by measures jointly taken by society as a whole, Weston will in appropriate instances support public measures for control of pollution.

[Signed] W. Britton

bearing on the success of its operations. Many of Weston's plants were large employers in small towns and consequently were heavily dependent on local government and townspeople for services and work force. Plant managers had traditionally been encouraged to take part in community affairs and given recognition for their activities. Britton had been thoroughly exposed to this philosophy and convinced of its merits during assignments in manufacturing early in his career. Extending it to encompass the physical appearance of the plant and the effect of operations on air and water seemed to him to be entirely natural.

The formality and timing of the policy statement were prompted by immediate business and organizational needs. Two specific developments in 1966 had influenced Britton in the months preceding the announcement. The first involved a major new facility in Division #2, the second largest division in the company and the one having the most severe environmental impact. The project, budgeted at over $80 million, was the first significant expansion in the division since it had been acquired by Weston in 1956. Two years prior to the acquisition, however, a similar, though smaller, complex had been constructed which incorporated a number of major, and at the time controversial, innovations in water pollution control. The engineer responsible for designing the earlier facility had since retired but his chief assistant, William Fredericks, was managing the construction of the new plant in 1966.

Fredericks had become convinced that his old mentor was correct in insisting on advanced pollution control technology on a later assignment as manager of an old plant that was to be put up for sale. Because of air contamination, the plant and others nearby were the subjects of intense public displeasure, which resulted in lawsuits and angry newspaper reports. Fredericks found the experience to be personally distasteful. Consequently, in 1964, when he was asked to coordinate the design and then manage the new facility, he sought approval for effluent control systems that in his view were sufficient to meet all foreseeable environmental demands. Although these systems added nearly $4 million to the cost, division management agreed to support him.

In 1966, the Division #2 project appeared headed for a $10 million cost overrun. One of the responses to the overrun suggested by business analysts in the division was a cutback in pollution control facilities. Fredericks fought for the controls, going so far as to say, "You take them out, and I'll leave as project manager." He eventually convinced Robert Rushmore, then General Manager of the Primary Operations Department, and John Franklin, then Division Manager, that it was better to spend the money as planned rather than wait for public complaint to force a less acceptable solution on the company later on.* The impressions retained from these deliberations were to have a wider impact on Weston in the future; Franklin became president two years later and Rushmore manager of the large Division #1 in 1972.

Britton was aware of both the pollution control program and the cost overrun. In review meetings he concurred with the decision to retain the effluent control equipment. As the largest single capital project in the company's history, it called for his attention in other ways as well. For instance, in January 1966 he delivered a speech to the Chamber of Commerce of the county in which the facility was being constructed. He pledged on numerous counts Weston's commitment to environmental protection. The content of that speech closely paralleled the policy statement issued seven months later.

The second development involved Walter Harris, Vice President and Director of Corporate Engineering. In early 1965, as Congress debated the Water Quality Act and amendments to the Clean Air Act, Harris began to feel that pollution abatement would soon be an important issue for Weston. He went to the Technical Planning Committee, composed of division technical directors and certain corporate executives, including Britton, with a proposal that an ad hoc committee be formed to monitor regulatory developments and act as a liaison with the operating divisions on ecological matters. Britton approved the idea, and a committee was appointed headed by the Corporate Director of Environmental Hygiene** and including Harris and a representative from each operating division.

With the passage of new environmental legislation in the fall of 1965, Harris felt that an ad hoc committee was insufficient. Conse-

---

*In 1975 the plant was considered to be a model in the industry from the standpoint of both pollution control and operating efficiency.

**Environmental hygiene at Weston referred to work safety and employee health matters and covered the effects of noise, heat, dust and other potentially hazardous working conditions.

quently, he again approached the Technical Planning Committee, this time with the proposal that a separate activity devoted to air and water pollution control be established in Corporate Engineering under his direct supervision. The idea was accepted, and early in the next year Harris asked William West, a metallurgical engineer with ten years' experience in the company, to take on this responsibility. West was then in an engineering section devoted primarily to advanced design and process development work geared toward Division #1. He had no direct experience in the pollution control field.

West began to familiarize himself with pollution control technology and existing regulations. He also attempted to survey the status of the company's activities in these areas by visiting plants and talking with engineering managers in the operating units. Very quickly he discovered that Division #2 had been incorporating environmental concerns in its planning for some time, chiefly because of Fredericks, and had developed a sophisticated technical capability in the field. The remainder of the company, on the other hand, was reacting to crises on an "emergency basis" as they came along.

West encountered difficulty in securing the attention of managers in the divisions; enacted regulations at the time were minimal, and few managers viewed the prospect as particularly significant. Moreover, the divisions were used to requesting answers to specific technical questions beyond the scope of their capabilities from Corporate Engineering. Now West came to them with "his" problems but could offer no demonstrated solutions.

After several frustrating months, West stated his difficulty to Harris: "We need a corporate policy on pollution. Without one, I can't buck the operating managers." Harris raised this issue with the Technical Planning Committee and found that it coincided with Britton's thinking. Britton then worked with Harris and West in drafting the policy statement which was reviewed by the committee and signed by Britton.

1966-1969: Awareness and Activity Increase

In the three years following the promulgation of the Policy on Pollution, activities were concentrated in three areas: the corporate executive offices, West's pollution control unit, and the manufacturing and engineering sections of Division #2. During this period, pressure on the organization from more stringent regulations and extended corporate commitment was building, ultimately forcing a redefinition of the specialist's role.

Corporate Executive Offices

Britton's concern about ecology extended beyond the protection of the air and water. In fact, his chief interest soon became solid-waste disposal, an issue that began to receive concerted national attention in 1967. The matter was of importance to a number of divisions, notably the large Division #1, because of problems created by the discard of company products by the eventual user. Weston had traditionally taken the position that remedies lay in more responsible consumer behavior, public education, and more effective means of waste collection. However, as public interest in tax and regulatory schemes grew and the potential impact on the manufacturer became more direct, Britton encouraged a more active company involvement.

Among Britton's first initiatives in solid waste was strong support for a study into the effect of Division #1 products on municipal sanitary landfill operations. The work was begun in 1967 by an industry association that included Weston as one of its prominent members and soon led to an association committee on Environmental Pollution Control. West was installed as committee chairman. Some months later, Division #1 sponsored "reclamation days" in selected communities by providing publicity and offering to buy returned products. Concurrently, the corporate research and development group was funded to investigate potential uses for reclaimed material that could not be economically recycled in the normal manufacturing process.

In addition to activities of this sort, the top officers of Weston made themselves available for related assignments outside the company. Franklin, shortly after becoming president in 1968,* accepted the vice-chairmanship of a national committee on resource recovery. Britton joined a state task force dealing with environmental protection, and division managers were encouraged to assume similar roles in industry and governmental committees.

Britton also stressed the continuing development of air and water emission technology. The reasoning given at management meetings

*Britton moved up to Chairman of the Board but remained the chief executive.

and before outside audiences was consistent, even monotonous, according to the vice-president of communications who helped prepare many of the addresses. Britton commented on one occasion:

> I think the businessman who doesn't pretty much keep up to the state of the art in the development of his physical operations is derelict in his responsibility to the shareholders. The more you delay doing things which are going to have to be done anyway, the bigger bill you're going to pay . . . Management, with the best of good intentions, is faced with difficult decisions in the face of these new demands. In the improvement of existing facilities, there is a need for a careful weighing of values. Many plants are vital to their communities, and some of them could become noncompetitive if loaded suddenly with substantial new costs. This could be an economic tragedy to those communities and, therefore, sweeping restrictions can have alarming consequences. In the building of new facilities the decision is simpler. The mandate of the future is perfectly clear. The installation must be pollution-free up to the fullest capability of present scientific knowledge. Nothing less will be tolerated.

Pollution Control Department

While Britton was expanding on this policy, West rapidly became immersed in the legal and technical aspects of pollution control. During the initial months he participated in hearings that were being conducted in several states on prospective air quality regulations and set up files that would enable him to track regulatory developments throughout the country. Although fragmentary and unevenly enforced, these first codes were an indication of the form that standards were to take and the procedures to be used to secure compliance.

Until well into 1968 a considerable portion of West's time was devoted to the two major expansion projects then under way in the company, the Division #2 facility discussed above, and a $27 million facility in Division #7. In the first instance his primary task was to coordinate the company's relationships with state and local regulatory agencies. Division engineers, under Frederick's guidance, designed, installed, and tested the pollution control systems specified in the construction plan.

West played a more active role in the design of the plant in Division #7, which lacked the technical competence that Fredericks brought to Division #2. He surveyed existing and potential environmental control regulations at state and local levels and brought them to the attention of the division engineering group. He performed ambient air tests, reviewed construction plans, and on numerous occasions participated in the specification of control equipment, including a water treatment system and a process for testing laboratory effluents. A means for limiting air pollution in the production process itself was not considered, however, because, as West recalled, "We didn't know how to do it." Nevertheless, the $1 million expended on environmental controls represented a step that was considered at the time to be in line with Britton's stated policy.

West also found that some operating managers in those states or municipalities with aggressive regulatory programs were coming to him for help in filing permit requests. Assistance took several forms. The regulatory agency generally required an emissions inventory. Since few plant engineers at that time knew how to perform and interpret stack or water tests, West was called upon to provide this service. Then if the tests reflected nonstandard conditions (as they often did), the facility manager and his supervisors wanted help in negotiating an agreement with the regulatory agency.

The evolution of the Pollution Control Department was significantly influenced by this early involvement in detailed operating problems. It soon became apparent to West that he could not, by himself, service field requests and continue to keep up with rapidly changing state and local regulations. Consequently, he secured permission from Harris to enlarge the department. By 1969, four pollution control engineers, all new to the company, and one technician had been added. West then had more time to devote to negotiating compliance schedules, tracking technological developments and resolving minor crises that cropped up from time to time.

As West worked on specific problems, he became familiar with the nature and location of the firm's more serious ecological difficulties. In general he found that, with the exception of Division #2, the company did not participate in industries having serious water pollution problems. On the other hand, air contamination was potentially a major factor for numerous divisions. Consequently, West investigated available air pollution control technologies: scrubbers, bag houses, and electrostatic precipitators. Since none had been applied to the manufacturing processes predominant in Weston at that time, he sought support for development projects and pilot tests which his department conducted in several plants. The initial results were not encouraging; scrubbers proved inadequate, and significant uncertainties remained with the other two. Moreover, a continuing survey of companies in similar situations revealed few efforts at innovation and little prospect of technical breakthroughs elsewhere. Thus, Weston moved toward commitments to invest in full-scale equipment with very meager technical assurances from the Pollution Control Department.

The original ad hoc pollution control committee had "died a slow death" in 1967. In its place West substituted a network of individuals, generally on division engineering staffs, who had some responsibility for environmental protection. The relationships developed by West with the operating divisions varied widely.*

Division #2: The priority given to pollution control here was relatively high. Moreover, division engineers were often more experienced than those in the Pollution Control Department. Thus, West was kept informed of the division's activities and participated in decisions involving regulatory agencies, but had little to do with technical or investment planning.

Divisions #5, #6, and #7: The Pollution Control Department adapted a more affirmative posture in its relationships with several smaller divisions in the Industrial Products Group which had relatively severe environmental problems but lacked the experience to cope with them. The corporate group took the lead in defining abatement programs and researching alternative means for implementing them. These divisions were, in effect, a testing ground for technical innovations and were consequently important factors in the evolution of the corporation's over-all response to environmental demands.

Division #1: The situation in Division #1 was very different; pollution control received scant attention at the division level during this time. The Pollution Control Department helped the local manager with permit applications and was occasionally called upon to resolve compliance problems as they arose. However, plant and regional managers in West's view tended to believe that

*Divisions #3, #4, #8, and #9 did not have significant pollution problems and consequently took little of the Pollution Control Department's time.

the ecological demands on their businesses were neither serious nor immediate.

Continuing Developments in Division #2

Fredericks did not have an opportunity to manage the new plant in Division #2. In January 1968, just prior to its start-up, he was promoted to manufacturing manager of the division's Primary Operations Department and given responsibility for all its facilities. The following month he made a presentation to Britton and Franklin in which he summarized the status of pollution control in Primary Operations. For each facility a history of investments was given, together with a five-year plan for additional expenditures necessary to remain safely within the range of forecasted regulations. A weighted measure of air and water pollution loads had been devised during 1967 by the Division #2 technical staff which now served as a convenient measure of plant performance as shown in Exhibit VI-2. In his presentation, Fredericks described the division's approach as follows:

A. Legislative surveillance: Continued surveillance of the status of legislative and corrective programs by Federal and State Government. A primary goal is active participation on committees organized for the purpose of defining criteria and enforcement of existing regulations. In pursuit of this goal divisional representatives in 1967 attended some 144 meetings devoted to air and/or water pollution considerations. Formal position statements were presented at six of these meetings.

B. Development of improved pollution abatement systems: In developing these systems we seek to introduce innovations which can effectively solve immediate problems, but also hold the prospect of reducing the long-term cost of installation and operation.

Restructuring the Corporate Staff

In January 1969 the Director of Organization Planning was asked by Britton to study how Weston was organized to deal with both solid waste and pollution control issues. The report, dated February 5, summarized the situation in these terms:

Environmental pollution efforts are fragmented. Ten different

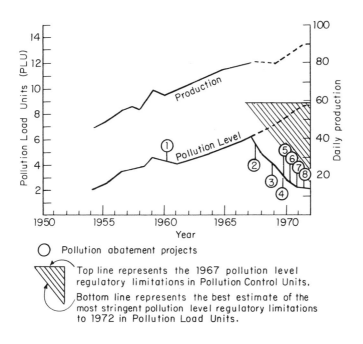

○ Pollution abatement projects

Top line represents the 1967 pollution level regulatory limitations in Pollution Control Units.

Bottom line represents the best estimate of the most stringent pollution level regulatory limitations to 1972 in Pollution Load Units.

units of the company* are working on the problem with varying degrees of intensity. There is no central coordinating authority involved with any phase of control responsibility.

The report suggested that "concerted corporate effort on all phases of environmental pollution control will necessitate the establishment of a central developmental and coordinating activity."

While the idea for a corporate environmental control office was readily accepted by Britton and Franklin, there were differences of opinion with regard to its function and authority. Franklin favored a single individual with a coordinative responsibility, while Britton was inclined toward a department with engineering support and the

---

*Included were five corporate staff groups (the Pollution Control Department, R & D, New Production Development, Personnel (health and safety) and Public Relations. Two departments in Division #1 dealing with solid waste, and three departments in Division #2 relating to air and water pollution.

authority to implement programs. Rather than resolve these issues at the outset, it was agreed that a manager should be appointed and, as he identified his needs, a final determination made on the scope of the department.

During the next four months consideration was given to the choice of the first Vice-President of Environmental Affairs. Manufacturing experience and the ability to work with the operating divisions were regarded as primary qualifications. Franklin was also concerned about the need he foresaw to relate effectively to the federal government as environmental legislation was formulated. The final selection was described by the Director of Organization Planning:

> Of those considered, Carl Winters was the only one interviewed for the job. Thornton [the Vice-President of Personnel], Franklin and I met with him. Only Thornton knew him because of a labor negotiation they had worked on together. However, his name was well known—he was one of the better plant managers in Division #1. He was also "expedient" in the sense that he wasn't running a big plant.

Winters assumed his new office in July and immediately became immersed in solid-waste activities in direct support of Franklin, who, as noted earlier, served as vice chairman of a national commission in that area. Since Winters had no staff at the time, he began to draw on West's department for support, though he did not become involved in its ongoing affairs. He also spent a good deal of time in Washington with technical people at such agencies as the Bureau of Mines, assessing the state of the art in solid-waste disposal and pollution control. He built a network of contacts in government that were to be of great value later in relating to the Environmental Protection Agency.

Toward the end of 1969 pressure mounted for Winters to give final definition to the environmental control function. Britton wanted to move quickly on the matter and became increasingly impatient with the delay. One issue was the disposition of the Pollution Control Department. Britton contended, "You've got to get the department out of engineering and demonstrate that it has some clout or it will never be effective." On the other hand, there was a clear feeling that Franklin did not want "an edifice" to environmental control built on the corporate staff. A second issue related to the location of responsibility for executing company policy. Winters argued in favor of limiting the formal scope of the new department, although his words were not totally unambiguous:

> It would have been easier to have centralized decision making. That argument was made to me at the time we were putting the organization together, but I resisted it because such a set-up would remove responsibility from the line managers. At Weston my job works whereas in some companies, it doesn't, because we have a clear policy—a responsibility in pollution which has the boss' support. I saw this job as coordinating the divisions' activities. The division managers see that I have support—I haven't known one of them to buck Mr. Britton on the policy yet. On the other hand, I have no veto power. I say that, but I don't really know if I do . . . and I don't want to find out.

In March 1970 West's unit became the Environmental Control Department (ECD) and was placed under Winters. The department was augmented by the transfer of the two-man Environmental Hygiene Section from the corporate personnel function on the grounds that the remedy to many health and safety problems ultimately lay in engineering rather than employee practices. Under the new arrangement, Winters reported directly to Franklin. His office was located on the floor with other corporate officers while ECD continued to work from the Weston technical center some seven miles away.

Introduction of Structure, Systems, and Procedures

Coincident with or shortly after the time that ECD was formed and the prominence of the environmental control function at the corporate level elevated, three administrative changes were introduced relating to organization, planning, and capital requests. In each instance, the intent was to systematize the response to ecological pressures and to extend corporate visibility into division activities.

Organization

The informal network of managers in the operating units relied upon by West was formalized in the spring and summer of 1970. Division managers were asked to assign responsibility to individuals in their units, if they had not already done so, for air and water pollution control, environmental hygiene, and solid waste. The designees were to serve as both a liaison with ECD and a focal point for division environmental activities.

Annual Business Plan

Also in the spring of 1970, the information requested in the business plan for 1971 was expanded to include forecasted capital expenditures and operating expenses for environmental control. The general format is illustrated in Exhibit VI-3. ECD was to review this portion of the division plans and submit comments to corporate planning for use in the annual budget review sessions in the fall.

Capital Allocation Requests

Finally, ECD was asked to review all capital requests over $50,000 for environmental impact. Comments made by the department were to be included in the dossier accompanying the project proposal when it was formally submitted by the division to the Corporate Management Committee for approval. Since the total annual capital budget approximated $80 million, several hundred requests exceeded the $50,000 minimum each year.

It was noted earlier that Weston's top management had sought to moderate capital expenditures in the late 1960s; the sum of division budgets for normal modernization and expansion was to be within internally generated cash flow. However, environmental control items appeared to fall beyond the scope of these intentions in 1970. Operating managers expressed the view that if a need could be demonstrated for equipment to meet anticipated regulatory or environmentalist demands, the funds would be made available. But as one manager commented, "We can normally substitute other projects for those shown in the plan without causing a fuss. But with ecology items, if we don't spend it as planned, we can't transfer the money to something else."

The special treatment for environmental control expenditures was not particularly significant in financial terms at the outset because the level of spending was small, but isolating these items in the capital budget tended to shelter them, temporarily at least, from the competition for funds.

EXHIBIT VI-3

Weston Business Plan
ENVIRONMENTAL CONTROL

I. *Major Programs & Problems*
This section should consist of a discussion of each of the major programs and problem areas for the Plan year in the following format:

Program	Location	Program Cost		Capital Expenditure
		RD&E	Total	

Comments:
The commentary for each program should include a brief description of the problem, recommended problem solution (in most cases this will be synonomous with the "program" under discussion), timing and involvement with other division and/or corporate environmental control function. The location can be either a plant, region, or the entire Division depending upon the nature of the program or problem and primary responsibility for the project.

Problems involving specific products or product lines in general should be included with the Divisional Level Activity. It is of particular importance in these situations to discuss the interface with other Divisions and Corporate activities.

II. *Anticipated Future Areas of Action* (optional)
This section should include a brief discussion of anticipated areas for close monitoring and/or action during the next two to five years. These areas will typically arise due to changes in emission standards and other legislative and regulatory criteria, product and process changes, and developments in technology. Where applicable, previous Weston experience in these respective areas should be referenced.

III. *Environmental Control Capital Expenditures by Location & Project*

Project	Location	Code	Amount
		1 - Process Effluent Control	
		2 - Environmental Hygiene	
		3 - Solid Waste and Litter	

Total Plan

continued

EXHIBIT VI-3 (cont.)

IV. *Environment Control Activities Cost Analysis*

	Process Effluent Control	Environ-mental Hygiene	Solid Waste & Litter	Total
Engineering & Development				
Operating Costs				
Public Relations				
Recycle Purchase Premium				
Other				
Total Plan This Year				
Total Last Year				

Transition: 1970-1972

During the following two years the effort devoted to environmental concerns in the divisions increased steadily. Based on estimates from various sources, the researcher counted at least 21 person-years allocated to these efforts by 1972, exclusive of ECD, of which approximately 11 were in air and water pollution, as shown in Exhibit VI-4. These figures understate the total time commitment because they refer only to managers with specific environmental assignments at group and division levels. However, the nature of the response to both corporate initiatives and external demands in this period tended to accentuate the earlier differences among divisions:

1. In Division #2 responsibility for environmental control had been assumed by senior managers, including the technical director and, of course, Bill Fredericks. Reporting to them were the manufacturing and technical people who assembled capital requests and performed engineering services in the plants. The division had been projecting pollution control expenditures for several years at this point and experienced little difficulty adapting its procedures to the new corporate reporting requirements. Since these projections had been derived, in part, from expansion programs in the business plan, capital requests routinely included attention to environmental impact.

2. In the Industrial Products Group (composed of divisions #5, #6, #7, #8, and #9) senior technical managers at group and division levels were assigned environmental responsibilities. Within a

Exhibit VI-4
Weston Industries
Divisional Environmental Affairs Staffing and Responsibilities

Division and Position	Air pollution	Water pollution	Environmental hygiene	Solid waste	Estimated time allocated (to the nearest quartile) (%)	Total time
PACKAGING PRODUCTS GROUP						
Division No. 1						
Director, Environmental Affairs				☆	100	
Technical Projects				☆	100	
Solid Waste & Reclamation				☆	100	
Consumer Education				☆	100	
Eastern Region				☆	100	
Midwest Region				☆	100	
Western Region				☆	100	
Engineer, Div. Staff	☆				75	
Engineer, Div. Staff		☆			50	
Industrial Relations			☆		25	
Noise Studies, Div. R & D			☆		25	8.75

continued

Exhibit VI-4 (cont.)
Weston Industries
Divisional Environmental Affairs Staffing and Responsibilities

Division and Position	Air pollution	Water pollution	Environmental hygiene	Solid waste	Estimated time allocated (to the nearest quartile) (%)	Total time
Division No. 2						
V.P., Technical Director	☆	☆	☆ a	☆	25	
Engineer, Tech. Staff	☆	☆	☆ a		100	
Engineer, Div. Staff	☆	☆			100	
Engineer, Div. Staff	☆	☆			100	
Industrial Relations			☆		25	3.50
Division No. 3						
Engineer, Div. Staff	☆	☆			25	
Customer Service				☆	25	
Industrial Relations			☆		25	.75
Division No. 4						
Engineer, Div. Staff	☆	☆			25	
Industrial Relations			☆		25	.50
INDUSTRIAL PRODUCTS GROUP						
V.P. Env. Affairs	☆	☆	☆ a	☆	100	continued

Exhibit VI-4 (cont.)
Weston Industries
Divisional Environmental Affairs Staffing and Responsibilities

Division and Position	Air pollution	Water pollution	Environmental hygiene	Solid waste	Estimated time allocated (to the nearest quartile) (%)	Total time
Engineer, Group Staff	☆	☆	☆ a		25	
Engineer, Group Staff	☆	☆	☆ a		100	
Industrial Relations			☆		25	2.50
Division No. 5						
Director, Engineering	☆	☆	☆ a		25	
Engineer, Div. Staff	☆	☆	☆ a		100	
Engineer, Div. Staff	☆	☆	☆ a		100	2.25
Division No. 6						
Director, Engineering	☆	☆	☆ a		25	
Engineer, Div. Staff	☆	☆	☆ a		25	.50
Division No. 7						
Director, Engineering	☆	☆	☆ a		25	
Engineer, Div. Staff	☆	☆	☆ a		25	.50

continued

Exhibit VI-4 (cont.)

Weston Industries

Divisional Environmental Affairs Staffing and Responsibilities

Division and Position	Air pollution	Water pollution	Environmental hygiene	Solid waste	Estimated time allocated (to the nearest quartile) (%)	Total time
Division No. 8						
Technical Manager	☆	☆	☆ a		25	
Engineer, Div. Staff	☆	☆	☆ a		25	.50
Division No. 9						
Manager, Plant Construction Engineering	☆	☆			25	
Marketing				☆	25	
Industrial Relations			☆		25	.75
International Division						
Engineer	☆	☆			25	
Marketing Staff				☆	25	.50
Approximate Totals	11.00		2.00	8.00		21.00

^{a} Includes technical aspects of health and safety only.

year they were able to assemble plans that West felt were reasonably comprehensive. They also initiated a number of innovations in pollution control technology that enabled their divisions to respond aggressively to escalating regulatory requirements. Most importantly, the issue appeared to have attracted general management attention.

3. In Division #1 considerable effort was directed to solid waste, signified by the creation of a department in August 1970 that was eventually to include seven people. However, air and water pollution control responsibilities were added to the duties of two staff engineers at section levels of the large technical department. From West's perspective, the division's environmental plans for 1971 and 1972 seriously underestimated the impact of future regulation and the magnitude of probable capital expenditures. Continuing problems were encountered by ECD in securing a place for environmental controls in the division's expansion programs. Only toward the end of 1972 did the division's posture begin to change.

Thus, 1970-1972 was a period of transition for Weston in the response at division levels to the pollution control issue. In the next chapter the circumstances which appeared to prompt this transition in the Industrial Products Group and in particular Division #5, the first unit to experience it, are described in some detail. Subsequent events are also portrayed which offer the reader an opportunity to compare the response of this unit with Division #1 under similar circumstances.

The Dynamics of Corporate Involvement

The Pollution Control Department had devoted most of its efforts to external affairs such as research on abatement technologies, regulatory surveillance, and mediation between operating divisions and government agencies. ECD continued and in some instances expanded these activities in response to increasing regulatory pressure.

With the passage of the Clean Air Act amendments, pollution control regulations began to undergo rapid and substantial change. As the reader will recall from Chapter II, federal law specified national standards for air quality and, later, water treatment, but implementation plans supported by specific emissions limitations were generally established by the states subject to EPA approval. Although a degree of uniformity was imposed by EPA, the detailed regulations often varied from state to state. Since Weston had over a hundred plants in 28 states, the work involved in monitoring changing standards, dealing with the increasing volume of permit applications, filing emission inventories, and negotiating with regulatory officials was enormous. The following example is representative of these day-to-day operating problems and the role played by ECD in resolving them.

One day in July 1972, West received word that a registered letter from a State Air Pollution Control Board had been received in the mail room and was being sent to ECD by messenger. While he waited for the letter, West speculated to the researcher that it was probably a denial of a permit application to operate a piece of equipment at the Wabash plant in Division #1. He traced the history of the project:

> In August 1971, we [ECD] learned that a capital request was brewing for some equipment to collect and process trimmings from a corrugating operation. The engineering drawings had already been done. When the CAR [Capital Allocation Request] came to ECD for review, we said O.K., but be sure to get construction and operating permits for it. The comments we put on the CAR evidently never got to the plant.
>
> In January I knew that the installation was being made but without a permit so far. So I went to the plant manager and said, "Let's get the permits." I also tried to get the plant engineering manager going. Finally in early April the plant people sent a request to build and operate the equipment to the local air pollution control office.
>
> A little while later, the state engineer came to the plant and saw that the thing had already been built and was about to start up. He said, "You've already violated one law by building it without a permit — don't start it up and violate another." They really got his hackles up. That was four or five weeks ago. The inspector sent in his report denying our request, saying he needed more information. Well, then the plant engineer goofed — he didn't check with us before he sent in the requested information and he made some errors. The state looked at it and said, "It won't work," and on the basis of the information provided the state was right. We then corrected the report here and sent it back. Meanwhile, the equipment has been sitting there idle.
>
> The problem is somebody said, "Let's do it" and went ahead

without checking. But we won't take responsibility from the divisions for proper performance in this sort of thing.

When the letter arrived, it was a permit denial, but for the Canton plant in the same division. West sketched the history of this project:

> The plant engineer in Canton had proposed an air pollution device to clean air from the production line enough so that it could be put back in the building. Although the plant manager apparently concurred, somewhere along the line the project got turned down. Carl Winters happened to hear about it because he knew the plant engineer and intervened. He took the project out of the normal flow of capital requests and went to the division manager and got it approved. Then the plant engineer didn't file the permit to build and operate it — an oversight on his part — until it was completed. Now this letter says it's been denied. In effect, they've asked for more information before granting the permit.
>
> It's unfortunate when this happens, especially because we're dealing with the same state regulatory agency and the same people in the agency. They don't understand the complexity of our organization, the fact that there are two independent plants, and so forth. They tend to think Weston is one big homogeneous company and this sort of thing is systematic obstruction.

While efforts to coordinate division compliance continued to absorb large amounts of ECD time, the scope of the department's activities expanded during 1970 into areas of more direct concern to operating management, in particular the investment decision process. One part of ECD's involvement related to the review of division environmental plans and capital requests. With respect to the latter, West noted that ECD took a stronger position on requests for pollution control equipment than it did on other investment proposals.

> We study the CAR [Capital Allocation Request] on let's say, a plant expansion before it's approved and attach comments — in the form of questions — that reflect any concerns we may have about the handling of air emissions, for instance, or noise. The comments are generally for the engineering people in the division because they're the ones who must react to them. But we have no veto power over the project nor can we force them to answer our

questions. However, we find that if we keep asking the same question, somebody may get tired of it and do something to satisfy us. On large projects, our comments are summarized along with those of other reviewers, such as planning and engineering, by a business analyst in the division before the CAR goes up for approval.

Our responsibilities on pollution control equipment is greater. In this case we have a technical responsibility to see that the money is well spent. In effect, we have the authority to stop or at least hold up requests which include environmental control equipment. Our job is to see first that the project is intended to meet standards and second that the equipment specified on the request is capable of doing what they say it will do.

Since a project of any consequence almost certainly entailed an environmental impact of some sort, Winters and West attempted to keep abreast of expansion programs through the division business plans and informal discussions with operating managers. They expressed the view that ECD was most likely to influence the project if they were involved while it was being defined. Success in gaining early access depended on a number of factors, including the immediacy of the regulatory threat, personal relationships at the engineering staff level, and the division manager's concern about environmental issues and confidence in dealing with them. Occasionally ECD was not apprised of a request until the completed forms arrived in the department on their way through the final approval steps. For most large projects, however, ECD had an opportunity to express an opinion on potential regulatory difficulties and the adequacy of the division's plans for environmental controls. Maintaining a balance between external demands and management needs was often difficult, as West noted:

> We [ECD] find ourselves in a "damned if you do, damned if you don't" situation a lot of the time. We get accused by the regulators of backsliding when we argue that the company is doing the best it can. Then, when we argue for a program inside the company, we get accused of giving money away. The operating managers sometimes fail to see that if they don't take steps now, the cost in the long run could be a lot greater. They hear the wolves barking, but they only notice the ones that get in and not the ones we're keeping outside.

In line with Weston's policy of decentralized responsibility, the division manager retained the right to resolve whatever differences of opinion might exist between his engineering staff and ECD for purposes of filing the capital request.

Considerable effort was devoted to tracking and analyzing division capital spending programs by the 10-person staff in corporate planning. While formal project requests were seldom flatly rejected, top management had been known to suggest that expansion proposals be delayed or given further study by the divisions. However, funding was rarely held up at this stage because of ECD comments unless a clear violation of an existing regulation could be cited.

Although there was officially no difference in the handling of capital requests for pollution control equipment, the director of corporate planning indicated that his staff did not have the technical or legal background to evaluate such requests and lacked the customary measures of worth (such as the discounted cash flow measure of ROI required on income-generating proposals). Rather than the lengthy economic justification frequently supporting other requests, these were typically covered by a single paragraph stating that the funds were required to meet existing or anticipated requirements. He commented that "our limited ability to make judgments on pollution control equipment forces us to rely heavily on Bill West. We assume the environmental plans will give him advance warning of the request so, if necessary, he can get involved in putting the project together."

Investment decisions were seldom as neatly compartmentalized as the paragraphs above might suggest. Moreover, differences in the priority given to environmental affairs among divisions often introduced added complexities. The following example is illustrative.

Through the efforts of regional engineering and plant personnel, Division #1 had successfully forestalled the Air Pollution Control Board in one county from insisting that control equipment be installed on the lines in its facility. They argued, with the support of others in their industry, that the available technology was not capable of meeting the standards at a reasonable cost.

Meanwhile, Division #6, which employed a similar production process, planned to enlarge its plant in the same county, the start-up date set for July 1972. However, the operating permit which had been filed with ECD's help had been denied because the plant failed to meet county ordinances on particulate emissions and plume opacity. On appeal, West was successful in overturning the first complaint, but the second continued to stand. Division #6 management then considered two alternatives: build the new equipment and restrict production in the entire plant to a level that would enable it to meet the plume opacity regulation until the control technology could be developed, or postpone the project entirely. Division management rejected the latter proposal, and the Air Pollution Control Board denied the former.

The Vice President of Environmental Affairs in the Industrial Products Group (to which Division #6 belonged) then uncovered a new design for a fiber bag house which *might* produce results that would satisfy the Board. Weston's bargaining position was strengthened because he was able to negotiate a delivery time of four months rather than the year required for many such installations. Meanwhile, Division #1 was formulating plans for an enlargement of its plant without the immediate incorporation of control equipment. (At the time Division #1 was awaiting the results of research being conducted by its industry association into the use of electrostatic precipitators.)

Two questions were suggested at the time by these events. First, would the fiber bag house work? And, second, what were the implications for Division #1 if Division #6 proposed the bag house as a solution that Division #1 had described as beyond the state of the art? Despite reservations in Division #1, the manager of Division #6, with ECD's support, elected to petition the Board for permission to build the added capacity, including the new control technology, and then to return for an operating permit after a suitable testing period. The Board promptly acquiesced. West commented on ECD's position: "Division #1 thinks this department sold them down the river. One manager even thinks we should have asked their permission before agreeing with the plant expansion in Division #6."

Although Winters kept in close touch with ECD's activities and raised the department's concerns on specific decisions to the attention of senior operating managers, he devoted a major portion of his time to external affairs. In addition to serving as staff for Franklin on solid waste matters, Winters actively pursued technical developments in pollution control. At one point he commented:

> I know what our competitors are doing. I care what our competitors are doing. I care what others think our competitors are doing. Because Company C has some way of reducing emissions, the government may ask why we don't have it too. There isn't

much going on that I don't hear about. The equipment suppliers use one client to sell the others. The industry associations take on some of this function, too. But with both technology and regulation changing very rapidly, it's hard to keep up.

Winters also brought the division environmental control representatives together periodically to discuss policy issues and developments of mutual interest. For instance, in 1971 he called them in to review the company's posture on "docilely" filing the information requested by EPA under the 1899 Rivers and Harbors Act.

Evolution in Top Management Concerns

In contrast to capital spending, the divisions received little credit for the operating expenses and depreciation incurred in environmental control when they negotiated performance targets with Britton and Franklin. Although these costs were estimated and displayed separately in the business plan, there were few hard data to evaluate because the accounting system was not set up to report actual charges to income associated with pollution control. Various managers estimated that annual operating expenses (including depreciation) amounted to 15 to 30 percent of the capital expenditures. Once again, the impact on the division budget was minor at first. Later, as capital expenditures grew, the burden of accumulating operating costs became noticeable.

As the 1973 plan was being assembled in mid-1972, the Corporate Planning Department noticed that for the first time pollution control equipment was "highly visible" in the capital budget; for some divisions the proportion was likely to exceed 20 percent of the total. Britton and Franklin began to ask: "Do the economics of the facility justify the investment?" Concern in the corporation was highlighted by a dramatic incident described below.

One of the large plants in the Primary Operations Department of Division #2 was beset by escalating environmentalist demands in the spring and summer of 1972. Because of its product line, the plant was a critical factor in the division's business strategy. On the other hand, while its location was very advantageous, the facility was relatively old, and division management was concerned that costs had "bottomed out" and were likely to increase. Moreover, it was felt that the existing equipment was progressively less capable of meeting new and more stringent customer needs at competitive prices. Consequently, on two occasions in the previous five years the division manager had approached the corporation on a $25 million modernization and expansion program. Each time he had been rebuffed, however, because the return he was able to promise was not very high and the industry appeared to be suffering from over-capacity and deteriorating prices. Nevertheless, with a capital base of only $12 million and low fixed charges, the plant had the highest return on net assets in the division.

Since 1968 Division #2 personnel had worked with the State Department of Natural Resources, one of the most aggressive such agencies in the country, on a program to reduce water pollution from the plant. In March 1972, the division manager agreed to an abatement schedule which committed the company to expenditures of $900,000 that year and an additional $1.5 million over the following four years. Then in June, several months prior to the passage of the Federal Water Pollution Control Act, the EPA regional office requested that Weston "voluntarily" reduce BOD* and suspended particle emissions by an additional 36 percent and 64 percent respectively. Furthermore, environmental groups were insisting that operating permits be given for only a year so that still more stringent controls could be immediately enforced thereafter. Division engineers calculated that the total cost of complying with the EPA request would now be increased to $8.0 million.

Division #2 management faced a dilemma at this point which precipitated a number of questions at the corporate level. Could a 67 percent increase in the book value of an old plant be justified without an economic return? If the expenditure were made, wasn't the division actually committing the corporation to the $25 million expansion program that had twice been postponed? Instead, shouldn't the division scrap the plant and propose a new one elsewhere? This final question had disturbing implications for the division's senior business analyst and the Primary Operations Department manager because they were aware that the $70 million required to replace the existing capacity would not, in the prevailing industry conditions, yield a return that would satisfy the corporation. There was also, of course, no assurance that an alternate location would result in lower pollution abatement expenditures.

The division business analyst commented at the time:

*BOD is a measure of the oxygen needed to break down dissolved materials in the water.

My department hasn't been that involved in pollution abatement requests before except in a broad planning sense. It's been the technical people who have said, "This is the year we have to put in a precipitator"; we can't add much to that discussion. But this one is different. Are investments in pollution abatement the tail wagging the dog? . . . We are given only so much money for capital expenditures so what we do here will influence what happens some place else. The final judgment will have to be made by the division manager.

After several months of analysis and uncertainty, the issue was tentatively resolved. EPA did not press its request following passage of the Water Pollution Act, although Weston continued to operate on the assumption that by 1977, the $8.0 million would be required anyway. The division analysis indicated that, with the exception of the central processing equipment, the plant was really quite efficient after all, and should therefore be retained with a modest $2.5 million investment in incremental capacity added to the abatement program. The division manager concurred and won approval for the necessary funding.

The questions raised by this incident were soon echoed in others. The Director of Corporate Planning commented on these developments:

I see more and more evidence that division managers are less reluctant to spend money on pollution control. They rely on their engineers and lawyers rather than sales and manufacturing. But one place that spending is beginning to be cut off is in plants that are considered to be question marks. The outlook for various plants has been discussed by Britton and Franklin in management meetings and the division manager asked to comment on them. He's in a position to feel where investments should be "reconsidered."

One division manager reflected on the same issue from a different perspective. "The corporation expects me to compensate for the cost of pollution control. In effect, they are asking me to look for opportunities to close down marginal operations which are headed for trouble in the environmental area or raise prices or try to figure out some way of making the pollution control expenditures pay off in productivity. They don't expect lower profits."

Evolution in Division #1

Toward the end of 1972 change became evident in the posture of Division #1 on pollution control. West reported that for the first time the division submitted an environmental plan which included a reasonably comprehensive assessment of future equipment needs and capital expenditures. He also reported that he was being alerted sooner to prospective capacity changes, and more rapid progress was being made in developing and implementing abatement schedules. Moreover, general management involvement appeared to be more prevalent.

A number of external forces may have contributed to the change. For instance, the economic implications of air pollution control regulations were by this time finally becoming clear. Furthermore, situations similar to the one described above in Division #2 were being forced on the manufacturing organization: Were plants to be closed or funds requested for pollution control equipment? A major reorganization in the division had also taken place; the regional general manager position was eliminated in July 1972, and functional reporting lines were established between the division offices and field units. In addition, the outgoing division manager was made a Group Vice President, and new sales and manufacturing managers appointed. The incoming Division Manager was Robert Rushmore. As the reader will recall, he had been in charge of Primary Operations in Division #2 six years earlier, at the time Fredericks was incorporating and defending the substantial pollution control expenditures in that division's large new facility. Finally, Winters returned to Division #1 as a Regional Manufacturing Manager and a Division Vice President.

In November, Rushmore set up a committee composed of his senior Sales, Manufacturing, and Technical Managers, Winters, and the new Corporate Vice President of Environmental Affairs to review where the division stood on pollution control. A week later he commented on the results:

> The first thing I found out was that we didn't have a plan. Now we're doing one. Paying for what it includes will have to come out of prices or our hides — and there's not much hide left. The costs are high but not so high that they'll take the heat off the budget; they'll be considered a cost of doing business.
>
> The engineering people put on a show for the committee last week. The technical director talked about air, water, noise and

heat, what we ought to do about each and how much it would cost. The meeting drove me up a tree. It was like they had just discovered pollution control. They were righteous about it — indignant at having to do anything.

But we've straightened that out now. Our capital program will be in the plan for next year. I'll participate in the decisions because of my background in Division #2. The marketing guy is there to understand the cost implications and how his prices might be effected in the future.

Two months later, Winters was promoted to be Vice President and Technical Director of Division #1, and then had responsibility for the engineers assigned to pollution control matters.

Evolution of Environmental Control Department

The organizational changes in Division #1 were part of a major restructuring in Weston announced in July 1972 that resulted in new managers for five divisions, the formation of a second product group to parallel the Industrial Products Group, and a major overhaul of the corporate staff. When the consultants who were engaged to perform the study gave their preliminary report to Britton and Franklin in a private session, they recommended that ECD report to the Vice President of Corporate Relations together with Public Affairs, Corporate Advertising, Press Relations, and similar functions. Britton strongly objected because he feared that the department would become, or others would think that it had become, an arm of public relations. As a result, ECD was assigned to the Vice-President of Administration, who also had charge of personnel, purchasing, organization planning, and corporate systems. ECD was one of several corporate staff offices that no longer reported directly to the President.

A search was then undertaken for a new Vice President of Environmental Affairs. After some months of discussion, John Herndon was ultimately selected. Herndon had been manager of a large facility in Division #2 and was credited with resolving some difficult personnel problems and significantly improving the plant's performance. His background was in industrial and labor relations rather than engineering.

While this search was being conducted, ECD lost one of its functions. As reflected in Exhibit VI-4, managers with responsibility for environmental hygiene in the operating units were often from industrial relations departments rather than engineering. In July 1972, the two specialists in ECD petitioned for reassignment to the corporate personnel function. Winters and West opposed the transfer for reasons that provided an interesting insight into the management of both their department and the occupational health and safety issue. West commented at one point:

> Environmental hygiene should be here [in ECD] to get the job done. It's basically an engineering function that has to do with reducing noise levels and eliminating unsafe working conditions. We go to the process engineer and show him his problems. Then if he becomes interested, things start to get done. Before, the IR [Industrial Relations] people would receive an employee complaint and they'd write a memorandum to the plant manager about it with a copy to engineering. Nothing would happen. We're talking about prevention programs which get involved with facilities construction or machine design and aren't the kind of people problems that IR usually deals with. Now we have the question again, where to put it? IR is handling parts of the company's compliance with OSHA [the Occupational Safety and Health Act]; there is some feeling that they should have it all.

Nevertheless, in the fall, based on the report of another consultant, the environmental hygiene section was returned to Industrial Relations. Some months later the Vice President of Administration commented:

> We've left that one [occupational health and safety] with the operating divisions. There is some staff in corporate personnel to help them if they need it, but we think it's really a local problem to be resolved at each plant location. We'll disseminate information and advice, but they'll have to handle the compliance reviews.

In December 1972, Herndon commented on the nature of his new assignment:

> The emphasis of my job is going to be solid wastes. We have a well-developed technology now for handling air and water pollution but not in solid wastes. Here we're dealing with public pressure, legislation, and programs such as recycling which may affect the product line and plant locations. For instance, there is some talk of a tax credit for using recycled materials. I take this to the solid waste committee and tell them to get with their business planning people and ask: "If this happens, what does it mean?"

. . . I'm trying to arrive at a position that will best serve the long-run interests of Weston. Should we have a formal policy on solid wastes? What are the implications if the divisions disagree?

The activities inside ECD were also undergoing change. West indicated that he was no longer as involved in pollution control technology as he was at the outset and was increasingly confident that the divisions were incorporating a concern for the issue in their facility planning decisions. ECD's role had become more heavily concentrated in managing the interface between the operating units and regulatory agencies and consulting on the ecological implications of major projects. The department's responsibilities were also gradually being expanded in two directions.

First, West reported that his involvement overseas was growing steadily: "The flavor of the policy is rubbing off on the International Division. Europe is about three years behind us on regulation. However, there is increasing interest in the division to apply the same technology over there, too, because it will probably be required eventually and it's more economical to transfer our skills."

Second, corporate management had become concerned about product safety, and Herndon was given the responsibility for exploring its implications. West commented in February 1973: "That's the next one. Congress passed the Consumer Product Safety Act in October, and we're trying now to get the divisions to establish a committee similar to the one on solid wastes. We may have to add someone here to spend full time on it."

ANALYSIS

Environmental protection was an active concern at Weston for seven years before the response to it appeared to be generally accepted among the operating divisions. That time span may seem excessive. Indeed, its length raises important questions about how rapidly the corporation may be expected to adapt to social demands, even those such as pollution control which raise few deep-seated prejudices or emotions. On the other hand, Britton pressed the issue in 1966, well before it was popular or supported by a credible regulatory mandate. Moreover, the managerial problems encountered in implementing the early policy were by and large overcome *before* the major dollar commitments were necessary. In other words the organization was prepared to manage the heavy expenditures expected from 1973 to 1980.

Adaptation

The response at Weston was decidely uneven; periods of turbu-lance were encountered in 1966, 1969, and from mid-1970 through 1972, during which the company's approach to environmental matters was re-evaluated. In each instance the chief executive took actions that altered the management of the process and permitted response to resume on a more comprehensive basis. If one imagined a trend line describing the concern for environmental impact in operating decisions (disregarding interdivisional differences for a moment), its shape would resemble Exhibit VI-5.

The explanation for this result lies in a diagnosis of the enabling and impeding forces which shaped decisions on environmental matters.[1] Tension was clearly evident on two planes and implicit on a third. The first involved efficiency; environmental demands were perceived to conflict with a narrower view of efficiency based on near-term economic performance. The second involved organiza-

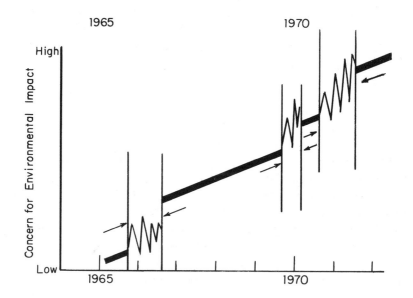

tional interests and competences; while some managers, by virtue of experience or assignment, favored increased attention to pollution control, others having divergent responsibilities and little understanding of the issue were inclined to resist it. Finally, the personal inclinations of individual managers most certainly varied widely on the appropriateness of environmental expenditures. These values inevitably influenced the decisions that managers were inclined to support. As the social issue matured, the enabling forces tended to be strengthened and the impeding forces weakened. However, it was the chief executive's initiative during the transitional periods reviewed below that determined how these tensions were harnessed and reconciled with operating procedures in the organization.

1. 1966

The Policy on Pollution was not written as a magnanimous gesture on Britton's part in the fall of 1966. Several events prompted his action, among them the construction of the facility in Division #2. This project was significant for Weston; funding it required nearly two years' cash flow after dividends, and occasioned a doubling in the firm's long-term debt. Although the division proposed and directed the project, corporate officers were vitally concerned that it be successful. Since the facility was to be located in a small community and had the potential for materially disturbing the surrounding ecology, the environmental issue could not easily be ignored. In a sense, the policy was first acted out in a context that drew and held the chief executive's interest.

Pressure for increased responsiveness was exerted by individual managers, though at this stage the proponents were not in positions traditionally accorded influence in setting corporate-wide policy. Both the plant manager, Fredericks, and the specialist in central engineering, West, needed support and ran the risk of being overwhelmed by management at division levels. Had Britton placed Division #2 under the gun for the cost overrun on the new facility (or had the division manager felt the overrun endangered his career or the funding prospects of some other project), the pollution control systems might well have been eliminated and with them the credibility of any policy made thereafter. For West, Division #2 represented a model that could be extended to other units.

The policy was also intended to help central engineering overcome resistance encountered in the operating units. The cause of this resistance could be traced in part to the decentralization introduced by Britton in 1962. For the previous four years the corporate staff had been rationalizing its relationships with the operating units. Direct involvement in Division #1 and much of the Industrial Products Group was being replaced by budgeting and control systems and management reviews. These same systems were also being applied to Division #2 and other units which had previously enjoyed relatively more autonomy. Middle-level managers had been treated to increasing doses of responsibility and accountability, a trend clearly contrary to corporate activities of the sort West was asked to undertake. To this was added the apparent remoteness of environmental protection legislation in 1966. Ironically, the Division #2 project may have sheltered the other divisions from incipient community demands because, aside from the new facility in Division #7, commitments for large capital investments were limited by cash availability until it was completed.

It is interesting that the policy and the initial interpretation given to it by Britton stressed the widely shared and more traditional value ascribed to community relations in the company. That was, of course, a reasonable way of formulating the problem and was true to his sensitivities and experience. Thus at the time the policy represented a plausible expectation that could be related to the efficient use of resources. Only later was its meaning expanded as a matter of "corporate responsibility" to address ecology itself.

2.   1969

For the next several years, the Pollution Control Department appeared to be sufficient. However, by 1969 the social demands it was designed to accommodate had grown to the point that change was deemed necessary. Although stiff federal legislation was another year away, it was increasingly evident that public support for ecology was likely to prompt more widespread regulation. In fact, the company was already struggling with state codes in various instances as the following chapter will illustrate. There were a sufficient number of isolated danger signals to warrant concern, though a systematic assessment of what they meant was unavailable at the time except in Division #2. In that division, the 1968 presentation assembled by Fredericks served as a clear indication of both the financial exposure and the planning and technical commitment required to cope with it. For Britton, this was the first systematic analysis of the problem and lent a note of urgency to his concerns about the remainder of the corporation.

Within Weston, the response to these growing environmental demands was becoming fragmented as various staff departments were drawn into it. Moreover, a related issue, solid waste, had assumed particular importance and required skills and attention that were then unavailable on the corporate staff. Meanwhile, an enlarged Pollution Control Department was exerting greater pressure on the operating divisions, on some occasions coming in conflict with operating management.

Thus, the impetus for change was building up, and the existing organizational arrangements and information systems were laboring under the strain. As the implications of public demands and Weston's environmental policy became clearer, resistance also became more pointed.

There were numerous reasons for resistance among the operating units. For instance, Division #1 had been under intense competitive pressure and was feeling the pinch on margins and market share. Its senior management was reluctant to encourage no-yield expenditures that were not obligatory. In the absence of encouragement from these managers, West found it difficult to persuade their subordinates in the field to consider future needs. Resistance might have been muted had the technology been available. However, since an economically feasible means for controlling air emissions from the production process had not been developed, responsiveness entailed experimentation, and that connoted money, engineering effort, and uncertainty. Capital stringency imposed by the corporation in the 1970 planning cycle constituted another inducement to hesitation; the divisions quickly became more protective of their call on investment funds.

Top management's response at this juncture was to consolidate and strengthen the specialist's role through the establishment of a Vice President of Environmental Control. Winters had ready access to top management and, through West's group, to operating conditions deep in the divisions. He was also given license to introduce planning and review systems to increase the attention given to the issue. By permitting pollution control expenditures to be isolated, Britton and Franklin temporarily appeared to set them outside the announced capital limitations in such a way that they could be

evaluated and influenced separately. In essence, corporate participation in environmental decisions increased. Yet, from Winter's
perspective the extent of his mandate was difficult to judge. Nearly
a year passed before his formal responsibilities were clarified and
before he assumed charge of the Pollution Control Department.
The new order was more tentative than the formal organizational
and systems changes suggest.

3.   1970-1972

External pressure mounted rapidly with the passage of the 1970
air quality legislation. The greatly increased volume of paperwork
and number of people with environmental control responsibilities
lent bulk to ECD's efforts; it became more difficult to ignore the
issue. Yet differences among divisions persisted for reasons at least
partially related to the individuals involved, the importance
accorded the specialist activity in each division, and the perceived
urgency of the external threat.

The individual middle manager appeared to have some influence
on the implementation of policy. For instance, Fredericks was
largely responsible for sensitizing the management group in Division
#2 to the importance of ecology. As managers from this division
moved on, notably Franklin to President and Rushmore to Division
#1, they continued to act on this sensitivity. The same could be said
of Winters as he returned to Division #1, ultimately in the key
job — from an environmental standpoint — of technical director.
The company tradition of promotion from within and interdivisional transfers tended to extend the influence of the promising
manager, and in this case facilitated the implementation of the
corporate policy.

Similarly, the location of the specialist in the division organization affected the tenor of the response. The appointment of a vice
president at the group level in the Industrial Products Group contributed to increased division manager involvement that will be
illustrated at some length in the next chapter. By contrast, the
section-level engineers in Division #1 bore the responsibility for
pollution control from a position that provided them with little
influence in setting division policy or defining major capital
projects. Not surprisingly, they tended to defer to the wishes of the
division's line management.

The final point—perceived urgency—is somewhat more complicated than it seems. As legislation was enacted there was less doubt among operating managers that pollution control would some day have an impact on operating and capital budgets. There were naturally some who felt that regulation would not apply to their operation, at least not in the near future. A more common attitude, however, was that since any standards would apply equally to the competition, there was little point attempting to meet them ahead of the rest of the industry. During a period of rapidly changing regulation and technology, this proposition was likely to prove costly. The rub came in not being able to add capacity on schedule, a penalty often more serious than the cost of the pollution control equipment. One such instance was recounted earlier in which a regulatory agency refused to issue a variance to the air quality code to Division #6 for a plant expansion. Then, when this division found a potential solution, a similar expansion project in Division #1 was turned down. The delay threatened immediate penalties on the latter's performance against its profit plan.

Variations among divisions could not simply be attributed to relative profitability. While the units in the Industrial Products Group were doing very well during these years, both Divisions #1 and #2 were encountering pressure on margins.

The more responsive the division was, the more likely ECD was to enjoy a productive relationship with operating management. Where division initiative lagged, ECD attempted to compensate by projecting the implications of coming regulation and taking positions on programs felt to be desirable. The difficulty experienced by ECD in doing so was manifested by its exclusion from investment decisions, late submissions of capital requests, difficulty with managers in the field, and its inability to influence weak environmental control plans.

During this period answers were sought to two related questions: Who was going to decide on the speed and extent of compliance efforts? And how were the expenditures to be accounted for in assessing division performance? The burden in each case was ultimately to fall on the operating manager, but with conflicting expectations; he was to live within the spirit of the corporate policy on pollution without sacrificing economic returns. In fact, no effort was made to account for the additional operating expenses incurred.

Top management's hope, of course, was that by placing him in this position, some means of compensating for the increased costs would be found, such as price increases, raw material substitutions, new products, and so on. The new "rules of the game" were not comprehensively and unambiguously published; instead, they were worked out and communicated as operating managers struggled to adjust to these apparently conflicting expectations.

The final outcome was in an organizational sense highly traditional. Reliance was placed on modest additions to staffing and systems; no further structural changes or corporate pronouncements were forthcoming after 1970. Over the previous several years, the forces impeding responsiveness had become less related to an awareness of the issue and more to the way response was to be managed. The thrust of top management's actions was to force environmental impact to be considered in business decisions. The operating manager saw that the result would be more to his liking if he could limit corporate involvement to its customary review function. For instance, managers in Division #2 in no way wanted to jeopardize the plant that had come under attack in 1972. Under existing market conditions, taking responsibility for the $8.0 million in pollution control expenditures was preferable to risking a corporate decision to shut the plant down.

By 1973, the role of the corporate specialist was being influenced by increasing division activity. As operating managers gained more experience with environmentalist demands and pollution control technology, they were less inclined to seek corporate help. From ECD's standpoint the precedents required to specify the corporate policy had probably been reasonably well established, and the procedures for planning and evaluating pollution control expenditures were rapidly becoming operational. Disengagement began to appear desirable, if not necessary. Concurrently, two other issues emerged as new challenges for the department; environmental protection in offshore subsidiaries and product safety. Though very different in many respects, they shared the characteristic of being at a relatively early stage in policy development and implementation.

The Response Process Summarized

The purpose of this first chapter on Weston has been to illustrate the broad sweep of the corporation's response to environmental demands. The three phases in the process were clearly evident, though, as one would expect in a specific situation, they were not neatly ordered as in the overview in Chapter V. Phase I appeared to begin with Britton's interest in the issue in 1965 and extended into 1970 when ECD was formally constituted. Phase II really occurred in two steps, the first coincident with the formation of the Pollution Control Department, also in 1965, and the second with the appointment of a Vice President of Environmental Control in 1969. The latter event seems more in keeping with the intent of the process classifications since it was closely followed by a series of events that included new information systems and specialist assignments. It drew to a close toward the end of 1972 with the transition in Division #1. Phase III also emerged piecemeal. Environmental control had become an integral part of the decision process in Division #2 around 1966. However, a more appropriate starting time to ascribe to this phase may be in mid-1970, when Divisions #5, #6 and #7 followed suit, for they did so in response to corporate initiatives. A summary of the process is provided in Exhibit VI-6.

As complex as this description of Weston's response may seem, it does not fully convey the intricacies of the experience. One would have to know a good deal more about the organization, the people involved and how they interacted, and the specific problems they confronted to truly understand why the firm behaved as it did. The next chapter provides such data in the context of a single critical episode that illustrates the transition to Phase III in Division #5 and set the stage for the transition in Division #1.

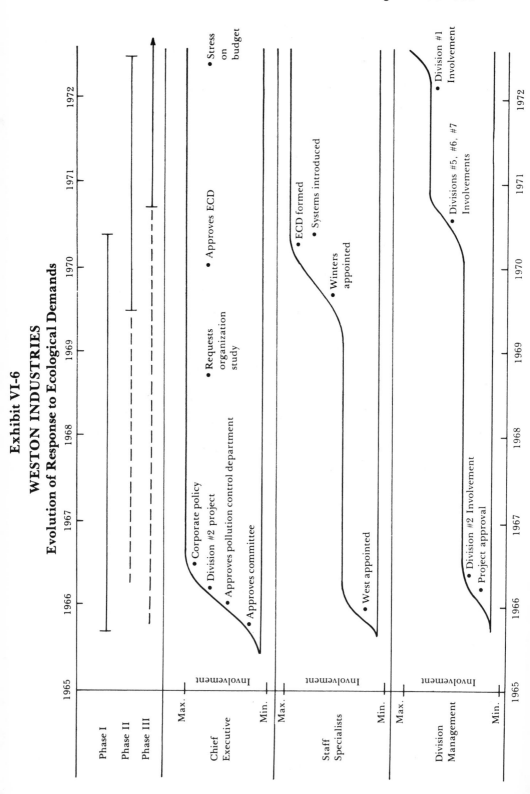

Exhibit VI-6
WESTON INDUSTRIES
Evolution of Response to Ecological Demands

VII
Weston Industries: Transition

As described in Chapter VI, by the mid-1960s Division #2 had progressed far ahead of the other divisions in its ability and willingness to incorporate ecological considerations in investment and operating decisions. A critical juncture was reached when other divisions began to follow suit. Beginning in April 1967, William West, head of the Corporate Pollution Control Department, and managers in Division #5 embarked on innovative efforts to meet regulations promulgated by the new Illinois Air Pollution Control Board (IAPCB). These efforts culminated in June 1970 in a capital request covering equipment for the Dolton plant. The project was thought to represent the first attempt to provide for air pollution controls on production processes in the industry. This episode had an immediate impact on the response to environmental issues in Division #5 and more generally in the remainder of the corporation.

The reader will find the two organization charts in Exhibits VII-1 and VII-4 (see p. 142) helpful in the following discussion; the first covers the period to March 1970 and the second from March 1970 to August 1972.

The Dolton Plant: 1967

The Dolton plant was located in a heavily industrialized suburb of Chicago. The facility had been constructed early in the century, and through the years little money had been spent on modernization. As a result, by 1966 the operation had become obsolete and inefficient although it continued to generate income on the basis of a stable product line and low fixed charges ($309,000 pretax profit on sales of $6,118,000 in 1966). The plant was one of four in the division and accounted for roughly 15 percent of its total volume.

Pollution Control Regulation in Illinois

Illinois was among the first states to consider stringent air pollution regulations. West, who had just recently assumed the new environmental specialist's position in central engineering, "cut his teeth" on the public hearings held during 1966. They were con-

Exhibit VII-1
WESTON INDUSTRIES
Partial Organization Chart
March 1967 - March 1970

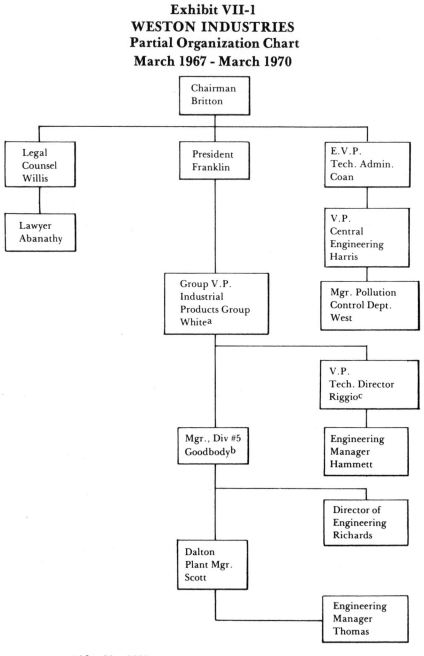

aAfter May 1968.
bUntil September 1968, then Bush.
cUntil June 1968, then Morrison. Riggio became Vice President
  of Venture Planning.

ducted against a background of mounting public concern over pollution created by the heavy industry on the southeastern fringes of Chicago.

On March 30, 1967, regulations covering particulates and smoke were approved by IAPCB to become effective 15 days later. They provided that if the standards could not be met within 60 days, a letter of intent was to be filed which promised that an abatement program acceptable to the Board would be submitted by April 15, 1968. Shortly after the regulations went into effect, 10,000 letters were mailed to industrial establishments requesting an inventory of emissions. An IAPCB official quoted in a Chicago paper, said that "special emphasis will be placed on pollution problems in heavily industrial metropolitan Chicago."

The Early Weston Response

On April 27, West received a memorandum from Greg Scott, the Dolton plant manager, which stated in part: "Mr. John Goodbody [the division manager] has asked me to advise him as to where we stand in relation to the regulations. Frankly, I do not know and, therefore, would appreciate being brought up to date on any programs to be initiated by Weston to insure the various Illinois plants meeting the regulations."

West indicated that he was looking into the matter and suggested a meeting to discuss procedures for filing the emissions inventory. As he was to do throughout the next two years, West kept Walter Harris, Vice President of Engineering, and Joseph Hammett, Engineering Manager of the Industrial Product Group (IPG), informed of his activities in Dolton. During the following six weeks, West performed some of the necessary stack tests and secured permission from the state to submit supplemental information after the June 15 deadline. By mid-August he had obtained the complete inventory and presented his evaluation to the division and IPG. The tests revealed that two of the three production lines were not in compliance with the particulate standards (see Table VII-1). Furthermore, owing to the composition of a coated product made on the second line, West also reported that fluorides were emitted into the air. Although the state did not have standards on gaseous effluents, he understood that they were being developed and felt sure that fluorine would be among the objectionable gases. West

Table VII-1

Particulates lbs/hr

Source	Allowable	Actual	Other emissions
Line # 1	5.4	13.0	
Line # 2	3.9	11.9	fluoride

also provided instructions to Scott for responding to IAPCB. Several days later, Scott submitted the inventory and indicated that the company would file an abatement program with IAPCB by April 15, 1968 as required.

In late October, at Harris' suggestion, West met with Hammett and several IPG engineers to discuss the alternatives available for the Dolton plant and the potential costs of meeting the standards. West suggested that on line #1, a bag house costing perhaps $150,000 was the most probable solution. The only practical method for removing the fluorides on line #2 was thought to be a wet scrubber. Although the scrubber itself was inexpensive, the process led to a water pollution problem because the fluorides then had to be removed from the water before it could be recycled or discharged. The total cost was put at roughly $250,000. A second remedy that was discussed and rejected was the discontinuance of the fluorine producing coated product line.

A Proposal for Modernizing the Dolton Plant

While pollution control expenditures were being estimated by West, Goodbody was talking about the need for a $1.5 million program to modernize the plant. He found little support for the idea until Lawrence White became Group Vice President in May 1968. White commented:

The Dolton plant had lots of problems. It was old and dirty. We were also having difficulties in the neighborhood. Precious metals are used in the production process, and not long before, robbers had broken in and shot the night watchman.

Britton [Chairman of the Board] wanted to shut it down. The plant had been in his territory once and he knew just what it was like. But I fought him on it. I could see trends calling for the production process we have there, and the plant is the only one in the company with that capability. Britton said, "Build a new plant," but frankly we couldn't have gotten a new one approved — I couldn't show the return.

With White's support, Goodbody, Scott, and Marc Richards, the Director of Engineering in Division #5, coordinated on the preparation of a capital request for the first part of the program, a $635,000 raw material processing unit. During 1967, sales and profits for the plant had declined 5 percent and 10 percent respectively to $5,818,000 and $278,000.

Preparation of the Pollution Abatement Program

From late October 1 until February 23, 1968, when West again met with engineers from IPG, little further was done on drafting the abatement program for the plant. During this period, a pilot test unit was being installed at the large Division #5 facility in Roan, New Jersey, under the auspicies of the Corporate Pollution Control Department to test wet scrubber technology as a method of removing both particulates and fluorides. However, because of long lead times and various complications, the first results were not expected until June, well after the date for filing the abatement schedule with IAPCB. After the February review meeting, an IPG engineer summarized the alternatives available for line #2.

1. Install a wet scrubber similar to the Roan, New Jersey, test model. This would solve our air pollution problem but would simultaneously create a water pollution problem which the plant can ill afford. A treatment system to precipitate calcium fluoride would be necessary and would be extremely expensive.

2. Installation of a limestone absorption bed similar to the unit experimented with by TVA (Tennessee Valley Authority) for fluorine removal. This is a pebble unit where fluoride collects on the limestone pebbles and can be removed by shaking. If this is only 70%-80% effective, it will still be within state requirements. This unit may not be suitable for our emissions.

3. A third patented, dry removal system was presented which did not sound as feasible as the others.

This second system seems to have the most possibilities; Bill West, and those present, feel we should make a pilot test at Dolton with this system for full evaluation.

If the limestone absorption bed pilot test were successful, West estimated a total installation time of 18 months for the full-scale unit. The situation for line #1 was simpler: "If the wet scrubber works at Roan, then it will work in Dolton."

On March 15, Peter Tucker, the senior engineer in West's department, formally proposed the pilot test referred to above to Hammett, with copies for Scott and Joseph Riggio, Technical Director of ITG, noting that it would take 28 weeks and cost $10,000. The proposal, however, was not acted upon by either the division or IPG.

As the April 15 deadline approached, company officials remained highly uncertain about how the standards could be economically met. Although West in particular was concerned about relations with the state agency, there seemed to be no alternative but to request a delay. Consequently, after clearing the contents with West, Scott petitioned IAPCB for an extension until October 15, 1968, for filing the implementation plan. Three months passed before Scott received a letter from IAPCB accepting the revised filing date.

By August it was becoming apparent that the wet scrubber at Roan was not producing satisfactory results. Moreover, West continued to meet resistance in his attempt to secure the division's cooperation for the limestone absorption bed pilot project. Hammett wrote to Scott:

> Based on some development work done by the Tennessee Valley Authority, Corporate Engineering has suggested an alternate method for removing fluoride from line #2 flue gas. This involves passing the flue gases through a hot limestone bed and removing residue by shaking. To set up and test a pilot operation of this method at Dolton is estimated to cost about $10,000 or $15,000. We believe this project should be approved before filing our plans with the State so we can include it as part of our program in reporting to the State.

He also noted that, in view of the apparent failure of the wet scrubber, another means might have to be found for controlling line #1 as well. Fiber bag houses appeared to be a logical alternative. If this method were chosen, however, the amount of chlorine gas that was emitted from the production process was then thought to present difficulties with corrosion. Hammett assured Scott that he recognized that substituting other chemicals for chlorine in the raw material would be costly, but suggested that "some testing be done as soon as possible since this will greatly reduce our pollution control problems."

As the October deadline for filing the abatement schedule approached, there continued to be considerable doubt about the technology. Neither Richards nor Scott was enthusiastic about Hammett's suggestions for cost and operational reasons, and had not as yet executed them. On the other hand, no alternatives had presented themselves. Consequently, the limestone absorption bed and raw material substitutions constituted the backbone of the plan eventually submitted to IAPCB. The dates and sequence shown in Exhibit VII-2 (see p. 134) were worked out by the Pollution Control Department and reviewed with Richards and Scott, who in turn obtained agreement from their newly appointed division manager, James Bush.

Reorganization in the Industrial Products Group

As these events were unfolding, Larry White had made two organizational changes in IPG that had some bearing on the autonomy of the four divisions in the group. The first involved the technical staff, as White explained:

> When I took over IPG one of my problems was that R & D expenditures were larger than profits. I found that consultants had made a study in '65 which said that the IPG technical staff should be decentralized as it pertained to engineering and the remaining R & D activities regrouped. Joe Riggio [then Vice President and IPG Technical Director] has made tremendous contributions to this company over the years. So in June of '68 I gave him a raise and made him Vice President of Venture Planning. Then I appointed one of his protegés, Stan Morrison, as Director of R & D and decentralized most of the engineering. My big problems were in Divisions #4 and #6 where we needed marketers, not engineers, to manage them. But we needed technical advice for the new men I was going to put in these divisions, and Riggio was to provide it.

Then during late summer of 1968 White replaced the manager of Division #4, moved Goodbody to Division #6 and appointed Bush as manager of Division #5. Bush had previously been a sales branch manager in Division #1, a department manufacturing manager in

EXHIBIT VII-2

WESTON INDUSTRIES

Air Pollution Abatement Program Filed with IAPCB, October 1968

AIR CONTAMINANT REMISSION REDUCTION SYSTEM OPERATION
LINE # 2

October 15, 1968	Begin the purchasing of the equipment necessary for the pilot air cleaning equipment.
June 15, 1969	Complete evaluation of pilot unit tests.
December 15, 1969	Complete design of the full-scale air cleaning system.
June, 1970	Have equipment at the plant site for installation.
September, 1970	Complete installation of equipment.

AIR CONTAMINANT EMISSION REDUCTION SYSTEM OPERATION
LINE # 1[a]

January 15, 1969	Complete evaluation of raw material substitutions to remove corrosive gases.
March 15, 1969	Complete evaluation of scrubbing unit at the Roan plant for application to this source.
June 15, 1969	Complete evaluation of pilot unit on source No. 2 as to its applicability to this source.

[a]The date for the completion of a system design for this source will depend upon which, if any, of the above, are applicable to this source. The time for design will be from 4 to 6 months. The time necessary for purchase and delivery of equipment is estimated to be an additional 6 months and the time for installation an additional 3 months.

Division #5 and most recently a general manager in an overseas subsidiary. As these changes were being made, IPG staff was drawing back from involvement in operations. Bush assumed his new job just prior to the submission of the compliance schedule for the Dolton plant and, through discussions with Richards and Scott, was cognizant of its contents.

Snags Develop in Implementing the Abatement Plan

Scott's letter of October 15 and the abatement plan were accepted by IAPCB in November, and the company was asked to report on

February 1, 1969, and every six months thereafter until the work had been completed.

As the first of these reporting dates approached in the summer of 1969, West became increasingly concerned about the division's commitment to the abatement plan. Moreover, the technical problems remained unresolved. The limestone absorber proved to be neither practical nor economically feasible, and the project, having finally been initiated in late 1968, was discontinued. Since no other means had been identified to remove the fluoride emissions, establishing control over line #2 remained in doubt. In addition, the wet scrubber test in Roan, having cost $70,000, was finally judged a failure in June 1969, which left the problem of controlling particulates on both lines unanswered as well. West then felt that three pilot tests in Dolton employing other technologies — high-energy venturi scrubbers, bag houses, and electrostatic precipitators — were essential. The division, however, replied that operating changes at the plant deemed necessary for productivity might delay any such tests for some months.

Consequently, West wrote to Richards on June 3 (with copies to Scott, Hammett, Bush, Harris, and Thomas Abanathy*) as follows:

> As you know, the Dolton plant has a commitment to the IAPCB to follow a timetable for determining the types and then installing the necessary air pollution control equipment on lines #1 and #2 . . . any changes to the program or to the timetable must be submitted to the authorities with justification for changes . . . our next report is due the first of August . . . I believe time is running out on us, and it would be highly desirable that we continue with the program as outlined. If it is your feeling that there is need for changes in the program, then I believe we should determine what these needs are and see if they will fit into the framework of the present abatement plan. If they will not, then determine what changes will be necessary and the substantiating factors behind it so that they can be submitted to the board for their approval.

Meanwhile in Division #5, Bush had been wrestling with the fluoride problem created by the coated product line. Although

---

*A corporate lawyer who specialized in environmental issues and who with this memorandum became increasingly involved in the Dolton situation.

regulations covering gaseous emissions had still not been issued, the apparent absence of a means for removing the noxious gases raised a difficult issue. As matters stood, there was little chance that the company could meet the abatement schedule on line #2. On the other hand, eliminating the fluorides by discontinuing the coated product line would cost the division $1 million in highly profitable sales. After discussing the issue with White, Bush reluctantly elected to withdraw from the business by year's end. This decision was communicated to West on June 5.

More or less concurrently, West also received a copy of a capital request sent to corporate engineering which indicated that Division #5 was planning to replace line #2 with a new one by April 1, 1970, and double the capacity in line #1 by July 1, 1970. Were the division to proceed with such an expansion, West was certain that the emission control pilot test installations could not be completed within the time frame established in the letter to IAPCB. In his view, the only alternative, if both expansion and abatement schedules were to be honored, entailed foregoing the tests altogether and proceeding with the riskier plan of installing full-scale control devices of a still uncertain design directly on the new lines.

On June 13 West submitted two memoranda to Richards. The first was written on the premise that the Dolton plant would not be expanded. It called for bag house and electrostatic precipitator pilot tests on line #1 to commence October 1, 1969, thus permitting purchase orders on the technology selected to be let by March 1, 1970, for a within-deadline September 1, 1970, start-up date. West concluded the memorandum by stating, "We will continue preliminarily on this project in this light until instructed otherwise." In the second document, West indicated if the expansion were pursued, the company should contract for an outside engineering service to take measurements on the existing lines and provide recommendations on the type of control equipment to be employed at the higher emission levels.

For the next several weeks the expansion program remained in limbo, though the division's interest in replacing line #2 appeared to ease. Then on July 17, Scott sent a telex to West and Richards, raising a more immediate question: "We are required to supply IAPCB with a report August 1. Who will supply information for the letter?" West was on vacation until July 28. In the meantime,

Richards had his engineering group prepare the letter for Scott's signature. It stated that the company planned to conduct the pilot tests recommended in West's earlier memorandum and noted that line #1 was to be modernized. Although the letter did not state that capacity might also be doubled, it indicated that the company was continuing to work toward the installation and operation of control equipment by September 1970. The danger in discussing the potential expansion at this point, in his view, was the possibility that IAPCB might object to it because particulate emissions would increase temporarily prior to installation of the control equipment. Consequently, the division was inclined to take the risk of not obtaining a satisfactory revision in the abatement program should the expansion plan be implemented rather than chance a delay in building capacity.

Abatement Technology is Completed

During July 1969, Corporate Pollution Control department engineers ran pilot tests with the high-energy venturi scrubber on line #1 at Dolton. They found that the equipment was capable of meeting the Illinois standards, but total costs, including those associated with water treatment, were unreasonable. As a result, further work on scrubber technology was discontinued following the completion of the evaluation in early September.

In October and November, corporate engineers initiated tests with electrostatic precipitators at Roan and Dolton in collaboration with Filco, an equipment supplier. The results appeared to be "relatively successful." Although, to the company's knowledge, the technology had never been applied to Division #5 manufacturing processes, in late December Filco indicated a willingness to submit a bid on the job which included the requisite performance guarantees.

The bag house pilot tests were delayed for a month due to the refurbishing and enlargement of line #1 in Dolton and were finally run on a comparable line in Roan. Because the tests were relocated, the results were not completed until February 1970. Preliminary evaluations, however, suggested that a bag house was also capable of reducing the effluent to specified levels. Consequently, the semi-annual report to IAPCB, filed on February 2, contained the following comment: "We are now faced with a decision between two technically feasible and effective systems and are presently making evaluations of both systems with vendors to determine the best system to be installed on this specific source." The company promised to inform IAPCB of its decision in 45 days.

With the test evaluations complete, a meeting was held on March 9, 1970, at the corporate engineering offices to select the control system for line #1 at Dolton. Those in attendance were West and three engineers from his department, Richards and one engineer from Division #5, Scott, and Hammett.

West surveyed the current state of the art in air pollution control equipment and presented the results of the pilot tests completed during the previous eight months. He then described three technically feasible processes—two employing fabric bag houses and one employing electrostatic precipitation—and provided cost estimates as shown in Exhibit VII-3. Rather than make a recommendation himself, West asked Hammett and the division personnel to decide on the approach to take.

Case II was immediately eliminated because both capital and operating costs appeared excessive. Richards argued strongly for the electrostatic precipitator in case III because it promised lower operating costs, greater ease of operation, and better "onstream" efficiencies than fabric bag house equipment. Scott agreed, noting that on the basis of his previous experience with other types of fabric filters, the estimate for operating costs in case I was too low. Hammett concurred in the views of the Division #5 managers. One important disadvantage of case III was discussed, as noted in a subsequent summary of the meeting; "There exists an 'unknown element' that always is associated with prototype applications; since to our best knowledge an electrostatic precipitator has never been used under these circumstances." Nevertheless, there was general agreement that the technological risk was worth taking. West was then asked to coordinate the pre-engineering survey at Dolton, prepare hardware specifications, and initiate procurement proceedings. Because of the technical uncertainties involved, the division concluded even before the meeting that a decision on line #2 should be deferred until the experience with line #1 could be evaluated. On March 19 the company notified IAPCB of its decision as promised and requested the necessary permit applications to construct and operate the control equipment.

While division and plant engineers were determining a location

Exhibit VII-3
WESTON INDUSTRIES
Alternative Pollution Control Technologies

Item	Case I $	Case II $	Case III $
			(Electrostatic precipitator)
	(Bag house)	(Bag house)	
1. Control hardware, shipping, and installation[a]	47,100	40,500	92,900
2. Auxiliaries (ducts, coolers, utilities, etc.)	69,000	101,900	56,000
Subtotal of 1 and 2	116,100	142,400	148,900
3. Engineering, approx. 12% of 1 & 2	14,000	17,000	18,000
4. Contingency, approx. 25% of 1 & 2	29,000	35,000	37,000
5. Total capital investment	159,100	194,400	203,900
6. Annualization of capital investment[b] 15/20 of item 5, 1st 5 years, $/year.	23,865	29,160	30,585
Balance of item 5, straight line 20 yrs. $/yr.	1,990	2,430	2,550
1st 5 yrs. annual capital investment	25,855	31,590	33,135
Remaining 15 years	1,990	2,430	2,550

continued

Exhibit VII-3 (cont.)
WESTON INDUSTRIES
Alternative Pollution Control Technologies

7. Annual oper- ating cost, 4/yr.c d	8,200	8,300	5,400
8. Total annualized cost (w/o capi- tal charges)			
First 5 years	34,055	39,890	38,535
Remaining 15 years	10,190	10,730	7,950

a Engineering cost estimates from vendors.
b Weston Tax Department.
c U.S.-HEW Publication No. AP-51.
d Two-year bag life.

for the pollution control equipment at Dolton, ECD engineers were preparing specifications and working with purchasing on the request for bids. Five vendors having experience in electrostatic precipitators were selected (including Filco) and four of them (one declined interest) attended a briefing run by ECD on April 23. A number of specification changes were made, and the vendors left with six weeks to submit their bids.

Meanwhile, an IAPCB official called Scott on April 24 to clarify the status of line #2. He asked if the control equipment was going to be used for both sources, or if line #2 had been shut down. Scott replied that on the basis of the information available to him only line #1 was covered, but that the product mix on line #2 had been changed to eliminate the fluorine emissions. Although the response appeared to be acceptable to IAPCB, Scott wrote Richards asking essentially the same question: What is the status of line #2? Richards' immediate reply was that in early April marketing had made a proposal which Bush was then considering that would result in the elimination of line #2 altogether and the substantial redesign and expansion of the third line in the plant. Were this done, pollution control equipment similar to that being specified for line #1 would then be installed on line #3.

While the division sorted through its expansion plans, difficulties emerged among some of the pollution control equipment vendors. The two largest companies withdrew from the competition, the first giving the following reasons.

We have reviewed it [the request for proposal] and noted that this is a new application for electrostatic precipitators. We were not able to determine the correlation factor of the data on the pilot unit with that to be used for the full-scale design. It would appear to us that a great deal more study will have to be done to determine the most economical base for an electrostatic precipitator.

The second vendor raised the following objections:

The pilot test data verified the extremely difficult nature of continuous efficient electrostatic precipitation on this application . . . Even using the pilot test criteria, we have no positive assurance that a design efficiency can be maintained over any extended period of time. The question of adequate rapping of the collection and discharge electrodes system could be an extremely difficult problem. . . . We do not feel that the data [are] available for our purposes in preparing a recommendation for a precipitator with a guaranteed collection efficiency.

On June 8, however, the remaining two vendors submitted proposals that purported to meet specifications. Their drawings were reviewed by ECD and Division #5 engineers, and on June 22 a meeting was held to select the winning bidder attended by West, Scott, two division engineers, the plant engineer, and the purchasing agent. The Filco bid was chosen, and a letter of intent authorized that was to be valid until August 1. The Filco proposal specified a schedule of six weeks for engineering drawings, six months for fabrication and delivery, and two months for installation. Consequently, if funding were authorized by August 1 and the schedule were met, the equipment would be in operation by mid-May 1970, or about six months later than promised in the October 1968 abatement plan.

Exhibit VII-4
WESTON INDUSTRIES
Partial Organization Chart
March 1970 - August 1972

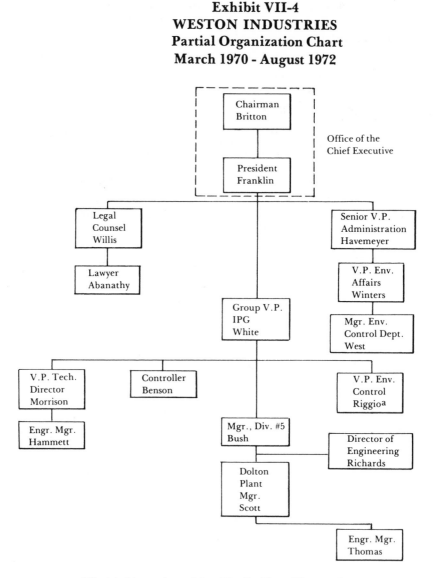

aRiggio's title was changed from Vice President of Venture Planning to Vice President of Environmental Control in June 1970.

Organizational Changes

It will be recalled from Chapter VI that at the end of March 1970 the environmental activities at Weston were reorganized. West's group was renamed the Environmental Control Department (ECD) and began reporting to the Vice President of Environmental Affairs, Carl Winters, rather than through central engineering. Winters and West had worked together for the preceding nine months on solid-waste matters, and Winters was generally aware of the Dolton situation. He had not, however, been directly involved in the decisions that had been made to this point.

A second organizational change occurred several weeks later in IPG. White had become increasingly aware of Britton's emphasis on environmental protection and he now felt that increased attention should be given to it in IPG. His concern had been triggered in particular by a proposal from a plant manager in one division to pump spent acids into deep wells. White asked Riggio to study the question and on the basis of his report vetoed the plan in favor of a method Riggio uncovered for reprocessing the acids. In June 1970 Riggio's responsibilities were specifically enlarged to include environmental affairs. He immediately began to press the divisions for the environmental plan prescribed for the first time as part of the 1971 business plan.

The Investment Decision

On June 23 a capital request for an electrostatic precipitator for Dolton was prepared by Richards and copies sent to ECD and IPG for review, with the expectation that it would be approved first by the corporate management committee at its July 20 meeting and then by the Board of Directors later in the month. The amount of the request, $240,000, compared favorably with the $250,000 figure included in the 1970 plan. It was simply justified by a seven-line paragraph indicating that the equipment was necessary to comply with the October 1968 pollution abatement plan.

On June 30 Riggio convened the first Environmental Management and Control Committee Meeting to review preliminary efforts in the IPG divisions to assemble the data on environmental control expenditures for the 1971 business plan. During this session the Division #5 capital request was discussed and some questions raised about the implications of the project. The next day Riggio expressed his concerns in a memorandum to Morrison (with copies to Hammett, Richards, and West). In part he wrote:

> I have been concerned about the Dolton program ever since learning that this is a solution and a commitment we have made sometime back. If I were more familiar with the details of the program which is to be implemented and the corrective measures, I might feel more comfortable and support the presentation of the capital request. . .
>
> I am suggesting that Joe Hammett, Marc Roberts, and someone from Bill West's Department come to grips with this and prepare the documentation that I am requesting so that we can put up a kind of defense during the Management Meeting and have reasons for it.

Riggio's memorandum coincided with the effective date of the Federal Environmental Protection Act of 1970 which was echoed in complementary Illinois legislation. Although the impact of the act would not be known for some time, it was clear that the IAPCB would be replaced by a new agency endowed with the powers called for in the federal act, and in all probability a new set of stiffer regulations would be forthcoming as well. As a result, it was conceivable that the Dolton plant would soon be subject to more stringent emission controls that the Filco equipment could not meet.

The next day West replied by outlining the considerable study that had already gone into the project and providing Riggio with additional detailed information. Before that memorandum arrived, however, Riggio had written another to Richards (with copies to West, Hammett, Morrison, and Bush) in which he said in part:

> Marc, as I told those that are involved in this Environmental Control, our General Manager, Mr. White is holding me to sort of make the final judgment as to whether we spend the large sums of money that are being requested and projected in the next few years in the area of Environmental Control. This particular proposal, as I understand it, is kind of final, and it is built into the request which Jim Bush proposes to submit for approval during July's Management Meeting.
>
> In that meeting will be Dr. Morrison, myself, and Mr. White, of course. Questions from across the table from the Corporate people will need answers and, in order to prepare for them, I have got to have more information. . .

I have the feeling that time is short and that we will not be
ready for the July presentation, in which case we may have no
alternative but to hold the presentation for a future meeting.

During the next several days, Riggio collected and analyzed the
data provided by West and Richards and then dictated a five-page
memorandum to West on July 8 (with copies to all concerned, including White and Jeffrey Benson, the IPG controller) summarizing
the questions that existed in his mind about the project as he then
understood it. The topics covered ranged from the implications of
future standards that might not be met by the contemplated equipment, to the status of line #2, to vendor performance guarantees.
The thrust of his thinking was contained in the following paragraphs:

> We will be asking for a large amount of money for just this one
> instance. This could be the forerunner and could set the stage for
> future commitments many, many times the dollar amount
> involved in this first installation. We, in IPG, and you [West],
> from an over-all viewpoint, must keep this in perspective. . .
> If we lack clear interpretation of Weston's Policy and/or lack
> some additional and essential data, it behooves us to ask for more
> time [rather] than to rush into a situation that may need
> amending soon after we go to our Management Committee and
> ask approval for $239,660.00 on July 20, 1970. . .
> I hope we can be unanimous in our decision. I propose that we
> do this on the basis of an "experiment" rather than even remotely
> suggest that this technology is a foregone solution as we approach
> our many lines and their solid particulate emissions.

West was away for a week, but Alex Lemke, the senior air pollution
control engineer, replied to some of the questions in a subsequent
memorandum. On the bottom of West's copy, Lemke noted his
interpretation of Riggio's feelings:

1. He is not convinced that Dolton line #1 is a serious contributor
   to air pollution.
2. He does not want to install *any* control equipment because of
   the profit impact.
3. He does not understand the seriousness of a Weston-IAPCB
   legal confrontation.
4. He is preparing for the possibility (admittedly remote) of poor
   control equipment performance.

On Monday, July 13, the pace quickened. Benson forwarded a copy of the capital request signed by White to the secretary, who assembled the agenda for the management meetings with the comment: "Riggio has written a long letter about this, and I want to see him when he returns . . . a slim chance we may withdraw it at the last minute . . . but, to be safe, it should be on the docket."

That morning, Riggio dictated a three-page memorandum over the telephone to Winters and Abanathy asking, "How do you think the Illinois State Authorities would react if we pleaded for more time (18 to 24 months) to come up with some more positive test and design information and/or new approaches?" He argued that in view of technical uncertainties, and other broader implications, the project was not yet ready to fund.

The following day Benson discussed the capital request and the stream of memoranda from Riggio with White. On the basis of the evidence available to him at that point, White felt that perhaps the division was moving too quickly to implement an untried technology. From conversations with managers in other parts of the company utilizing similar manufacturing techniques, especially those in Division #1, he knew that the events in Dolton were viewed with some concern. Would the state insist that comparable action be taken elsewhere? In any event, he decided to have the capital request removed from the management committee docket. To Riggio (with copies to all concerned) Benson wrote: "Based on your recent letters and recommendations, I have reviewed the subject capital request with Larry White and it will be withdrawn from the docket of the forthcoming management committee meeting."

This verdict had not long to stand. Winters immediately communicated with White and stressed the criticality of moving ahead with the program. He maintained that relations with the state were already strained by delays, and the company should not prolong further an effort which had already extended over more than two years. Moreover, he argued that Weston was ahead of the industry and would probably not be affected by stiffer regulations for some time. Once again Benson wrote to Riggio: "Today's bulletin. Based on Carl Winter's strong convictions in this matter, the capital request is being put back on the docket for next week's management committee meeting at which time I would suppose that a final conclusion will be reached regarding this expenditure."

The capital request was approved by the management committee on July 20 to clear the way for a response to the state. A meeting was then called by Riggio for July 23 to review all aspects of the Dolton situation. His lengthy memorandum, distributed the previous day, revealed that he continued to favor seeking an 18-24 month extension of the abatement program. He contended that additional time was needed to study and develop more specific data and design parameters not only for electrostatic precipitators but for bag houses and scrubbers as well. Of particular importance, in his view, was research into the possibility of linking both emission sources to the same control unit, thereby arriving at a more economical result.

The review meeting, attended by Riggio, West, Abanathy, Richards, and Scott, produced no conclusive changes in the plan. Richards and Scott were concerned about the report to be filed with the Illinois Environmental Protection Agency (successor to IAPCB) on August 1 and were anxious to move ahead with the program as then defined. Given the increasing strength of the environmental movement, there was considerable doubt in their minds about obtaining further variances, and the division could ill afford to have the enlarged Dolton plant closed. Richards also had a proposal for line #2 which was not covered in the existing plan. By running a low-margin, commodity item on the line until a decision was made on control equipment, the particulate emissions would fall within the state limitations for nine months of the year. On the other hand, Riggio continued to press for consideration of a device having the potential of linking the two sources. It was finally agreed that Riggio would prepare a second set of specifications based on his evaluation of the requirements and have this sent to the two vendors who had submitted bids previously.

On July 24 Riggio called William Newell, the corporate purchasing agent, to discuss the procedures for obtaining the new bids. Later in the day Riggio forwarded the modified specifications to Purchasing and required that the vendors be asked to have their bids in by August 4. He indicated that the changed performance requirements would "greatly lessen the task for the vendors." Newell also understood from this conversation that he was to cancel the letter of intent with Filco.

The report that Purchasing had been asked to cancel the outstanding letter of intent produced an immediate response in the division. After talking with Richards, Bush met with Winters and Newell and then sent the following memorandum:

July 27, 1970

Mr. W. R. Newell
cc: Mr. J. D. Riggio
    Mr. C. G. Winters
    Mr. W. N. West
    Mr. M. C. Richards

ELECTROSTATIC PRECIPITATOR FOR
DOLTON, LINE #1

Bill, confirming our discussion this morning with Carl Winters, I have instructed you *not* to cancel our letter of intent with Filco — as Joe Riggio apparently asked you to do Friday. Please do nothing formal re any Division #5 bid or letter of intent, present or future, without my approval.

In addition, it was agreed you would ask Filco for a two-week extension on their letter of intent to:

    (1) Enable us to double check their ability to perform.

    (2) Enable them to consider the revised specs proposed by Joe, for which we would like another bid (if possible, and prior to August 15th).

It was also agreed you would ask for bids on Joe's proposed specs from the other two firms who originally bid on the project.

And finally, in a subsequent phone conversation with Marc Richards, it was agreed we should not be late with our letter to the Illinois authorities (due August 1st) so Marc would write it for Scott's signature. . . .

JAMES E. BUSH

Newell reported the following day that he had called three vendors and had given them the new specifications over the telephone. The immediate reaction in each instance was that it would be impossible to design a precipitator capable of meeting the requirements.

On August 1 Scott signed a letter to the Illinois Environmental Protection Agency outlining the progress being made by the company to implement the abatement plan. A revised completion date for the precipitator on line #1 was set at May 15, 1971. For line #2, the company stated that it was modifying the mix of products run on the line so that for nine months of the year it would operate within the tolerances set by the code. For the remainder of the year, the company requested the Agency's temporary "indulgence" until experience had been gained in the operation of the equipment on line #1.

During the following two weeks the equipment suppliers were unable to produce an acceptable design for a unit capable of handling both emission sources. Consequently, on August 14 Filco was issued a final purchase order.

Additional complexities continued to arise in the next several months. For instance, under the new regulations, a formal variance procedure, accompanied by public hearings, was required to cover the delay in meeting the 1968 abatement plan. However, the major decisions with respect to the Dolton plant had then been made, and the company moved steadily ahead to implement them.

Subsequent Events

As work on the electrostatic precipitator at Dolton was being completed, a more consequential problem was developing at the Roan facility in New Jersey. Roughly 65 percent of the division's volume was produced on the eight lines in the Roan plant. Because of the varied nature of the division's products, there was little overlap in capability between this plant and the other three in the division. As a result, the Roan facility was a vital part of over-all Division #5 operations. It also served as headquarters for the engineering and manufacturing service departments.

Response to Ecological Demands in New Jersey

On February 9, 1971, the New Jersey Air Pollution Control Bureau (NJAPCB) conducted public hearings on revisions to the state pollution control code. West and Ralph Petit were in attendance. As a member of the IPG engineering department, Petit had participated in the early phases of the Dolton project before White reorganized the technical function and decentralized the engineering portion of it. Now he worked for Richards in Roan, a major portion of his assignment relating to pollution control.

At the hearings, the research director of the industry association to which Division #5 belonged stated that the proposed regulations were more stringent than could be accommodated by the current state of the art. Nevertheless, after the meeting he agreed with West and Petit that the standards would be implemented more or less as proposed, with special problems to be handled through a variance procedure. Were this to occur, all of the lines at Roan would be out of compliance by wide margins. Moreover, whereas the Illinois code had the effect of requiring Weston to eliminate 90 percent of the particulate matter, the New Jersey code implied the removal of about 95 percent. The following day, Petit summarized the situation for Richards and concluded by noting: "Since we will require a variance for all our lines as soon as this regulation takes effect (which could be as soon as June 15), I believe now is the time to decide what we are going to do in Roan to establish a definite program and timetable."

In fact, the New Jersey regulations were not announced until January 27, 1972, just under the deadline set in the Environmental Protection Act for the promulgation of state implementation plans. The standards, to be effective March 27, 1972, were not significantly different from those discussed a year earlier. In the intervening period, Division #5 engineers took emissions inventories in the Roan plant and continued to examine the possibility of linking multiple sources to one pollution control device. Further information was obtained from the equipment at the Dolton plant which had been put into operation and was then operating with moderate success.

Within three weeks of the announcement of the new standards, Petit had the data available to solicit cost estimates for single and multiple source designs from Filco. Although a conference could not be arranged with the state until June, Petit continued to work on the engineering specifications and the as yet unresolved issue of combining emission sources in one control device. On the basis of his work, letters were sent to seven vendors in late May asking them to quote on both configurations for lines #1 and #2.

With additional engineering inputs in hand, a decision was made in late June on the nature and timing of the abatement plan as follows:

Lines	Installation Date
1-5 (combined)	December 31, 1973
6-7 (combined)	August 30, 1974
8	To be phased out or equipment installed by July 1, 1975

The decision to proceed with combined emission sources was made in discussions involving Riggio, Richards, and Petit. A critical influence was Riggio's study into control technologies employed overseas. In fact, he had located a Japanese supplier, MATCO, that in his view offered particularly attractive design and cost advantages.

Meanwhile, West had been coordinating the company's approach to the state regulatory agency. Although state officials had indicated an interest in considering all Weston facilities located in New Jersey together, West had succeeded in preserving the distinction between divisions by arranging separate compliance reviews for each. He did so because Division #1 was not nearly as far along in developing a plan as Division #5. In fact, ECD had been requested to draft a variance petition for Division #1's two New Jersey plants that would stretch out the installation of emission control equipment to August 1976. Little more had been done by the division to that point.

Consequently, West's relationships with these divisions during the summer of 1972 were very different. He kept in touch with program development in Division #5 but did not become involved in engineering or investment decisions. He was able to deal from a position of relative strength in filing permits and presenting an abatement plant to NJAPCB. On August 28, with Riggio's urging, the division decided on a MATCO unit, and West and Abanathy promptly approved the construction permit application completed by Petit. Within two weeks, the application was accepted by the state, and immediately thereafter a capital request for $1,123,000 was sent through channels for final approval. West added ECD comments approving the engineering and regulatory aspects of the request, and it was placed on the docket for the October meeting of the Board of Directors.

In contrast, West became embroiled in a controversy in Division #1. The regional manager was anxious to spread the cost and effort of installing control equipment over the normal rebuild cycle for individual production lines in the plants. He contended that the state would accept an abatement program which specified that portions of an operation would remain out of compliance beyond the July 1, 1975, deadline required under the Environmental Protection Act. West, Abanathy, and the company's New Jersey attorney felt that such a plan would be rejected even though only two of twelve lines in the plant were to be put under controls after that date. Several months passed, and little progress was made on the development of an abatement plan. Finally, West arranged a meeting for August 17 which he hoped would be attended by the regional manufacturing manager and the two plant managers, as well as the division pollution control engineer, the regional engineering manager, Abanathy, and outside legal counsel.

To West's consternation, the three manufacturing managers did not attend the August 17 meeting. During the session, the termination date remained in contention. The division engineers maintained that the expenditures should be spread over the longer period, and they argued that the company should test the state's feelings about an extension. Eventually, their view prevailed. Then, despite prodding from ECD, another month passed before the regional manufacturing manager accepted his subordinates' plan and division engineering began to develop equipment specifications.

During this time, the regional manufacturing manager commented to the researcher:

> I'm foot-dragging—if that's what you call it—because the equipment we're talking about is brand new, and the first on the market are often half-baked affairs. I'd rather wait until someone has built a better one. . . The company will grant us the money. That's no problem. But the depreciation gets charged to the plant. The capital expense rationale is forgotten pretty fast by the corporation. We were going to expand the Somerset [New Jersey] plant this year. . . Now because of the added cost of the pollution control equipment, we may not. We don't get enough more capacity to justify the cost.

In the meantime, West had found state officials unwilling to accept compliance dates beyond July 1975, because such an action would place them in violation of the National Environmental Protection Act. A final ruling remained in doubt, however, because the plant in question was located in an area that met the national secondary ambient air standards. The company's position was that under these circumstances the state was not required to disturb existing operating permits which, for the two lines, did not expire until 1976. Consequently, the Division #1 abatement plan was filed as originally formulated and as of June 1973 had not yet been finally accepted or rejected by the state agency.

By December 1972, Division #1 engineering was on the verge of selecting a domestic equipment supplier to construct the first electrostatic percipitators to be installed in the division's New Jersey plants. At this point Riggio made a strong plea for the use of MATCO devices such as those installed at Roan. He had been so impressed by the cost and design features of the MATCO percipitators that he had secured White's interest in pursuing a licensing agreement with the Japanese firm, whereby Weston would market and arrange for the manufacture of MATCO equipment in the United States. After a period of questioning, Division #1 agreed to install the MATCO Product, and IPG found itself on the way to being in the pollution control business.

Management Reactions

At various times during the concluding months of the events described above, the managers involved talked with the researcher more generally about their concerns. The following comments are illustrative:

West: (*Manager of the Environmental Control Department*)

I may not always agree with Riggio on the details but that's really beside the point. He makes things happen in IPG. This situation is in contrast to Division #1 which has shown no interest in a Riggio-type position at the division level. Because of that, I'm forced to go through Winters to the division manager and then down through the organization to get things done, and this makes it uncomfortable. Trying to influence the regional managers (in Division #1) directly has been very difficult. The result is that pollution problems get treated as technical issues, not as business problems. They don't get general management attention. The division manager may care but he isn't going to tell the regional managers how to run their businesses. There isn't anyone in the technical group involved with the issue that has enough influence to get it considered.

White: (*Vice President, Industrial Products Group*)

I operate without an administrative manager in IPG. That may seem inefficient because more people report to me, but I get involved in my businesses. Here Riggio reports directly to me. He gives me a monthly status report on each plant, and whenever there is a new pollution control equipment installation, I arrange to see it operate. So the organizational dynamics are simplified—there are fewer filters. . .

It's tough on the division managers. We say do both; make profits and keep up on the pollution control. And we're facing some heavy expenditures to 1975. But the spending is sort of like good house-keeping—it goes with a good profit record. You have to believe there are benefits. For instance, we have a very efficient operation now in Dolton that is giving us better profits than ever before.* The modernization program was responsible for it, but that wouldn't have happened if we'd been scared by the pollution control regulations, and shut the plant down.

Riggio: (*Vice-President, Environmental Control, Industrial Products Group*]

White said, "Let's get this one [environmental control] on the road" . . . like any new development, you can't put the whole organization on it. Somebody must wear two hats, and I was chosen. Because of my background I could cover most areas without much outside help. I also knew the people in the organization to interface with, and have structured this through the engineering departments in the divisions.

In New Jersey, when others were going for variances, we asked the state for permission to do the whole plant. We got our permit back in ten days. They were looking for someone to innovate; I don't know if the state has other companies doing it, but they seemed surprised by our request. We're not *trying* to be first. Instead, our mission is to get the job done right. . . looked at from

*Sales and profits for the Dolton plant in 1971 were 34 percent and 246 percent respectively above those reported in 1967.

a competition standpoint, if you put in a bad system, you're in trouble on costs. So we learn by doing and not just by knowing what others are doing—if that were all everyone did, nothing would happen.

Bush: (*General Manager, Division #5*)

The Dolton problem came at us early and hard, and we had to improvise to meet our commitments. But now we have more confidence because our system seems to work . . . The corporation was breathing down my neck on that one to make sure I didn't make a mess of it. We felt a lot of pressure from Division #1 to do it right. They have a lot of plants in Illinois and, even though we had worse problems, they thought if we screwed it up with the state, they could have been in trouble, too.

Basically, we don't have to rely on Riggio and the Environmental Control Department any more. I'm well organized with Richards and Petit, and we're big enough to do the job ourselves. On the first one in Dolton, I got involved in putting the program together to learn the technology. But now I've left it pretty much up to engineering to handle. . .

The only time I might get into trouble with the corporation is if I try to protect an underutilized line which still provides a contribution. Recently, I've been looking at whether we ought to discontinue parts of our business. . . The corporation depends on us [division managers] to shut down the unprofitable businesses. Now they're charging us with interest on our investment. We're still responsible for the bottom line and they're not expecting us to run a less profitable business. We are supposed to compensate for these additional costs. . .

Approval on the capital requests for pollution control equipment is just about automatic now. We have some choices as to method and timing, but the money has to be spent sooner or later. We spend about $4 million a year in this division on capital items and sometimes as much as $7 million. The request for New Jersey obviously means that we can't stay within the average figure. But the request itself doesn't worry me very much—not any more than one for $9,000. The evaluation isn't anything like the one that would go into another project of similar size.

Richards: Engineering Manager, Division #5

We have no trouble making decisions in this division. We come to an agreement among ourselves and stand together . . . Jim Bush has total responsibility, but on this one [pollution control] he has asked me to make the decisions. I get his approval but he doesn't interject himself into it like he does in other cases. We follow the same routines now with the capital requests for pollution control equipment that we do with anything else—except that we have this ultimatum from Britton that no one get into trouble—so we get the money. If I had a regular request for $1 million, it would take six months to put the economic analysis together. This one [for New Jersey] was on a half a page. It was easy to do, and I'm sure it will sail right through . . .

We're responding immediately to the law—others are not; [another company] is actually challenging the law. We're not helping them much by doing something they say is beyond the state of the art. But we want to spread the capital investments over a number of years. I wouldn't want to be caught with a $5 million capital request in 1975.

ANALYSIS

The Dolton plant incident triggered a significant transition in Weston's approach to environmental demands. Although the critical events may have occurred during a six-week period in June and July 1970, what happened before and after that period is an integral part of the story. The antecedents provide an apt illustration of organizational behavior in a Phase II setting. The subsequent events in New Jersey portray significant changes in the approach to pollution control in Division #5 that had not yet been mastered in Division #1. As a result, the full sweep of the episode from 1967 to 1972 is relevant to this commentary.

The Antecedents: April 1967-May 1970
The difficulty of implementing social policy is suggested by the time required to respond to the environmental demands placed on the Dolton plant. Fully eighteen months were devoted to the development of an abatement plan filed with the state in October 1968. At that point the company was compelled to make schedule commitments without a definite idea of how they were to be met. Another twenty months were required to settle on the technology and an equipment supplier, and even then significant questions remained about the final outcome. Why did the response take so long? The reasons can be only partially ascribed to technological uncer-

tainties. More important from a management point of view was the fact that a variety of organizational problems had to be resolved.

Consider first the context in which the original abatement plan was written: The number of unknowns that were confronting West as he picked up the problem in April 1967 were certainly enormous! What were the emissions at Dolton? How could they be controlled? How amenable was the state to delay? What additional regulations were forthcoming? And so forth. Both the division and IPG immediately looked to West for the answers. They viewed his task quite simply: to find some way of satisfying IAPCB without disturbing the operation or forcing it to absorb appreciable added expense. Thus, West took the initiative in performing stack tests, instructing the plant manager how to respond to the state, experimenting with control technologies, and ultimately drawing up the compliance schedule. At the time, he appeared to have assumed a large share of the responsibility for the results.

The division, of course, had its own problems. The Dolton plant was clearly in trouble on performance grounds, and division manager Goodbody was in danger of losing it. If he wanted to win support for his modernization project, he could not afford to make a big issue out of pollution control lest his superiors view it as another reason for closing the plant down. At the same time, division preoccupation with saving the plant and pushing ahead with its overhaul may have contributed to the persistent delays encountered by West in obtaining cooperation for the limestone absorption bed test during 1968. The concurrent decentralization of the technical function in IPG to division levels tended to disengage Hammet, Engineering Manager for IPG and the one with whom West had been collaborating, from active involvement in operating problems. In fact, Hammet had no better luck than West in speeding the limestone tests. Thus, West became increasingly dependent on his relationship with the division engineering staff.

From the filing of the abatement plan in October 1968 until June 1969, West was under increasing pressure. As one technology after another failed to show promise, the plan began to look unattainable. When the division announced that the plant was to be expanded, the chances of meeting the deadline while still following the prudent course of running pilot tests just about disappeared.

Once again division management placed highest priority on the issue of greatest concern to them — having sufficient capacity — and forced the Pollution Control Department to work around it. The same inclination pertained to disclosing the extent of the expansion; risks for the division were measured in very different terms from those for the corporate specialist. On the other hand, under the influence of White, the Group Vice President, Bush agreed to give up $1 million in revenues by discontinuing the product line which caused the flouride emissions. For obvious reasons, the division manager did not respond with the same degree of alacrity to advice from the corporate staff that he did to his immediate superior.

West continued to bear the primary burden of implementing the plan until a technical solution had been found that was acceptable to Division #5 in the spring of 1970. He was, however, careful to let division engineers choose the equipment type from among several alternatives. It is interesting, though hardly surprising in view of the corporation's posture on operating budgets and capital spending for pollution control, that the division selected the configuration which promised the lowest operating costs and best operating efficiencies but the largest initial investment. This choice also involved the greatest chance of technical failure, but then both West and the supplier had warranted that an electrostatic precipitator would perform satisfactorily. In a sense, the stakes for these third parties in the success of the equipment were higher than for Division #5 personnel who, after all, were not directly responsible for the technology.

Consequently, even though the capital request was prepared by the Division Engineering Manager, and submitted through customary channels, the question of securing approval appeared from the division's perspective to be a *pro forma* exercise that was more West's concern than theirs. Bush's chief interest lay in protecting the Dolton plant; as long as the program was satisfactory to the state, his needs were largely met. For West, on the other hand, the program represented the culmination of three years of effort and called for him to put his reputation for handling technical and regulatory matters on the line.

Trauma: June-July 1970

Trauma was occasioned by the reinsertion of IPG in the decision process. The intervention of Riggio, the newly appointed IPG Vice

President of Environmental Control, and ultimately White, was
prompted by corporate-wide concerns that expanded the implications of the decision beyond the narrow limits of the Dolton plant.
For more than a month Riggio hammered on both ECD and the
division. Had alternative technologies been adequately considered?
What precedents were being set for the far larger expenditures to
come? And so forth. Twice he went one step further and temporarily interrupted the decision, first by having the capital request
withdrawn from the management committee docket and then by
insisting on consideration of a dual source design.

Needless to say, Riggio's challenge was disconcerting to those who
had an interest in the original proposition. From West's viewpoint,
the labored but finally completed task of equipment specification
had been challenged, as had ECD's role generally in IPG. Bush was
aware that implementation of the abatement plan under the best of
circumstances was already certain to be late. If time were taken to
consider all of Riggio's objections, the additional delay might cause
a shutdown or some other harsh countermeasures from the new
Illinois Environmental Protection Agency. The rebuttals to Riggio — by Winters in reinstating the capital request, and then by Bush
in nullifying the cancellation of the letter of intent with Filco — were
indications of these concerns. The episode was unusual at Weston
and had three immediate consequences.

First, Bush asserted his responsibility for and authority over capital requests pertaining to pollution control in Division #5 facilities.
Officially this had always been the case, though in practice ECD
had guided the Dolton project subject to division-imposed constraints.

Second, there was now little question that White was actively
interested in the pollution control issue. It was also clear that a
manager who slighted it or could not provide adequate justification
for proposed investments was likely to be overridden and criticized
in the process. Since Riggio was not prepared to defer to ECD, the
division could not expect to escape accountability by relying on
ECD advice either. In essence, it was prudent for the division manager to take responsibility for the quality of the analysis and the
judgments resulting from it as well. Although nowhere explicitly
stated, some modest portion of his performance appraisal could
fairly be ascribed to the handling of environmental control decisions.

Third, division engineers had been drawn into the decision and, through working with ECD, had learned a good deal about the technology and the procedures for dealing with regulatory agencies. As a result, Bush had his own specialists to call on in resolving future problems and did not have to rely on staff reporting to his superiors.

The Aftermath: August 1970-1972

The significance of the Dolton incident becomes apparent in Division #5's approach to the New Jersey regulations. In contrast to the earlier Dolton experience:

1. Regulatory changes were monitored by division staff and the response to them anticipated in an internally initiated abatement plan.

2. The division performed the necessary emissions tests and managed the development of technical alternatives, this time incorporating Riggio as an adviser.

3. ECD was involved in presenting the plan to the state regulatory agency and reviewing the division's proposed course of action, but otherwise did not seek to intervene in the project definition.

4. These steps resulted in a program that was to bring the Roan facility into compliance well within the time frame prescribed in the regulations, despite the incorporation of another important design innovation and more stringent standards than had previously been met in the industry.

Thus the task of responding to the pollution control issue was added to the problem-solving repetoire of Division #5. The division manager had become involved and was prepared to accept responsibility for the difficult decisions that would be necessary to accommodate the social demand in the profit plan without compromising the spirit of the corporate policy on pollution.

The transition from a corporate- to a division-initiated program was not accomplished without cost. Beyond the allocation of money for control equipment and division specialists such as Petit, Bush accepted the burden of anticipating and in some fashion compensating for the environmental demands in the division's business strategy. To the extent that social responsiveness diminished his flexibility to add capacity, request investment funds for other projects, or retain certain product lines, this task became a good deal more difficult. The costs of increased job complexity and reduced operating flexibility are not easily measured. To the manager on the firing line, however, they are very real.

With due allowance for the growing maturity of the environmental issue from 1969 to 1972 and ECD's increased sophistication in dealing with it, the response in Division #1 developed in a fashion that resembled the earlier one in Division #5's Dolton plant. Division management looked to ECD for assistance in negotiating a compliance schedule that met the operating needs of its facilities. Although West did not specify the timetables or become involved in technical matters as he did in Dolton, he was clearly the motivating force for the first nine months of 1972. The regional manufacturing manager was "foot-dragging," because he was reluctant to assume the added costs and risks of a nascent technology before it was absolutely necessary. Consequently, West was not able to obtain agreement internally for a schedule that safely avoided regulatory questions.

Yet the episode in Division #1 did not result in trauma. The division environmental specialist lacked the influence or the mandate from division management to contest the region's position had he wanted to do so. West could not override this position either. Moreover, the corporation was in the midst of a major reorganization, noted in Chapter VI which proved particularly unsettling for Division #1. The regional manufacturing manager was to report directly to a new vice president of manufacturing whose feelings on pollution control were as yet unknown. In addition, Winters, who had taken a strong stand in the Dolton case, was preoccupied with his move back to Division #1.

Thus the organizational pressures contributing to trauma in the Dolton plant incident were largely absent in the case of Division #1; only West was common to both. In their absence, the regional manufacturing manager assumed a posture that he felt was entirely appropriate for the business and expected by his superiors—i.e., do not request funding for "unproductive" projects unless absolutely necessary. The corporate policy was not sufficiently precise to rule on the decision one way or the other, and ECD did not have (or want to use) the muscle to override his judgment.

Instead, transition in Division #1 appeared to result from structural and management changes in the division itself. The visible support given to the issue by Rushmore, the new division manager, assured that it would assume a far higher priority in the thinking of managers in the field. Also, by the end of 1972 the regulatory machinery was so firmly in place that the operating manager had far less latitude to decide on a program independently of public expectations.

VIII

Business Products Corporation: Response to Demands for Equality in Employment

Business Products Corporation (BPC), with sales of about $2.0 billion in 1973, produced a range of industrial and consumer products and services. Growth in sales and profits had consistently exceeded 12 percent per year during the previous decade, and top management placed strong emphasis on the continuation of this performance. For the most part, growth had been achieved by the proliferation of products developed through a sizable commitment to research and sold by aggressive, worldwide marketing organizations. A number of acquisitions had also been made during the 1960s which extended the scope of corporate activities into new but related fields. Despite a broad product line, BPC was characterized by a dominant technological thrust.

Until 1969 BPC was organized for the most part by function; vice presidents for sales and manufacturing reported to an executive vice president of operations, who in turn reported to the president, as did those responsible for research, finance, personnel, and various other administrative services. There were also several smaller units directed by general managers who were accorded a greater measure of autonomy from the large central staff. A major reorganization was undertaken in 1969 that included a relocation of the corporate offices and a sharp reduction in the size of the staff. Several acquisitions were also consummated at this time, and a divisionalized organization structure adopted throughout the company. Altogether, six divisions were created, some of them divided into two or more separate business units. The effect of the restructuring was to remove the top officers and their immediate staff from involvement in operations, a transition that was to have a very definite impact on efforts to hire and advance minorities and women.

Although the 1969 reorganization was the most significant in the period of interest to us, there were frequent changes in reporting relationships and responsibilities at operating levels. For instance, the sales organization was divided into regions, also in 1969, each region headed by a general manager supported by functional managers for personnel, control, operations, and so forth. In 1972 the largest product division was broken up into separate "divisions" predominantly responsible for marketing, manufacturing, and development. Each of these units maintained a full complement of personnel and financial services. Consequently, operating managers were frequently called upon to fill newly established positions and perform according to standards that were still under development.

A detailed budgeting and control system was employed by BPC to negotiate "stretch" performance targets and monitor results. The pressure to meet performance commitments was characterized by operating managers as "intense." For instance, when volume lagged behind expectations, it was not unusual to find expense budgets cut and hiring freezes temporarily imposed. One corporate staff executive commented, "At BPC I believe line managers respond very quickly to direction; they understand the goal-setting process and will do their best if they feel it's a company priority."

Owing to the company's rapid expansion, managers willing and able to assume increasing responsibilities were rewarded with accelerated career progressions and bonus incentives. The average age of the BPC manager was consequently quite low. During the late 1960s, a number of senior operating positions were also filled by experienced executives hired from other firms, a practice deemed necessary on a one-time basis. It was anticipated that, in the future, top management would be increasingly obtained through internal development. Lateral transfers and even demotions were not unusual among middle managers. The organization could be described as aggressive and competitive. To protect the individual, the chief executive instituted a policy whereby he personally reviewed the termination of anyone employed by the company for more than seven years.

Early Activities: A Focus on the Community: 1964-1967

In early 1964, Walter Sherrill was hired by BPC to establish a personnel research unit that would, among other duties, be responsible for organization planning. Shortly after he arrived, Sherrill was asked to review the status of minorities in the company and in the city surrounding its headquarters. He was also nominated to serve in a community organization that secured and distributed scholarship funds for black students.

These assignments were undertaken specifically at the request of John Harrison, then Chairman and President of BPC. Harrison had long maintained that the responsibilities of business to society extended beyond the narrow limits of producing goods and services. He was deeply involved in community affairs himself (his grandfather had been mayor of the city) and had engaged BPC in a number of programs to advance education and the arts. By this time both Harrison and the company had a reputation for holding an enlightened view of the role of the corporation in facilitating social change.

The results of Sherrill's early investigations were not encouraging. He found that less than 2 percent of the employees were black in an area where blacks accounted for 7 percent of the population, and almost none were to be found in the marketing units located in the field. Although there were no official barriers to entry, neither were there efforts to increase the proportion of minorities in the work force. As for the city, Sherrill quickly learned that its placid demeanor should not be confused with contentment in the ugly but little noticed ghetto.

That summer the city was buffeted by severe rioting. The disturbances, among the first in the country, came as a shock to community leaders such as Harrison who had taken pride in the city's low unemployment rate and seemingly progressive attitude. He immediately encouraged his managers to discover how the company might help to alleviate the plight of the minority population, and indicated that the company should be prepared to work with responsible parties in the community.

Within a few weeks various approaches to preparing unemployed minorities for entry-level positions in production were being explored by the vice presidents of manufacturing and personnel and their subordinates. Union leaders were also included in the discussions and gave their blessing to the idea. During the spring of 1965 a proposal was prepared by Personnel Research for an experimental training program, dubbed Project Advance, to help twenty culturally deprived individuals meet BPC employment standards. The proposal indicated that "in practice, this will mean selecting near misses on our present standards. After we have developed a proven training program, we can attempt more extensive rehabilitation with greater likelihood of success."* Project Advance was to be directed by a program leader from Personnel Research and was estimated to cost $85,000.

While the proposal was being discussed and eventually approved, two further developments emerged. First, BPC applied for inclusion in Plans for Progress, a government-sponsored program to encourage corporations to expand employment opportunities for minorities. Participation necessitated more detailed reporting of employee demographics by racial background than had previously been required; sixteen reporting units were specified by BPC with a separate break down by geographical area.

Second, a militant action group, JUSTICE, was formed in the city with widespread support from the black community. Led by William Browning, then Manager of Personnel Practices, BPC representatives opened a dialogue with this organization and were successful, despite initial confrontations, in building a working relationship with its leadership. The principal item on the JUSTICE agenda was employment. They were appreciative of Project Advance, but indicated that the program was not large enough to have a significant and immediate impact on their constituency. Browning called Harrison's attention to the JUSTICE suggestion for a substantially larger commitment to hiring the underqualified. Harrison's reply stated in part: "While my heart is with it, this is a tremendous jump in aspirations. Is it manageable? Let us not go so fast that we lose control. . . Do we have these openings which will be permanent? Nothing would be worse than to start them and then have layoffs a year from now." Although the recommendation was not acted upon then, BPC agreed to collaborate with JUSTICE in recruiting qualified minority applicants and studying employment standards.

Project Advance ran from December 1965 to March 1966 and was judged to be highly successful. Sherrill was then asked by Browning to draw up plans for further minority training programs. In early July, Personnel Research proposed a moderately enlarged Advance II and a parallel program to fill entry-level clerical positions, both to commence in October at a combined cost of $165,000. With an

---

*In the process of interviewing and testing candidates, those found to be already qualified were to be hired.

eye on the possibility of renewed civil disorders, the report stated that, "because BPC will have no ongoing program for the inner city through the tense summer months, we feel it desirable to communicate throughout the city our plans for the fall." However, no sooner had the expenditures been approved and JUSTICE informed, than the authorization was abruptly canceled. A major product introduction was encountering difficulties at the time with the result that budgets were slashed throughout the company. Browning, who had recently been named Vice President of Personnel, informed JUSTICE of the situation and won their forebearance for a delay.

In February 1967, clearance was given for Advance II to be rescheduled for the summer and fall of that year. Harrison and Graham Moore, who had moved from Executive Vice President to President in May 1966, also jointly announced that, economic conditions permitting, the company expected to employ 150 more minority persons from the city in the next year. This commitment represented a doubling of the minority representation and was the first of its kind entered into by BPC. Sherrill described how many of the new employees were recruited: "Advance II was starting up at the time that JUSTICE was sending busloads of blacks to neighboring companies demanding employment and demonstrating when it wasn't offered. When they came to BPC, we opened the doors and hired 80% of them, many directly into the work force rather than Project Advance. What would have been confrontation turned into a thing of beauty."

Later in 1967 JUSTICE approached BPC to support the establishment of a minority-owned business in the inner city. The concept was favorably received by top management (Harrison was then serving on a congressional panel appointed to recommend legislation to assist minority enterprises). The Personnel Department enlisted the assistance of senior manufacturing and procurement managers who, together with JUSTICE, sifted through business propositions to find one that met community development needs yet had a potential for profit. In May 1968 the study team's proposal was accepted by Moore and shortly thereafter a federal grant was obtained to sustain the venture in its infancy and permit it to offer training for the hard-core unemployed. BPC offered consulting assistance, and an agreed-upon level of purchases for the initial four years at a premium price if necessary.

BPC's formal relationship to the new business extended to 1973. At one time, as many as six consultants — mostly specialists from diverse functional areas — were assigned to the venture. Sherrill served on its Board of Directors and was responsible, through a full-time project manager on his staff, for BPC's participation. Despite periods of strife and changes in personnel in both organizations, the business appeared to turn the corner in 1970, and the BPC consultants were gradually withdrawn. After the excitement and publicity accompanying its start-up, however, interest in the venture waned in the BPC organization. Indeed, in early 1970 Sherrill wrote to Browning, "We do not believe there is a full awareness, within BPC, that paying a premium price on an interim basis is part of the support we should provide the venture. While there is not overt resistance, there is a lack of understanding among management members who are new to BPC or long-time BPC people who have not previously been involved." The BPC commitment was duly reconfirmed, but the emphasis in minority affairs had by this time been focused almost entirely on employment within the company.

Efforts to Increase Minority Employment: 1967-1969

In the summer of 1967 Sherrill hired Andrew Jenkins to coordinate BPC relations with the black community and to provide professional expertise in minority relations. Jenkins had a long and distinguished career in civil rights dating back to the Roosevelt administration. Although he reported to Sherrill and was in a formal sense far removed from the Chief Executive, Jenkins nonetheless had impromptu contact with Harrison and from time to time over the next two years gave briefings on minority programs to the executive group. An abbreviated organization chart is shown in Exhibit VIII-1.

When Jenkins joined the company, Personnel Research was attempting to diagnose why an extensive minority recruitment campaign had failed in the Software Systems Division, a small unit in Buffalo, that had of its own volition expressed a desire to increase minority representation. Neither the division nor Sherrill had been able to pinpoint the source of the difficulty. After a trip to Buffalo, however, Jenkins quickly concluded that the division's message was simply not reaching the black community, at least not in an acceptable form. He commented: "The company was incredibly naive in

Exhibit VIII-1
BUSINESS PRODUCTS CORPORATION
Partial Organization Chart
July 1967-March 1969

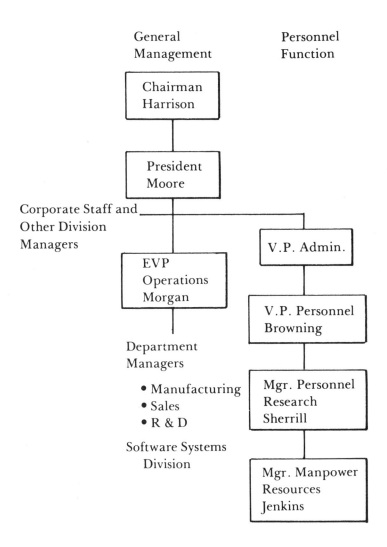

those days. There was very little understanding of the power structure in the black community. There was also a tendency to equate
blacks with the hard-core unemployed." Jenkins offered to bring
community leaders together for frank discussions with division
management about the company and its approach to minority
affairs. The suggestion was accepted and implemented with
excellent results; the minority applicant flow increased sharply, the
number of blacks on the division's payroll nearly doubled in the next
six months, and managers gained a greater understanding of community needs.

Although the Software Systems Division experience was an
acknowledged breakthrough, it was not immediately replicated in
other locations. Up to that time little effort had been made to elicit
the support of operating managers for augmented minority employment, and most felt under no compulsion to act voluntarily.
Personnel Research reported at year-end that the earlier goal of 150
black hires in the headquarters city was within reach but threatened
by a general slowdown in work force additions. In the field
marketing organization the number of blacks had inched up from
74 to 83 (.9 percent), though only 1 percent of the new hires were
black. Some of the smaller divisions appeared to be in fairly good
shape but others lagged, in one case to the extent that no minorities
were employed at all. Despite the success of the inner city programs
and the acclaim received by the company for its efforts, the priority
accorded minority affairs by operating managers, with a few
exceptions born of personal conviction, remained low.

During 1968 corporate attention began to be focused inward.
Top management's commitment to improving opportunities for
minorities in the company was stated emphatically, and for the first
time pressure was exerted on the organization for improved
performance in this area.

Personnel Research — essentially Sherrill and Jenkins — were
attempting to develop a formula for fixing minority hiring targets in
early 1968. They were also working on a proposal for minority
recruitment based in part on Jenkins' experience in the Software
Systems Division. These efforts were soon merged with the search for
an answer to a more immediate question: What goals should BPC
accept in the National Alliance of Business JOBS program? Moore
had agreed to serve as city chairman for the program and had every

intention of setting a high standard for others in industry. He naturally looked to Sherrill's group for staff assistance. Although NAB appeared to be principally interested in the hard-core unemployed, Moore insisted that BPC set targets for qualified minorities as well. On that basis, and with Moore's detailed approval, a target of roughly 1,300 qualified minority and hard-core* hires was recommended by Personnel Research, two-thirds of them to meet existing entry standards. The net additions by year-end were estimated at about 800 minority employees. Provision then had to be made for passing this commitment down to the operating units, developing an information system to reflect progress, and offering recruiting and training assistance as needed.

For some months, Personnel Research had felt the need for a strong corporate statement that would establish BPC's commitment to minority employment. Jenkin's had specifically stressed the need for it in a discussion with Harrison that spring. Finally in May 1968 as the NAB pledge was completed and two weeks prior to Moore's appointment as chief executive, a letter signed by Harrison and Moore was sent to all BPC managers stating in part:

> . . . despite a stated policy that seeks to fulfill our obligations to society, and even though the significant steps we *have* taken have been publicly praised, our performance is still far from a shining beacon of corporate responsibility.
>
> We know, of course, that many Negroes — fearing rejection — simply don't apply to BPC for jobs. And of those who do apply, many fail to meet our usual standards of qualification. But those factors obviously cannot be used as excuses. They are, rather, the very problems which BPC must and will attack in the future.

The letter outlined three action steps. First, BPC was to "heavily intensify" the recruitment of blacks and other minorities, in part through extending the approach developed for the Software Systems Division to other units. Second, selection standards and training programs were to be systematically reexamined to remove damaging entry barriers that tended to screen out all but the most qualified individuals. Third, training of unqualified minorities was to be increased, based on the Project Advance experience, and incorpor-

---

*About 15 percent of the hard-core figure was non-minority.

ated into the existing hiring process. Responsibility for implementing these plans was spelled out as follows:

> The full and unqualified cooperation of all BPC managers is
> expected in reaching our minority hiring goals. Corporate Per-
> sonnel has been given the responsibility for implementing our
> plans, and for establishing an accountability system through
> which top management — beginning immediately — can regularly
> assess progress in all divisions, departments and subsidiaries of the
> corporation.

During June, Sherrill communicated preliminary minority targets
in terms of gross hires to personnel departments in the operating
units and requested implementation plans from them. During the
next several months, as these plans were written and reviewed in
Corporate Personnel, the over-all goals were increased by about 6
percent. As Sherrill put it later: "We had a package including the
Harrison-Moore letter, the targets and Jenkin's program that the
field units couldn't refuse."

Also in June, Jenkins launched "Project Inform" in Atlanta. He
picked that city because he "wanted to show what could be done in
the South" and was confident that the results would be favorable. In
the following months, he traveled across the country arranging
meetings between spokesmen in the black community and BPC
managers in the field. Sherrill reported to Browning in October that
preliminary reports indicated "an unusual degree of success" in the
marketing organization. As of August, the percentage of minorities
among new hires, often in branches which had less than 1 percent
minority representation, ranged from 10.6 percent in the Midwest
Region to 36.8 percent in the Southern Region. Although Project
Inform was not solely responsible, it was clearly having a beneficial
impact, and consequently plans were made to extend it substantially
beyond the initial test sites.

Meanwhile, Personnel Research designed a comprehensive system
to be installed by each personnel office to record information on the
employee selection process and specifically the disposition of minority applicants. Pilot work was also initiated in the Software
Systems Division to examine and revise entry qualifications for
hourly and lower-level exempt jobs. Concurrently, Advance III was
implemented, this time with government funding and with a somewhat larger enrollment than in previous programs.

By early 1969, Sherrill was able to report substantial progress in minority relations. Over-all minority hiring was running at 107 percent of target for the first six months of the plan, with roughly equal success in qualified and hard-core categories. The various support activities offered by Personnel Research were also being implemented more or less on schedule with apparently satisfactory results. The planning and control systems had proved adequate, although improvements were clearly warranted. For instance, no provisions had been made for a net additions forecast or explicit turnover assumptions, and various inconsistencies proved troublesome in the treatment of hard-core hires and the breakdown of the figures by subunit. Remedies for these shortcomings, however, appeared to be well within reach.

On the other hand, the Personnel Research Department's performance in other areas was lagging. Although the weight to be given to minority relations in the department's priorities had been revised upward to 35 percent in May 1968, in fact the time alloted to it had been substantially higher. Consequently, work on a management development program, weighted at 25 percent, was behind schedule, and sales personnel selection studies had been in part recast as minority-related projects. Sherrill also reported to Browning that "although efforts made earlier in the year to upgrade confidence in MPS (Manpower Planning Systems) were successful, the concentration of efforts in the minority relations area was extremely disruptive. . . user confidence in MPS and related systems is at a low point."

Despite these shortfalls, Sherrill received strong support for the progress in minority relations from Browning and anticipated a comparable commitment to the area in 1969. Each of the established activities was continuing, and several new training programs were to be initiated. A new question was also being raised: "Are Negro employees on the BPC exempt payroll advancing as rapidly as their white peers?" A preliminary study was completed in March, based solely on personnel records, which proved inconclusive. Since over 50 percent of the black exempts had been hired during the previous two years, a formal comparative study of career paths was viewed as premature. Not surprisingly, the data indicated a sharp imbalance in the levels attained by black employees on the exempt payroll; none had reached the confidential payroll, and over 50 percent were in the lowest three grades which accounted for only 16 percent of all exempts. On the other hand, there was also ample evidence of promotion activity.

Also in March, Richard Poole, an eleven-year veteran from manufacturing, was appointed Manager of Minority Relations on Sherrill's staff. He was to coordinate BPC activities and serve as the lead consultant to the inner city business described earlier that was then just getting into production. Jenkins, who was reportedly experiencing some difficulty adapting to the BPC organization, reported to Poole and continued to devote most of his efforts to Project Inform and external relations. With the first year of the "intensive minority hiring program" to end on June 30, an immediate concern for Sherrill related to the formulation of new targets for the operating units. It was probable that the company would move to a calendar year planning cycle in this area which left the last six months of 1969 in limbo.

Reorganization

BPC launched into a major reorganization in early 1969 that changed quite dramatically the context in which the minority relations program was managed. The first indications of change occurred in January with the creation of regional offices in the marketing organization of the core business, each with the capability of discharging staff functions, including personnel. At the same time, one of the smaller divisions moved from the headquarters location in the Midwest to New Jersey. Several weeks later a major acquisition was consummated that for BPC heralded entry into a new and challenging field. The most significant development, however, was the announcement in March that the corporate offices were moving to New York in September of that year and responsibility for operations was to be decentralized in a restructured divisionalized organization.

The core business, now called the General Products Division (GPD), was placed under Brian Macauley, who had previously directed sales and marketing. There was an abundance of new faces among the senior managers under him who had been recruited in the preceding months from other large corporations. Macauley, in turn, reported at the corporate level to Howard Morgan, Executive Vice President-Operations, another executive relatively new to BPC. In effect, Harrison and Moore were intent on stepping back from operations and turning their attention to the broader issues of leading an increasingly diversified and multinational corporation. The importance of comprehensive controls under this arrangement was signaled by a revamping of controller's organizations at both corporate and division levels and the installation of more exacting measurement systems.

There was a good deal of uncertainty during these months among middle managers in GPD about reporting relationships and the implications of the new structure for policies and responsibilities. That the "old BPC" was being replaced by some new form was clear enough, but the practical consequences of this transformation became apparent only as positions in the new organization were filled and problems were encountered and resolved.

It was nonetheless evident that the reorganization portended a recasting of the personnel function. A manager from the firm acquired in February was named Corporate Vice President of Personnel, and the existing corporate group then became the Personnel Department for GPD. Browning was to report through an Administrative Vice President* to Macauley as shown in Exhibit VIII-2. However, since staff in the new corporate office was to be limited, the disposition of the company-wide functions directed by Browning and his staff remained in doubt.

Problems Emerge in Minority Relations: 1969-1970

The reorganization temporarily put a halt to the development of further programs in minority relations while responsibilities and objectives were clarified. Toward the end of May, in the course of summarizing the activities in Personnel Research for Browning, Sherrill commented on the Intensified Minority Hiring program: "On an interim basis, GPD should work toward establishing hiring targets. However, on a longer-range basis, this becomes a corporate concern and should be picked up at that level, at least from the standpoint of determining the appropriate level of company-wide activity." At about the same time, Sherrill also provided Browning with an "advanced word" about the minority relations area to the

*This manager had formerly been Vice President of Manufacturing and was intimately involved in the early minority relations programs. Several months after the reorganization, however, he left the company.

Exhibit VIII-2
BUSINESS PRODUCTS CORPORATION
Partial Organization Chart
March 1969-July 1970

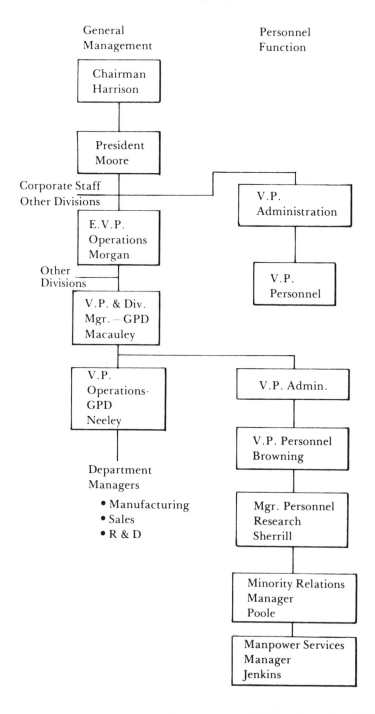

effect that some black employees were critical of it without, in Sherrill's judgment, trying to understand the nature and purpose of the program. Sherrill was concerned that such criteria might be heard out of context by "the new management group."

By July, Sherrill was able to report that, for the nine months ending March 30, BPC had met 110 percent of its minority hiring target, a result that drew specific praise from Harrison. A further government funded hard-core training program, now for 180 people, was also approved. This activity had become sufficiently routine that the GPD manufacturing organization was set up to handle all phases of it except a few contractual arrangements. In retrospect, it was significant that Personnel Research initiated a study during this period based on in-depth interviews with minority exempt employees to ascertain their needs and attitudes toward the company. More extensive efforts to delve into the trouble spots uncovered in the earlier review of personnel records were being held in abeyance, however, pending the establishment of new targets for minority hiring.

During the summer, Sherrill agreed with the other division personnel managers that minority hiring targets for the last six months of 1969 would be at the rate achieved during the year which ended on June 30. The final figures for 1968-69 reflected over-all performance at 116 percent of plan, the intake in the "qualified" category (vs. hard core) running higher at 128 percent. Meanwhile, Jenkins continued to tour the country arranging Inform sessions, roughly two-thirds of the GPD field offices having been visited by Labor Day. Although not uniformly successful, the program on balance continued to receive positive comment as a means of engaging the company with the black community.

As the summer wore on, Personnel Research devoted increasing effort to a number of "crash programs" for GPD management that were unrelated to minority affairs. For instance, turnover had become a problem among sales and customer service employees in a number of offices; Sherrill's department was asked to design training programs and interview employees on the sales compensation package. Another study related to selection test validation for these same job categories. Management's concern was prompted by the fact that GPD had introduced two major new products during 1969 and was struggling to complete a still larger project for introduction early the next year. By fall the principal new item on Sherrill's agenda was an "operational analysis" within this product development team.

In October, Sherrill removed Poole from the inner city enterprise as part of a management realignment that was designed to reduce BPC's active involvement in its day-to-day operations. Since Poole was not to be replaced, Sherrill also eliminated the minority relations section in the department, a sacrifice that left him feeling understaffed. Performance in minority hiring for the previous year was reviewed with corporate personnel and, as Sherrill noted in a memorandum to Browning at the time, "it is now their responsibility to distribute the report."

As the fall wore on and the expected guidance from the corporate Personnel Departments on targeting for 1970 did not materialize, Personnel Research went ahead on its own with a procedure through which goals were related to a reasonable increment over 1968-69 results. Unlike the preceding years, however, the operating units submitted their own estimates rather than a response to centrally determined targets. Sherrill indicated that from his perspective, "No provision was made for minority relations in the corporate move to New York; the legacy was not passed on. As a result, a void was created in GPD."

The report compiled from interviews with minority exempt employees was completed in December and distributed to top management. The analysis suggested that minorities had a generally positive attitude toward BPC but that many also expressed reservations about the true equality of career opportunities for them in management ranks. The conclusions, although moderately critical and suggestive of how much had yet to be done, were not alarming. Harrison immediately posed two questions to Browning: "Have you planned to make some report back so that the black people who are most interested in the questionnaire know that we are taking it seriously? Has it been decided what policies we will follow to improve the situation?" Three weeks later, after consulting with Sherrill, Browning replied that "the major policy change we see as necessary to improve the situation is to require a performance review of every minority employee to determine whether he is promotable and what training or assistance would facilitate such promotion." Other activities noted as in the planning stage included a target of 13 percent blacks among new college hires and a variety of other personnel programs. He also wrote that survey findings and plans were to be discussed with the participating employees.

During the first months of 1970, Personnel Research was scrambling to assemble the Affirmative Action Plan for GPD which was prescribed for the first time by Executive Order. Corporate personnel, in conjunction with the legal department, issued criteria for preparing the document in the divisions. A significant difference between this and earlier plans filed by BPC under Plans for Progress was in the reporting detail; demographic data were now required by job category (offices and managers, professionals, sales workers, and so forth). Such data were not built into the existing personnel reporting system, and time-consuming revisions were necessary simply to permit submission of the plan in April.

Meanwhile, rumblings of discontent among black exempt employees at GPD headquarters became increasingly evident. Browning expressed sympathy for many of their needs and a sense of frustration at being unable to move on the issues. The March feedback session on the Personnel Research survey appeared to raise the level of awareness and promote a feeling of unity among the employees involved. In late March one of the participants put his thoughts down in a letter to the manager on Sherrill's staff who conducted the session. In part he wrote: "While BPC may be slightly ahead of its contemporaries in hiring practices, it has yet to escape the stigma that most other companies have . . . that it hires black Americans, provides them with opportunities, but does not advance them even when they have better qualifications than their white counterparts."

Then on April 22, approximately 50 black exempt employees signed a letter to Harrison and Moore in which they portrayed what they perceived to be a wide gap between BPC as they knew it and the promise contained in the earlier Harrison-Moore letter. Citing statistics on blacks in management (many of them the same or updated versions of the figures in the Personnel Research document of March 1969), they concluded that "proclamation has not become process at BPC. Simply stated, BPC has not honored the May 1968 statement for equal opportunity."

Moore elected to respond first by meeting alone on May 8 with two representative groups of five black exempt employees. Moore believed the meetings to be quite constructive, and several days later the black exempts replied that in their view "a renewed and apparently positive awareness now exists." They also advised that a "steering committee" had been selected from among their number to represent their interests in future discussions with management. Moore also met with the GPD management group to review the minority employment program. Then on June 2 he wrote to each of the signatories to the April 22 letter, reaffirming his personal commitment to equal opportunity and indicating that although progress since 1968 had been substantial, much remained to be done. He also stated that the Affirmative Action Plan contained programs, including the review of each minority employee's performance, which he intended to see implemented. The letter was received cooly by the black exempts, who felt that it did not address the issue forcefully enough.

While these events were unfolding, several changes in management occurred. At the corporate level, the Vice President of Personnel was terminated and replaced by Philip Adler, a lawyer who had joined BPC in 1960 to work on acquisitions. After six years, the last two under Moore, Adler left the company to write and engage in community activities, returning as Director of Business Development in 1969. Though he professed little experience in personnel, he was persuaded to accept the position by Moore's insistence that social awareness was at that time the most critical element in the job. At GPD, Browning resigned. His successor, Frank Thomas, an experienced personnel executive from another large corporation, arrived at the end of July. In the ensuing realignment of the personnel function in GPD, Thomas reported directly to Macauley, the Division Manager, and Sherrill was placed under a former peer, Dudley Jackson, who in turn reported to Thomas. As a result of these changes, the managers with specific responsibility for minority relations in GPD slipped further down in the organization. The new organization is shown in Exhibit VIII-3.

A Further Attempt at Decentralization: 1970-1971

In mid-June, a week after Moore's letter to the black exempt employees was mailed, Macauley called a meeting of all GPD department heads at which he reviewed the developments of the preceding two months and emphasized the critical need to implement the program contained in the April Affirmative Action Plan and line man-

Exhibit VIII-3
BUSINESS PRODUCTS CORPORATION
Partial Organization Chart
July 1970-June 1972

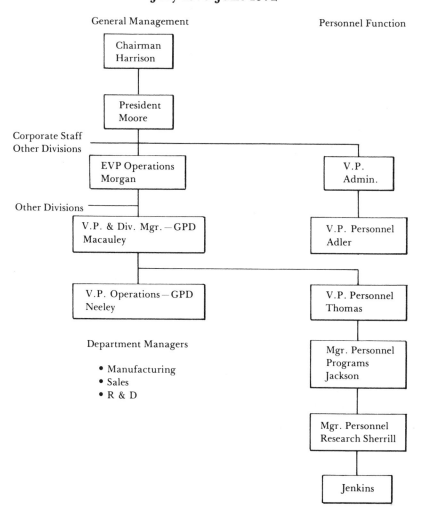

General Management   Personnel Function

Chairman
Harrison

President
Moore

Corporate Staff
Other Divisions

EVP Operations
Morgan

V.P.
Admin.

Other Divisions

V.P. & Div. Mgr. — GPD
Macauley

V.P. Personnel
Adler

V.P. Operations — GPD
Neeley

V.P. Personnel
Thomas

Department Managers

• Manufacturing
• Sales
• R & D

Mgr. Personnel
Programs
Jackson

Mgr. Personnel
Research Sherrill

Jenkins

agement's responsibility for seeing that results were achieved with staff support. A week later Sherrill met with GPD personnel managers to discuss implementation and indicated that he would follow-up with each of them on specific targets and timetables.

Several days later, Adler inquired into the status of the performance reviews that Moore had promised for the employees receiving his letter. Sherrill reported that while this step was being taken on an interim basis by the departments involved, a more basic revision was needed in the existing career development and performance appraisal system that would extend to all minority employees and eventually to the entire work force. Shortly thereafter, Jackson issued instructions for a Personnel Evaluation Report (PER) to be completed on a "crash basis" for each minority exempt employee. The reader will recall that Browning and Sherrill pointed to this need in the former's letter to Harrison in January 1970.

In early July, a budget crunch hit General Products Division as a dip in the economy threatened the attainment of profit goals. Non-replacement hiring was frozen, overtime curtailed, travel strictly controlled, the use of consultants discontinued, and so forth. In some instances there were layoffs. The potential impact on minority hiring targets was obvious. Less noticeable was the dilemma described by personnel managers, who then had the added burden of managing and seeking support for an Affirmative Action Plan without ready access to new resources.

As the summer of 1970 ended, responsibility for minority relations activities in GPD were reconsolidated; Sherrill was to be held accountable for the development of Affirmative Action Plans and statistical monitoring systems, the handling of discrimination complaints and hard-core training program evaluations, and the design of a division strategy for dealing with the black exempt protest. It was hoped that centralized direction would facilitate and improve GPD's response to mounting pressure, including for the first time government compliance reviews. (While a federal audit of GPD headquarters had been successfully completed during the summer, the St. Louis sales office had not responded promptly to a city request for a program and was ruled out of compliance.) Sherrill then won approval for the addition of another person* to assist in the specification of reporting systems and Affirmative Action Plans.

*At year end 1970, Sherrill had five men in his department; two allocated to minority relations (Jenkins and the new hire) and the other three to Personnel Re-

During the fall, Personnel Research concentrated on the design of an information system to monitor performance in minority and female hiring and advancement. Following discussions with the government compliance agency, it became clear that a computerized system would be required. For the next eighteen months the department worked with the personnel units in the field and the data-processing group, ultimately developing a system that was cited by the compliance agency as a model. Sherrill also attended to the more immediate problem of extricating the St. Louis sales office from its difficulties with the city by negotiating a commitment calling in part for an increase in minority representation from 7.6 percent to 20.2 percent of the total work force over the next 27 months.

In accordance with the prevailing posture on division autonomy, Adler did not take part in on-going minority relations activities in the operating units. From the information available to him at the time, the divisions were moving ahead with the implementation of the Affirmative Action Plans. Moreover, an October report on minority representation as of June 30 (prior to the hiring freeze) reflected excellent progress in a numerical sense. Yet, Adler and others among corporate management remained uneasy about the underlying conditions that had provoked the black exempt employees to question BPC's commitment to equal employment.

At year end 1970, Sherrill's attention was focused on obtaining hiring commitments from the operating departments to include in revised Affirmative Action Plans. He had already completed the remainder of the plan for all units but the marketing regions, and they had been provided with an over-all format. The intent was to use the manpower plan already submitted with the 1971 financial budget as a basis for establishing minority hiring targets. The targets in turn were to be keyed to the percentage minority representation in the relevant labor market as prescribed in the government guidelines. Sherrill prepared a memorandum for Macauley's signature, authorizing the personnel staff to solicit agreements on the hiring rationale from department heads so that specific targets could be calculated as the manpower plans were approved. Because of delays in budget approval and the time taken in reviewing the

---

search projects such as employee selection methods, survey programs and performance appraisal standards.

plans, however, official hiring targets for 1971 were not in force for the marketing organization until May of that year.

The impact of minority-related activities on operating budgets was a vexatious issue for the GPD personnel staff. For instance, the general manager in the Northeast Region indicated that his recruiting program, estimated to cost $16,500, had not been funded in the Operating Plan. He asked Thomas if incremental funds were to be provided, adding: "We will support any national effort to the utmost of our ability, but it is going to cost money." Thomas replied that cooperation with GPD staff might effect some savings but that "at this time there does not appear to be any possibility of supplemental budgets for minority recruiting as such costs should be part of the regular personnel budget."

In mid-April 1971, Sherrill surveyed the support given by the regional general managers to the Affirmative Action Plans. For the most part, he found that they had endorsed the plan and had instructed their branch office managers to cooperate with the Regional Personnel Manager in its implementation. Sherrill termed the response "adequate," pending a review of subsequent progress against targets. A change also occurred in the top management of GPD at this time; Macauley moved up to a newly created post of Group Vice President, and Henry Neely became manager of the division. Neely joined BPC in late 1968 and had most recently been GPD Vice President of Operations.

During the late spring, pressure for change in the approach to minority relations was building from a number of sources. As the figures on year-end employment were compiled, it became apparent that for the company as a whole, the gains in minority representation made in the first half of 1970 did not hold up during the hiring freeze in the last six months. In fact, compared with the prior year, total employment declined by 0.5 percent while the number of minorities declined 5.7 percent.

More disturbing to corporate management, however, were its independent findings which tended to confirm the existence of attitudes and subtle barriers to advancement cited the previous spring by the black exempt employees in GPD. These findings also indicated that many managers considered BPC's position to be Harrison's and Moore's personal commitment that was not necessarily binding on them. These findings were being discussed as rumblings again became audible in the GPD organization, this time among minority sales and customer service employees in the Baltimore-Washington branch office. Once more, the difficulties centered on advancement and upward mobility. Black caucuses had been formed in each city, and, although the branch manager and the regional personnel manager were meeting with them frequently and were desirous of containing the problem in the region, the situation appeared to be potentially explosive. In this context the corporate role in minority relations was redefined.

Extended Corporate Staff Involvement: 1971

In June a Management Resources Department was formed under Adler and charged with the dual responsibility of minority relations and manpower planning, executive development and training. The position was filled by Frank Wesley, who, while personnel manager of the Northeast Region in GPD, had gained a reputation as a fast-moving, decisive manager. He commented on his initial reaction to the offer:

> I told Phil [Adler] I wasn't the right person for the job because (a) I'm white, (b) I understood the problem but wasn't at all sure I could empathize with it, and (c) I wasn't that convinced the corporation was committed to pushing the issue through. Phil said that he couldn't help it if I'm white, that empathy hadn't worked in the past, and that I should talk to Moore about commitment. When I talked with Graham [Moore], I asked him: "Some day when I run out of solutions, I may come to you; will you help?" He said, "yes."

Wesley had been in his new job for only a few days when the black exempt employees in Baltimore voiced their grievances in a letter to Moore, stating that they had found regional management to be unresponsive. The allegations were sufficiently disquieting that Moore asked Adler and Wesley to investigate and prescribe such corrective action as appeared necessary. For the next several weeks Wesley burrowed into the specific charges in detail, concluding that the actions of local management had been justified in some instances but not in others. The latter case was personified by a former army colonel who had not been promoted to an available customer service manager's slot despite a record that would normally have won the job. In general, discontent stemmed from a perception that minorities were not being advanced in accordance with their relative abilities.

In the course of this study, Wesley developed the "gateway job" concept. He said:

> I got basic. If our objective is to have minorities in upper levels of management, the important question is how did those who are already there get there. For instance, all of the regional managers had been branch managers at some point. Branch managers are usually drawn from district sales managers (DSM's) or customer service managers (CSM's). The DSM's and CSM's are the gateways in marketing that open up avenues for promotion. The gateway job provides experience that's essential for the next position and also an opportunity to demonstrate skills in a way that is easily measured and highly visible. Each functional area has them. For instance, in control the route to senior positions is through financial analysis rather than accounting.

From a quick perusal of the GPD marketing organization, Wesley found that minorities occupied less than 1 percent of the gateway jobs; he recommended (and Adler concurred) that this figure be increased to 6 percent* by the end of 1972. In fact, at the time Adler forwarded Wesley's write-up of the gateway concept to Thomas, he noted, "I described this approach to the Baltimore black employees last week. They're fully aware of it and extremely interested." Shortly thereafter year-end targets were negotiated with each of the regions for minority DSM's and CSM's. At the conclusion of his investigation in Baltimore, Wesley made a number of recommendations to regional and branch office management, including a promotion at the earliest opportunity for the former colonel, which they agreed to implement.

In April the personnel group in GPD had begun to place renewed emphasis on minority advancement, first through formalizing and updating the Personnel Evaluation Reporting (PER) system which was designed to highlight promotability and development needs among minority exempt employees, and second through a management training effort on topics ranging from minority awareness to selection methods. Sherrill also proposed an elevation in the report-

---

*Six percent was the target then being used in BPC for exempt positions and represented the percentage of minorities among individuals with 16 years of school according to the 1960 census.

ing level of minority relations in GPD and the creation of a specialist position in each marketing region. His recommendations were deleted at Thomas's suggestion, however, in favor of simply adding an exempt position to the existing division staff.

While special programs were certain to absorb time, Sherrill indicated in a July report to Jackson that the first and second priorities for Personnel Research in 1972 were likely to be the completion and monitoring of the division's Affirmative Action Plans. He anticipated that although changes in government reporting requirements would probably make target setting a good deal more complex, by working with the operating units during the fall the plans would be completed by the end of the year. In the meanwhile, close tabs were kept on progress made in the regions on meeting gateway job commitments. At the end of September Thomas sent one regional manager who expressed doubts about meeting the targets a memorandum, composed by Sherrill, urging him to hire outside if necessary.

As Personnel Research grappled with the administrative machinery in the large GPD organization, Corporate Personnel became increasingly impatient. In mid-October Wesley criticized the division plan for responding to earlier corporate suggestions. In general he indicated that insufficient attention had been given to upgrading the minority relations function and building progress in this area into the performance evaluation of managers at all levels. The covering note from Adler to Thomas was more pointed: "The thrust of Frank's comment is that more immediate and forceful action can and should be taken. I agree with that thrust. I am concerned that too much of the GPD approach is analytical, logically progressive and systematized but not geared to quick end results . . . What is needed now is some concrete, productive actions, both visible and fruitful . . . and this progress can be accomplished despite budget pressures once minority relations progress is recognized as having the top priority that we give it."

On that same day, Adler gave wide distribution to a second Wesley report, this one summarizing a one-day audit of the Southern Region conducted in late September. On balance, Wesley's assessment of the situation was negative. Although the region appeared relatively certain to meet its gateway job commitments and was utilizing the PER system effectively, it was far behind on the over-all

1971 Affirmative Action Plan targets. Wesley's diagnosis pointed to unrealistic targets that were late in being set, and a regional cost-cutting program that curtailed the payment of personnel agency fees, limited recruitment budgets, and froze nonreplacement hiring. Moreover, he found a wide disparity in minority employment among branch offices and a time lag in division reporting that he considered excessive. The audit concluded with the following statement: "At the present time, the [GPD] Personnel Department works through the Regional Personnel Department and the line manager is 'off the hook.' "

Corporate criticism had an immediate impact on the personnel group in GPD. While Sherrill took issue with the tenor of Wesley's reports and indicated that they did not reflect full cognizance of the division's efforts, he nonetheless agreed that greater line management involvement and a clearer relationship between minority relations and performance evaluations were highly desirable. The question remained: how to secure those elusive benefits? Jackson urged that the importance of moving quickly on minority advancement into upper management ranks be stressed to Neely (the Division Manager), and the implementation of the PER system accelerated with Neely's visible support.

The first tangible reaction, however, came from senior GPD marketing management immediately after Wesley's audit. Sherrill was then about to visit the regions to work with the marketing organization on commitments for the 1972 Affirmative Action Plans. David Marlin, the newly appointed GPD Vice President of Marketing, informed each regional general manager that he expected their cooperation and that their performance was to be judged in part on how effectively the plans were implemented. More graphic support was forthcoming as a direct result of Wesley's audit of the Southern Region. Marlin ordered the region to implement a minority recruiting schedule supplied by Personnel Research, the estimated cost of $24,000 to be absorbed in the region's budget. Moreover, once a branch had received recruiting assistance, hiring was to be restricted to "minorities only" until performance had significantly improved.

Then, in late October, Neely was briefed by his personnel staff on the importance of showing progress in minority advancement. He first requested an analysis for each of the nine managers who reported to him of the three exempt pay categories in their departments. The analysis reflected a dearth of blacks among the 5,000 exempt jobs, particularly in the upper two exempt categories, and the disparities existed in all departments. With responsibilities fixed and peformance summarized in familiar pay category terms, Neely then asked his subordinates for specific plans to improve their records. By December he had commitments for attaining a 6 percent minority representation in the specified categories in all but one organization within one to three years. Neely also drew up for Sherrill a "closed loop" reporting system that he felt was necessary to monitor results in terms of actual "net additions" versus plan.

By the end of the year, 1972 Affirmative Action Plans for GPD were in place which, in Sherrill's view, contained aggressive objectives. Approval had also been secured for a minority relations specialist in each marketing region. Finally, Personnel Research reported a 22.5 percent increase in over-all minority employment in the division during 1971 and a hiring percentage that was almost up to plan. Although field marketing missed its targets by wide margins, the proportion of minorities in that organization nonetheless increased by more than 50 percent to 8 percent of the total work force. The other units exceeded more modest targets.

Corporate Intervention
The improved morale evident in Personnel Research with the completion of the 1972 planning cycle was soon dashed as corporate intervention was again forthcoming in response to employee demands from two sources. The first was a request from the black caucus for another meeting with Moore at GPD headquarters, this time to discuss a far-reaching program it had developed to improve opportunities for minorities and in particular black exempt employees. The second was a new and potentially more damaging series of charges from the black sales and service personnel in the Baltimore sales branch. These situations surfaced in December as the top management group was adjusting to Harrison's sudden death. In a transition planned for some time, Moore became chairman and Morgan was elevated to President and Chief Operating Officer.

Baltimore
Corporate management heard nothing further about the Baltimore flare-up of the previous June (other than the encouraging news

that a number of black salesmen were recruited with the assistance of the Baltimore caucus) until word arrived in December that a suit was being filed with EEOC. In December, however, corporate personnel became aware of a pattern in the assignment of sales territories that appeared to discriminate against minorities. A quick check with region headquarters revealed that the sales force had recently been organized by product line in addition to area and the more sophisticated lines were given to the more experienced sales people, who in this instance were white. In addition, there were signs that the corrective steps agreed to earlier with Adler had not been fully implemented; for instance, the retired colonel had again been passed over for promotion.

Adler immediately called these developments to the attention of both Morgan and Macauley. The former felt the situation warranted corporate investigation and action. On the other hand, Macauley was inclined to view it as basically a GPD problem and maintained that without a role for division management, the prospects for resolving this and future incidents at operating levels would be impaired. The outcome of the discussion was a decision to dispatch a joint investigating team composed of Wesley and a division representative. To stress the importance accorded minority relations, Wesley suggested that the GPD choice be a line manager ("someone we can't afford to send") rather than a personnel executive, and consequently Bruce Henniger, a former regional manager and then national service manager, was drafted.

For a week Wesley and Henniger worked over the Baltimore employee records, quantifying as many of the findings as possible. Their report indicated a pattern of lower starting salaries, less training, and fewer remunerative territories for blacks in the sales force. Moreover, although the region had performed well in hiring minorities, it had not moved ahead on various other aspects of the plan, including redress for the retired colonel, whose case it now appeared had been blatantly mishandled. Wesley communicated these results to corporate management.

Within hours of receiving this news, Morgan was on a plane to Baltimore, accompanied by Marlin, the GPD Vice President of Marketing. With Marlin taking the lead, but with Morgan's presence clearly felt, the basis for assigning sales territories was revised, compensation and promotion arrangements were made for the aggrieved employee, and further emphasis on minority relations was agreed to by the region. Some months later Marlin had the Baltimore branch manager transferred to a staff job and instituted changes in the regional organization which were widely interpreted to be related in some measure to the handling of minority relations. He also cautioned the other regional managers, "Don't let this happen to you."

GPD Headquarters

The black exempt employees at GPD headquarters explained their plan for improved minority relations to Moore, Morgan, Macauley, Adler, and Neely in December 1971. The recommendations were based on the desire for accelerated development and promotion of black exempts and specifically included a request for at least 10 percent black managers and professionals in the top two exempt categories, an identification of 25 or more black candidates with top management potential, and the inclusion of accountability for minority employment and advancement in the performance appraisals of individual managers at all levels in the organization. (A commentary on the employees' plan prepared for corporate management by Personnel Research summarized the various programs already existing in GPD and the recently formulated target of 6 percent minorities in the top exempt pay categories. It also indicated that no black exempt employees had yet been identified as candidates for branch manager and that fewer than the targeted figure had been designated as promotable to the top pay categories.)

The BPC response was formulated under Moore's direction. He commented later:

> I was increasingly frustrated by the lack of movement of minorities in the organization and to a lesser degree by the broader employment figures. As I went to meetings around the company, I looked at who was in the room. I was also listening to the blacks' complaints and had to agree with many of them. It was difficult to get a handle on the main issues. Opposition was there, but no one would speak it openly; it was subtle, and to get at it one must penetrate behind the numbers.
>
> Middle management may not always agree with me. They may say, "That's O.K. from where he sits, but he doesn't understand my problems." The other jobs they were supposed to do were the

ones they had traditionally been judged on, and I'm sure many thought these were tough enough. We were asking them to take on a difficult assignment that many felt ill-equipped to handle.

In January, Moore again met with the black caucus, this time to discuss the company's plan. Although shunning numerical commitments, he indicated that many of the caucus's suggestions would be implemented. In addition, a Minority Advisory Council (MAC) was announced, to be composed of a dozen minority employees selected by the company (specifically corporate personnel was to choose them based on recommendations from division personnel managers). MAC was to review the operating units' Affirmative Action Plans and serve as a source of advice and council to corporate management on minority affairs. The response from the caucus was "mixed."

Division Response

The response in GPD to the corporate interventions in January was generally negative, particularly in the personnel function. One manager commented at the time:

> We are under intense economic pressure, and corporate is in a punitive role. They are not being supportive. They want results and are using the boss's ear to get it. Power is being used unfairly. We aren't getting the resources to do the job and they aren't taking into account the pressure we're under . . . Now top management people are in Baltimore and GPD has been pre-empted. This tells the employees to go right to Moore, and our effectiveness is destroyed in the process.

Subsequent Events

The Minority Advisory Council met with Adler and Wesley during the first week of March and proceeded to dissect the Affirmative Action Plans that had been completed in GPD the previous December. In terms Wesley described as "constructive" the council then made a variety of recommendations to Moore for intensified programs in the operating units and, in particular, higher targets for minorities in upper positions. Rather than using the percentage of new hires as a basis for setting objectives, they suggested, and Adler and Wesley agreed, that setting targets for *net* additions was preferable. They also recommended that additional funds be allocated to operating management to implement the programs.

As these discussions were concluding, a major reorganization was announced that restructed GPD. In essense, the division was divided into two units, more or less along functional lines, each segment to have a full complement of staff services. Marlin became Division Manager for the Graphic Systems Division (GSD) and reported directly to Macauley as did Neely, who retained manufacturing and development. In the personnel function, Thomas and Jackson remained with Neely. Scott Parsons, formerly Manager of Personnel Operations, became Marlin's personnel manager. Until a Manager of Minority Relations was located (to whom Jenkins would report), Parsons' manpower resources manager doubled in that capacity. Sherrill resigned to accept an attractive offer elsewhere. The revised organization is depicted in Exhibit VIII-4.

In this setting, Adler and Wesley met with senior GPD operating managers and their personnel staffs and presented the new minority hiring and advancement targets based on the discussions with MAC. Wesley described what happened.

> They [the operating managers] said, "You've changed the targets in mid-stream!" Since organizational lines had been changed and net adds were now to be used for targeting, the numbers had to be recast to show new responsibilities. In some cases the higher numbers were accepted, in others compromises were negotiated. We took the position, can you meet the targets and what do you need in the way of supplemental funding to do it? The total came to $600,000. It took Moore two seconds to approve the budget.*

The response in GPD to these events was muted, however, by the reorganization and the imposition of revised minority targets. Much of the energy devoted to the issue was consumed by renewed attention to the PER system and by efforts to gear up for an expanded minority recruiting effort. The personnel reporting system was fully computerized during the first quarter, and provision was made for monthly statements for operating managers to supplement the quarterly figures requested by Corporate Personnel. It was June,

*The size of BPC should be kept in mind. After taxes, this figure amounted to less than half a cent in earnings per share terms.

Exhibit VIII-4
BUSINESS PRODUCTS CORPORATION
Partial Organization Chart
June 1972-April 1973

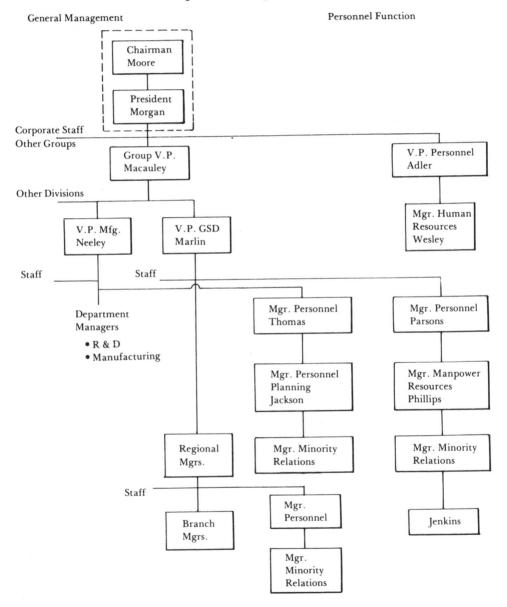

however, before the new targets were finally approved, although there were clear indications that the higher figures were being taken seriously prior to that time.

Several special programs were initiated or accelerated at the division level but stalled prior to implementation. For instance, the minority awareness training seminar that Jenkins had had on the back burner for over a year received a flurry of attention. However, the first audition revealed serious weaknesses, and it was put back into development. A proposal was also made by Personnel Research for the design of a management practices survey—essentially a minority relations audit—to be conducted in the sales branches. Although both Wesley and Adler were enthusiastic about the idea, funding limitations and the reorganization caused execution to be postponed.

Corporate Intervention Renewed

For some months Adler had been discussing with Moore and others the need for emphasizing the importance of minority relations by incorporating it specifically in management performance appraisals. Moore was now prepared to act upon this suggestion. In April he made his thoughts known to senior operating executives, and in early July a letter was addressed to all BPC managers on the subject of equal employment which stated in part:

> The most significant change this year—the one that is basic to all others—is to place responsibility for achieving equal opportunity objectives where it rightfully belongs: with operating management, with each of us. Achieving these objectives is as important as meeting *any other* traditional business responsibility.
>
> It follows, of course, that a key element in each manager's over-all performance appraisal will be his progress in this important area. No manager should expect a satisfactory appraisal if he meets other objectives but fails here.

Then during August and September 1972, the Graphic Systems Division, the marketing arm of the former GPD organization, plunged into another incident which ultimately involved Morgan. This time it was sparked by four black women employed in a small service unit in the Midwestern Region who leveled charges of discrimination at their immediate supervisor. The episode is recounted in detail in Chapter IX and need be mentioned only briefly here.

Corporate attention focused on the controversy initially when it was aired in the media with intimations that "national demands" were also at issue. As regional management struggled to diagnose, contain, and resolve the problem, however, Morgan became concerned about a broader question of equity. What rights did the individual — in this case the first-line supervisor — have in the face of accusations and protest damaging to the company?

The episode was altogether different from the earlier one in Baltimore. This time, once regional management became aware that a problem existed and might be serious, response was immediate and forceful, though, as it turned out, not particularly successful. Indeed, Morgan's concern was more with the dangers of over-reaction to a poorly understood situation than with a failure to demonstrate good faith efforts to implement policy. In the end, division and regional management were left to sort out a means of improving minority relations and demonstrated an eagerness to do so. However, Morgan made the final decision on the supervisor and in the process passed judgment on the handling of the entire affair. His decision had the effect of overturning the wishes and actions of five levels of management beneath him and was at the time greeted with displeasure and even disbelief.

Division Response

In the ensuing months, a variety of activities were observed in GSD that were initiated in direct response to this latest incident or received renewed impetus from it. For example, the minority awareness training program was taken off the shelf, refurbished, and within a period of several weeks was being delivered on a schedule that was to carry it to all managers by April 1973. The management practices survey was also funded with Marlin's active support, and the first branches were examined in December 1972. The importance given to the surveys at the time was signaled by the assignment of Henniger, now a Vice President, to head the task force responsible for its implementation.

Attempts were made in the waning months of 1972 to accord minority relations greater weight in the performance evaluation process. In several of the sales regions, the quotient was made explicit; 15 percent of a manager's performance was attributed to equal employment activities. Then, as approval for the 1973 targets was communicated in February, Marlin extended this weighting to all managers in his organization with 20 or more employees. He also praised those of his direct subordinates who had met their targets in 1972 and criticized others who had not, writing in one case, "I am extremely disappointed with the results achieved [in your organization]. Stated simply, this type of performance cannot be tolerated and marked improvement is expected during 1973."

The procedure adopted for revising the Affirmative Action Plans was also modified in GSD. The basic plan was no longer assembled at division level and specific targets negotiated with the regional personnel officers. Instead, the general manager at each sales or service location was held responsible for generating a plan that was reviewed and defended up the line. Additional support was available in the regional offices because the position of the minority relations specialist was upgraded and an additional person added to work specifically on recruitment.

Despite the obvious and intense pressure to meet numerical commitments, a more subtle change seemed to be occurring in the attitudes of operating managers. The problems they had been confronting in minority relations became at the same time more familiar and more pervasive. One manager commented: "Much of what we've been seeing are deep-seated problems in management practices. Our minority employees are our best early warning antenna; they are fantastic for sensing when something is wrong. However, they often reach the wrong conclusion and ascribe it to discrimination when really it's something in the personnel system that is just plain dumb. Sloppy performance appraisals, insufficient training, and poor career counseling are broader problems that affect everyone."

The Changing Role of the Corporate Staff

Wesley expressed satisfaction with the results achieved in 1972. Over-all performance in minority placement for BPC, measured against the budgets revised in midyear, revealed the following record:

	Percentage of Target
Total employment	154
Gateway jobs	123
Stock option jobs	112

The number of minorities on the payroll jumped by 1,800, which increased the percentage representation from 10.4 percent to 13.4 percent. Moreover, the pool of talent rated as having the potential for advancement into higher-level exempt positions had expanded significantly, and the targets for 1973 suggested that conditions would continue to reflect rapid improvement.

In March 1973 Moore sent another letter to all BPC managers, congratulating them on their achievement and asking for their continued support in the years ahead. The reaction to the letter on the part of the black caucus in the old GPD organization was negative. With a new set of proposals in hand, its leadership requested a further meeting with Moore. This time the invitation was declined, and the caucus was invited to discuss the issues with division management.

Direct corporate involvement in the 1973 planning effort as it pertained to minority relations was greatly diminished. Adler and Wesley met again with MAC to review the operating unit targets. Although some changes were suggested by the council and subsequently negotiated with the divisions, the dislocations were modest. Also, there was no supplemental corporate budget in 1973; the divisions were expected to pick up the cost of equal employment activities in their business plans, and in fact no attempt was made to determine the total amount attributable to these activities.

During the fall of 1972, Corporate Personnel became increasingly anxious about BPC's exposure in a related but separable area: equal employment for women. As early as October 1970, Sherrill had been approached by representatives from NOW (The National Organization for Women). Beginning with the 1972 Affirmative Action Plans, entries were required for female hiring and advancement, and additional stress was placed on these targets in the 1973 planning cycle. Nevertheless, it was clear that the programs for minorities had been the predominant concern at both corporate and operating levels.

Attention to equality for women was given emphasis by two developments — the tremendous settlement in the AT&T discrimination suit* and the emergence of female caucuses in two of the operating divisions. Wesley and others were alert to the possibility that BPC, because of its record in minority relations, might be viewed as an inviting target for regulatory or private interest groups. Wesley had hoped to postpone detailed investigation of the status of women in the company until the third quarter of 1973, at which point he felt the minority issue would be well under control. His timetable, however, was advanced by six months.

Wesley first conducted a brief survey from the computerized personnel files, asking such questions as, for example, how many women with college degrees were in non-exempt jobs. He then added a woman to his staff who had previously been a customer services manager in the GSD marketing organization. Further statistical studies were requested from the operating units. With these data as background and with the assistance of a consulting firm, corporate personnel conducted an in-depth investigation of women's attitudes and needs in the fall of 1973.

As the field work for this book was completed, Moore was awaiting the results of the study. Although he had affirmed the corporation's intent to implement a policy of equality in the employment of women, he had not taken explicit steps to dramatize this concern. In his letter to BPC managers on minority relations earlier in the year he had written, "Full utilization of women in BPC, every bit as important as the matters I deal with here, is a subject to be addressed separately in a subsequent letter." The time was approaching for that promised communication to be issued.

ANALYSIS

As in the case of environmental protection at Weston Industries, roughly seven years elapsed between the initial attention given to equal opportunity in employment and the clear indication that a process for delivering it to minorities was being implemented in the operating divisions. During this period, the company's definition of

*As noted in Chapter II, AT&T was ordered to make lump-sum payments of some $15 million to 15,000 minority and female employees and give raises aggregating $23 million to another 36,000.

the problem changed as the underlying issue of civil rights and equality matured in society. What first emerged as a matter of providing sustenance to the ghetto by training the hard-core unemployed ultimately became the more subtle and difficult task of truly integrating the organization at all levels. It is naive to judge the actions of the mid-1960's by 1973 standards — to say, for instance, that the early policy assumptions were demeaning to those it was intended to help or did not take cognizance of subsequent demands. The more important questions are ones of adaptation. Were these assumptions changed on the basis of new understanding, and was there a process for converting revised policy into action? The answer for BPC is certainly affirmative, though adaptation was at times painful and costly in terms more human than financial.

Adaptation

Responsiveness at BPC was sparked by demands born of individual experiences and fed by the promises contained in or imputed to preceding corporate initiatives. Though the company was naturally influenced by the progressively stringent planning and reporting requirements of government agencies, pressure from these sources was not the driving force. Rather, specific and generally spontaneous events played the key role in determining the course of efforts to formulate and implement policy. The nature of the analysis below parallels the one employed in Chapter VI for Weston Industries. Five periods of particular stress and change were evident, each characterized by conflicting pressures on the organization and each resulting in actions that shaped the response process in subsequent months.

1964

The riots of 1964 produced among the top management group at BPC a sensation of innocence lost. Harrison had forged a reputation for his company of social consciousness that was violated by the sudden eruption of forces only vaguely understood and up to that time largely ignored. BPC had not been in the vanguard of the civil rights movement; for instance, Plans for Progress, the accepted corporate response of the day, had already been in operation three years by the time the company joined it in 1964. The explanation, however, appeared to lie in a preoccupation with managing a rapidly growing business rather than a disaffection with the issue. Indeed, awareness prompted almost immediate involvement.

The urgency of attacking the sources of urban malaise which led to the disorders defined the problem for BPC. It was "out there," and Harrison accepted and communicated to his management group a responsibility for helping in some way to find the remedies. The most obvious opportunities were in training and employment for the disadvantaged and participation in community affairs. To a large extent, Project Advance and the relationship with JUSTICE were based on the individual initiative of operating managers. Harrison's visible interest provided encouragement and support for those who were similarly disposed. The fact that they were fairly numerous and in key positions was perhaps due to the cohesiveness and shared values in an organization which in those days was a good deal smaller than it was in 1973, and in more intimate contact with its chief executive. On the other hand, there were no attempts to involve indifferent managers, nor was there a necessity to do so. The programs were conducted apart from the ongoing business and posed few operational difficulties. They could also be turned off and on as they were in 1966 in the face of a profit squeeze.

Until 1968, the focus continued to be on problems external to the firm. Aside from periodic budget curtailments, constraints to action were most clearly imposed by a fragmentary understanding of the black community. It is hardly surprising that Jenkins, the first full-time specialist, was a man with a civil rights background and the qualifications that promised to help overcome these constraints rather than the organizational ones that followed. Harrison encouraged openness and innovation but caution as well, and in retrospect the physical impact of BPC's community-oriented activities was comparatively modest. Yet, unlike many corporations, BPC avoided failure; Sherrill approached the redefinition of purpose in 1968 with a widely publicized record of success that fortunately was also shared by numerous operating managers.

1968

The Harrison-Moore letter of May 1968 was an important milestone, for it brought the problem "in here" and signaled the end of a reliance on voluntary action. The driving forces continued in part to be external. The report of the Kerner Commission had an influence on top management thinking, as did the need to generate hiring objectives for the program of the National Alliance of Businessmen. There was also a growing awareness that the issue was not confined to the plight of the hard-core unemployed but extended to minorities deprived of opportunities for participation in skilled and management jobs as well.

The plan for intensified minority hiring sketched in the Harrison-Moore letter rested on two assumptions: first, the moral imperative contained in the notion of equality was a sufficient inducement to elicit the support of operating management; and, second, corporate personnel had identified the programs that would permit the plan to be implemented. Both assumptions were entirely plausible. Individual managers had devoted enormous effort, much of it on their own time, to activities in the community. This provided at least some evidence to suggest that the commitment to corporate responsibility voiced by Harrison, and more recently by Moore, was commonly held in the organization. Moreover, the problem had now been recast as locating, hiring and, if necessary, training minorities in large numbers. If the plan had general support, these became in essence technical matters for the personnel function. Project Inform and Project Advance appeared to offer immediate and proven sources of staff support.

For a time it appeared that the plan had worked; the number of minorities hired by the company actually exceeded the intake targets which themselves represented a vast increase over anything BPC had attempted in the past. An important transition had also occurred: the issue was firmly supported by Moore as he became chief executive, thus eliminating any doubts that may have existed about the continuity of top management interest. Corporate Personnel under Browning had installed systems and offered assistance appropriate to a specialist activity. Although minority representation was still very low and line management for the most part remained bystanders, there was nonetheless cause for optimism at year end, 1968.

1969

The initial approach to minority relations ultimately collapsed under the weight of expanded and more complex demands. In the two years that had passed between the 1968 letter and the black exempt employees' appeal to Moore, the issue had grown to include and even emphasize advancement opportunities for minorities already on the payroll. Demands of such intensity were unexpected by Harrison and Moore; for a time momentum had been lost, and the company became vulnerable to attack. The major event during this period was the reorganization in the spring of 1969. The new divisionalized structure dramatically altered the context in which the minority relations activities were conducted and raised new barriers to responsiveness without compensating measures to overcome them.

The reorganization physically and symbolically removed impetus for the minority relations program. The gulf between GPD and the corporate offices opened so quickly and seemed to be so unassailable, that questions arose, particularly in Browning's personnel group, about whether the commitment continued to have the priority accorded it in 1968. Exhortation ceased, and the new corporate personnel officer failed to give heed to the issue at all. Thus, when corporate guidance on 1970 hiring targets was not forthcoming, it became increasingly obvious that the divisions were to proceed on their own initiative.

Few of the managers holding key positions in the new GPD organization had participated in the earlier community programs, and a number of them joined the company after the Harrison-Moore letter. As they took charge of the division, the financial planning and control system became more exacting and heavily relied upon to measure performance. Meanwhile, the Personnel Research Department was far behind or in trouble on projects offering immediate payoffs to the business, e.g., sales force turnover and selection studies, manpower planning, and so on. In contrast, the minority program was exceeding numerical targets and absorbing inordinate amounts of time. The obvious prescription was a reallocation of the department's effort, a step which cut back the *corporation's* involvement in minority affairs at just the time that the nature of the problem was changing.

Personnel Research was aware that resentment was building up among black exempt employees and had proposed that their records be reviewed to ascertain promotability and training needs. Such a task required the broad support of operating management—support that did not materialize until *after* the problems had been dramatized for Moore. In addition, Personnel Research put highest priority on compiling the Affirmative Action Plans, clearly a departmental responsibility, rather than efforts to influence promotions and training directly. In short, the influence of the specialists in GPD had rapidly diminished, and the evidence was there for all to see; the position of minority relations manager had been eliminated, hiring targets had been set by personnel managers in the subsidiary units with minimal division review, and no major new programs had been initiated since Project Inform (which by late 1969 was in its waning days).

The atrophy of the minority relations program cannot readily be ascribed to bad faith on the part of division management. At a later time, for instance, Neely actively sought to increase the attention paid to minority advancement among his subordinates, and Macauley firmly supported the company's commitment to the minority-owned enterprise. On the other hand, the reorganization introduced another level of general management and a new emphasis on controls which appeared to have a very significant impact on management's thinking. One simple lesson was clear: specialist capability at the division level could not be relied upon to garner the resources necessary to adapt to changing demands in the absence of explicit corporate support.

1970

Moore's response to the letter from the black employees in April 1970 is enlightening. Rather than replying that the proper point of appeal was division management, he chose to collect first-hand data himself. The corporate honor had been challenged, and his action very clearly reaffirmed top management's commitment to the spirit of the 1968 statement. Yet Moore preserved the division's responsibility for implementing corrective action by accepting the GPD Affirmative Action Plans as the remedial program. His choices may have been limited, of course, because at the time there was no specialist on the corporate staff to propose alternative measures. The Affirmative Action Plans were also a new programming technique, the limitations of which were not then fully appreciated.

The outcome was at best bittersweet to members of the Personnel Research Department in GPD. While they no doubt welcomed the renewed corporate support, they were likely to be held by operating management at least partially to blame for the fact that the protest occurred at all. In any case, Browning left the company, and the minority relations function was buried still deeper in the division personnel department.

Moore also began to reshape the corporate role; from then on division minority relations activities were to be centrally monitored. Adler's appointment as Vice President of Personnel, and his investigation of attitudes among black exempt employees were the first indications that Moore intended to take a hand in managing the response process. the conclusions of the study, coupled with the growing indications that the Affirmative Action Plans were either insufficient or incompletely executed, contributed to a further augmentation of the corporate staff through the creation of a Human Resources Department. The capability then existed to intervene in the affairs of the operating units as well as to offer alternative plans and directives.

The 1970 experiences suggested that the earlier assumptions guiding implementation were not entirely valid. First, good faith appeals were not compelling in the face of adverse budgetary conditions. During the weeks in which Sherrill was assembling the program to support the Affirmative Action Plans, division management was vigorously cutting costs. Since no provision was made for exempting or protecting expenditures and time allocated to minority relations, the program, not surprisingly, suffered as a result. The pressure on the budget and the personal stakes in achieving it were the predominant forces influencing the operating managers. Second, the issue had again been redefined, this time in terms of promotions, performance evaluations, and bonuses, as well as recruiting and training. The personnel function was not capable of implementing programs that affected career progressions without broad organizational support.

1972-73

The forces producing the climax observed in 1972 were already plainly visible in the fall of the previous year. First, employee activism had spread as more minorities were added in entry-level exempt jobs, and specific problems cropped up in locations other than GPD headquarters. The value of direct appeals to Moore had been demonstrated by his reaction in the spring of 1970. Second, the enlarged corporate staff had defined its own plans, in particular the "gateway job" concept, and was placing increasing pressure on the operating units to produce quick results. Moreover, reviews and audits of division performance prompted more criticism than praise. Third, the frustration in the chief executive's office was increasing, a factor likely to be initially encountered and perhaps magnified by those interested parties in close proximity to him, notably Adler and Wesley.

Personnel Research in GPD was, as the boxing commentator puts it, "bobbing and weaving" from 1970 until late 1971. Consolidating minority relations under Sherrill had the near-term benefit of insuring that the division could respond appropriately to growing government requirements and legal matters, but it further removed the issue from operating management. Then efforts to develop targets for 1971 ran afoul of budgetary limitations and delays in setting the over-all manpower plans. To make matters worse, the numerical results for 1970 were disappointing. The GPD personnel function was vulnerable, and it, rather than division or regional general management, absorbed the brunt of corporate criticism. With some urgency, Thomas, Jackson, and Sherrill sought and obtained greater involvement from Neely, the division manager, in setting targets for 1972 and fixing responsibilities on line management. However, the revitalized program was too little and too late to forestall the incidents which brought corporate intervention.

Within a year after these interventions, however, three fundamental changes were observable in the process governing the response to minority issues:

(1) The attention accorded minority relations by operating managers in planning and personnel decisions had increased significantly. The personnel function continued to administer the reporting systems and did the recruiting, but target setting and implementation had been taken over by managers with departmental or operating unit responsibilities. Rather than the "top down" commitments imposed on the organization in 1972, the process displayed signs of being converted into one built on primary commitments made at operating levels.

(2) A relationship had become apparent between the handling of minority relations and the individual manager's performance evaluation. The relationship was not necessarily well understood, though it

was perceived that one's career could be hurt by being caught in an unfavorable light during a publicized dispute.

(3) Corporate management had not relented on its insistence that financial plans be met. In essence, the divisions were asked for superior performance in both areas. The ambiguity inherent in multiple goals, issued with no mention of acceptable trade-offs between them, had been transmitted down to managers at the branch level.

As these changes took place, the corporate specialists withdrew from active involvement in directing the process and turned their attention to the emerging problems of providing equality for women.

The Response Process Summarized

The BPC experience with the implementation of equal employment for minorities may be restated in terms of the phases in the response process. This has been done schematically in Exhibit VIII-5. Phase I extended from the time of the civil disturbances in 1964 to the Harrison-Moore letter of 1968, which clearly stated the company's position on equal employment and focused attention inward. Phase II began in the functional organization that existed in 1964, lapsed during the reorganization in 1969, and was reentered in 1970. Although the specialists continued to function in the divisions during this interim period, they were not present at the corporate level and hence were not available to the chief executive for his deployment in managing the process. Operating management had been formally involved in minority affairs since 1968, when the first full-scale hiring targets were established. However, Phase III did not emerge until initiative for the implementation of corporate policy was seized by division management following the corporate interventions in 1972.

In the next chapter, the last and perhaps most dramatic of the corporate interventions is examined in detail. The evolution of policy and implementation has been sketched in broad terms above; a description of the Elmsford incident in this historical context provides a sense of the dynamics involved in the transition to Phase III.

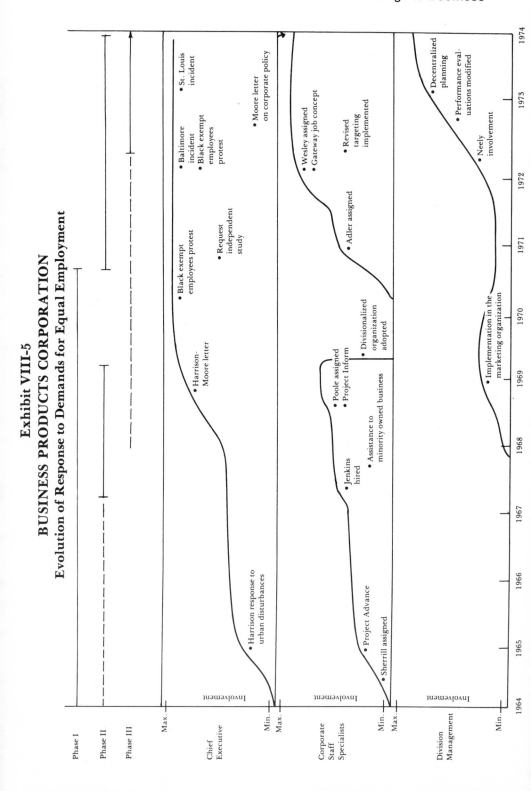

Exhibit VIII-5

BUSINESS PRODUCTS CORPORATION

Evolution of Response to Demands for Equal Employment

IX

Business Products Corporation: Transition

During the summer and fall of 1972, a minority relations problem erupted in a small service unit in (the Graphic Systems Division of the Business Products Corporation (BPC). As noted in Chapter VIII, this incident was actually the third of three such incidents that appeared to figure prominently in the implementation of corporate policy on equal opportunities for minorities. I have elected to report on it at some length. Without a reasonably full understanding of the drama and complexity of such situations as this, it is difficult to appreciate their impact on subsequent events. As the reader proceeds through this chapter, the organization chart in Exhibit IX-1 will be a valuable guide.

The Graphic Systems Division

The Graphic Systems Division (GSD), with sales of about $1,200 million was the marketing arm of the core business in BPC that historically had provided the corporation with consistent growth and the resources to finance new activities. The division's offices were in Indianapolis, the site of most of the production facilities that were managed by the manufacturing division. Sales, distribution, and customer service activities in GSD were conducted through five regional organizations, each directed by a general manager. Thus Daryl Roman, who became manager of the Chicago-based Midwest Region in May 1971, was responsible for about $250 million in sales and 3,300 employees.

Toward the end of the year, Roman negotiated with division management sales targets and expense budgets for the region which ultimately were included in the plan agreed upon with corporate management. It was customary in BPC for the chief executive to expect and to receive "stretch" commitments from the operating units. For the first several months of 1972 the Midwest Region had ranked fourth in sales performance against plan. Improvement was steady, however, and by the end of July Roman was able to report that his organization had nudged into first place by 1 percentage point at 91 percent of plan on a year-to-date basis.

Exhibit IX-1
BUSINESS PRODUCTS CORPORATION
Partial Organization Chart

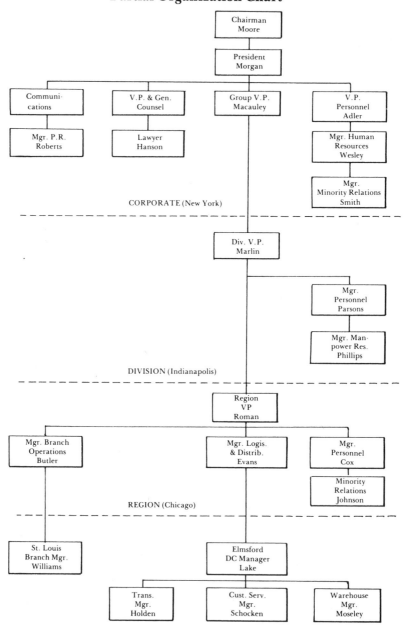

The Elmsford Distribution Center

The Elmsford Distribution Center was created in early November 1970 in the wake of a decision to phase out the national distribution service in Indianapolis and assign that function to dispersed facilities reporting to the five regional sales organizations. Included among the major functions of a distribution center were the following:

> To warehouse, ship, and invoice customers for GSD supplies. (The warehouse was force-fed and stock levels were managed centrally.)
> To warehouse and ship all but a few of the largest machines.
> To warehouse machines returned for overhaul pending notification of overhaul schedules.

The work force was largely clerical and female. For instance, of the 32 employees at the Elmsford facility, four were managers, eight were warehousemen, and the remaining 20 were women working in traffic, customer service, and inventory analysis. An organization chart for the unit is provided in Exhibit IX-2.

Being relatively close to Indianapolis, the Elmsford facility was among the last of the dozen to be authorized. During the 18-month period between the announcement of the phase-out and the move to Elmsford, the Distribution Center Manager, Peter Lake, had operated under difficult conditions. Forced to vacate his old quarters in the modern GSD building on three days' notice to make room for a new marketing group, Lake relocated the remnants of the national service warehouse in a rundown, rat-infested loft in the Indianapolis central city. Work force turnover in the warehouse was over 300 percent per year; the better-trained employees moved on to more skilled jobs in the BPC manufacturing facilities around Indianapolis, and the rest suffered from the varied afflictions of ghetto residents. On one visit to the warehouse, he recalled that 14 of the 23 employees were absent for one reason or another.

When the operation was transferred from Indianapolis to Elmsford, its management team, composed of the managers of traffic, customer service, and the warehouse supervisor, was also relocated. Shortly before, this, however, Lake had approached his supervisor, Alex Evans, Midwest Regional Manager of Logistics and Distribution, with the request that Joseph Schocken, then 30, the Manager

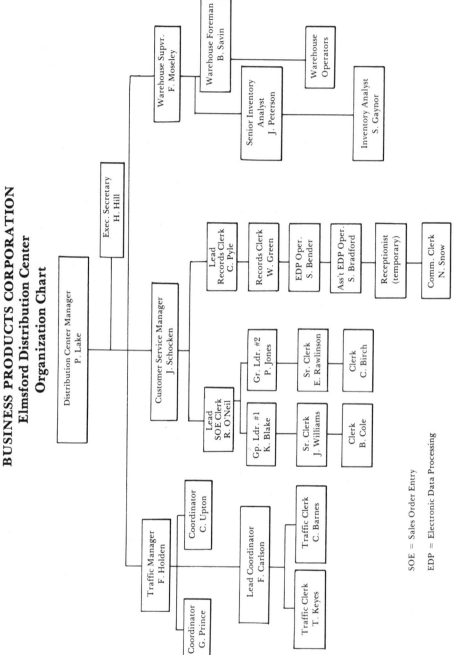

Exhibit IX-2
BUSINESS PRODUCTS CORPORATION
Elmsford Distribution Center
Organization Chart

SOE = Sales Order Entry

EDP = Electronic Data Processing

of Customer Service, be reassigned to some other job and not with the Distribution Center. Evans agreed. At that time Schocken had been working around Lake for three of his six years at BPC, one and half of them as Lake's subordinate. He had been put on probation by his previous superior from September 1968 to March 1969 (a long time in BPC) for marginal personnel skills, and was viewed as moody and erratic, though hard-working and loyal. On the other hand, his technical and operational skills had been rated high.

Evans explored the reassignment opportunities for Schocken in Indianapolis for two months to no avail; in essence Evans was told, "You've got him, his record is cloudy, he's yours." Schocken, too, had at first been reluctant to move to Elmsford, citing family reasons, but when he was told that his job could not be guaranteed otherwise, he agreed to relocate. He was not told, however, that Lake and Evans had sought to sever him from the Distribution Center management team. Tragedy struck Schocken not long after he settled in Elmsford. During a company seminar, which he had not wanted to attend but was persuaded to do so by the region, his wife committed suicide.

The first months in Elmsford brought little relief for the management team. The capital request for a new facility had languished in Indianapolis for over a year, with the result that the Distribution Center was located for 15 months in temporary quarters. In this case, temporary quarters meant six trailers fastened together and parked in a middle-class suburb not far from where the permanent building was to be constructed. Conditions were "primitive." The trailers were cramped and broken up into numerous little working areas. The septic system froze from time to time, causing the toilets to fail during the winter months, and it was not unusual for the temperature differential between floor and desk level to be 30 degrees.

In this situation Lake had two major tasks. The first was to manage a volume of work that was 50 percent larger than it had been in Indianapolis, because new territories had been added without the relinquishment of old ones. For some months operations were conducted in both cities, and Lake recalled that he could not get his entire management group together for weeks at a time. The second task was to build an organization. This process was complicated by several factors. First, BPC had instituted a corporate-wide hiring freeze in the late months of 1970 due to lagging budget-actual financial comparisons. As a result, until the new year the work force was interviewed by Lake and his managers but hired through a third party as temporary help. This created a good deal of uncertainty and some resentment among the new people, who did not see why they should not be entitled to all of the fringe benefits normally accruing to BPC employees.

Further, the applicant flow obtained through initial advertising in the Elmsford area was entirely white, in keeping with the profile of the surrounding communities. Lake, desirous of operating in the spirit of the corporate minority relations policy, sought minority candidates in greater St. Louis. Since there was a GSD sales branch there with experience in recruiting minority employees, Lake worked through it to identify, interview, and test minority applications. Not having facilities or staff for testing, Lake selected much more informally from among applicants coming to him directly in Elmsford. When the Distribution Center's doors opened, five of the thirteen temporary employees, including Lake's secretary, belonged to a minority group.

Despite physical and economic obstacles, the organization appeared to Evans and Lake to be developing nicely. The caliber of new personnel was considered excellent, and a pioneering spirit took hold that helped them through the uncomfortable winter of 1971. Reducing the backlog became a challenge prompting a high level of commitment and motivation. Lake described some of his activities:

> In a way, the trailers had a positive influence in the sense that we tried to pay attention to the employees in lots of little ways. You know, name plates for their desks, roses for girls out sick. One time we were without toilets for 7 days. By coincidence, we had a Muzak system hooked up the first day. I went around the office being a clown telling them, "What do you people want, both toilets *and* Muzak?" There was a common enemy and everyone pulled together to work down the tremendous backlog. The trailers may have put us in awkward positions, but they made us do some good things, too.

In the fall of 1971, Lake again approached Evans with the suggestion that a transfer out of the Distribution Center be considered for Schocken. Evans discussed with Daryl Roman the possibility of moving him to the Midwestern Regional Office in a staff capacity. The matter was given some study but nothing came of it. However, the Manpower Resources Plan at year-end recommended that he be moved at the end of 1972 to a position in which his operational skills would be more central to his job. In the meantime, Schocken continued as Manager of Customer Services at Elmsford, responsible for roughly a dozen women employees.

In mid-1971 construction on the new Distribution Center facility finally commenced. As the work progressed, Lake took pictures and displayed them in the trailers as a sign that better times were ahead. Performance indicators in the Distribution Center reflected steady improvement from the first months when Elmsford had the worst record in the country. Evans commented on his evaluation for 1971: "Elmsford got the job done in 1971. And without much administrative support from the region. We asked from both supervisors and employees a tremendous amount of effort. I can remember writing in Lake's review, 'He's great at jerry-rigging. Give him any task and he can do it and keep his people motivated and committed. But the critical question is, can he run a refined operation?' "

When the Distribution Center moved to its new quarters in February 1972, Lake felt that the time had come to tighten discipline, especially for attendance and lateness, which we had not emphasized as strongly earlier because of the poor working conditions. He "rattled the cage" from time to time, stressing that customer service, the Distribution Center's primary concern, depended on employees' being on the job. While he did not want time clocks, he made it clear that time cards were to reflect tardiness as well as absences. The employees responded by achieving an absentee record of only .9 percent for the first half of 1972, which was considered extraordinarily low. Both Lake and those who reviewed the performance of the Distribution Center took this as a good indication that morale and dedication continued on a high level.

After the move to the new building had been completed, Evans reviewed the functions of the Distribution Center. He found that customer service and traffic were "coming on strong," the warehouse was improving, and the equipment control group was the best in the country. When the center was established, Evans and Lake agreed that the functions should be put in first-rate order sequentially, and now only inventory control posed a problem. In May, responsibility for this function was shifted from customer service to the warehouse manager, and a specialist from Evans' staff conducted a study which pointed to the need for an additional inventory clerk. Evans concurred with this recommendation and suggested to Lake that he pick the very best person in the Distribution Center to be the lead clerk, with special emphasis on her analytical skills. At the end of May, Lake reported that a woman in traffic who had been with the center since it opened was his choice. At the time, Evans asked if her transfer would create a problem for the current clerk, a black woman, also one of the original employees. Lake responded that he felt that he would be able to "console" her. The correctness of Lake's choice appeared to be confirmed in the following weeks as the inventory control function exhibited steady improvement.

By July the region could point to the Elmsford Distribution Center with some satisfaction. Its performance was then among the best in the country. Evans recalled that Roman had complimented him after a visit that month to the facility, saying in effect, "They should all be like that one." It was generally noted that the visitor was impressed with the friendliness apparent in the work environment.

Minority Relations—Some Early Rumbles

Behind the commendable operating results and the pleasant atmosphere, Evans and Lake had on several occasions become aware of dissatisfactions expressed by several of the black employees. However, in the context of the myriad problems encountered and for the most part being overcome, they were viewed at the time as either understandable or relatively insignificant.

The first involved the resignation of one of the original minority employees, Susan Wilson, in March of 1972. Schocken indicated that he had placed her on probation for absenteeism in late 1971, her record at the time reflecting more than twice the number of lost hours as the next highest employee. In February she had an automobile accident and lost several more days. There was some evidence to suggest that the temporary disability form filed after she returned, and presumably signed by a physician, had been falsified, though this suspicion was not discussed with Wilson at the time. Then in March her doctor advised her that, in view of other medical problems, she would probably be absent quite frequently in the near future. At this point, she was counseled by Lake regarding the possibility of a leave of absence and also questioned about the earlier medical form (which she denied falsifying). She then resigned. As these events unfolded, Lake kept Evans informed.

The Wilson episode did not end there, however. Just before she left, and without Lake's knowledge at the time, she filed a suit with the Missouri Equal Employment Opportunity Commission,* charging BPC with forcing her to resign under duress. By this action she became something of a martyr to the other black women. Hannah Hill, Lake's secretary, had several long discussions with him about the handling of her case. Hill emphasized the numerous problems Wilson had: poor housing and transportation, an illegitimate child, and so forth. Lake retorted that, in view of her record, he had been justified in his actions. Moreover, he suspected that she had resigned rather than chance an investigation into the authenticity of the disability form.

Several weeks later, Shirley Gaynor, another of the original black employees, had a two-hour session with Lake in which she lodged a complaint against Schocken. She maintained that he was a racist, and she provided a series of incidents to support her contention. Lake had had previous discussions with other (white) employees about Schocken's insensitivity toward the needs of the people in his department. As Lake listened to Gaynor, he had the feeling that he was picking up further evidence of Schocken's managerial weakness. Nevertheless, after this meeting he spoke to Schocken "briefly and honestly" about what had happened, but with no more emphasis than on earlier occasions.

The next straw in the wind involved Evans. In May, GSD held an "open house" at Elmsford to inaugurate the new building. Hannah Hill came with her husband, Nathan Hill, a black activist and community organizer in St. Louis, who was currently involved in establishing a drug rehabilitation center (The Black Community House). Nathan Hill took Evans aside and "laid it on him." In the noise and confusion it was hard for Evans to understand all that was being said; he did not entirely grasp Hill's outside affiliation, though he knew Hannah Hill was his wife. Much of the monologue

---

*Owing to a backlog of cases, the state had not yet considered the Susan Wilson case at the time of the protest described in this chapter.

related to the problems Hill was having in St. Louis, to his need for financial support for his drug rehabilitation program, to a fundamentally racist society, and in vague ways to the existence of racism in BPC. However, Evans heard no specific charges leveled against the Distribution Center. In the next few days, Evans relayed the sense of his conversation to the Regional Personnel Manager, Michael Cox, and checked with Lake, who indicated that he knew of no serious racial problems in Elmsford.

Then in late May the lead inventory control clerk's job was identified and filled by a white woman from traffic, as described above. When she was hired, Shirley Gaynor had expressed an interest in inventory control, and Lake had assigned her to the one slot then available. Her performance over the next year and a half was satisfactory. However, while she was seen as very intelligent, Lake felt she had a "narrow" view of the job. She was difficult to counsel and was viewed as disruptive in the work force; management, as Evans put it, "couldn't come to grips with her." The woman transferred from Traffic, who, along with Gaynor, had been a Grade 3, received a two-grade promotion. Gaynor had not received a promotion since being hired, nor had she been interviewed for the lead job. As Evans put it, "She hadn't received much training. No one had ever given her a job she couldn't do." Gaynor consequently felt she should have been made lead inventory control clerk.

For the next two months little of significance to management transpired in minority relations. Evans commented, "We didn't see Hannah's criticism as serious. She is a very sophisticated person. From a look at her résumé, it's pretty clear she is way overqualified for the job she's in. She can be leveling criticism but in such a pleasant way, you might not catch it." As Lake's secretary she also had access to the personnel files and to most of the information flowing into and out of the office.

A Nightclub Affair

On the evening of Thursday, August 10, Sam Johnson, the Regional Manager of Minority Relations, flew to St. Louis to preside over an open house held at a local motel for minority candidates for service representative positions at the sales branch. His visit came at the conclusion of a four-day advertising campaign on radio stations popular in the black community.

Just before Johnson left he stopped to speak with Cox. Toward the end of their conversation, Cox mentioned in passing the discussion he had had with Evans about the latter's meeting with Nathan Hill. Cox said he thought Hill might be a minister—the Black Community Church (House)—who wanted BPC to contribute to his drug rehabilitation program. He also indicated that Hill had had a meeting with the St. Louis Branch Manager, Bradford Williams. In any event, Cox asked Johnson to get in touch with Hill to find out more about the drug rehabilitation program and whether Hill might wish to help identify minority candidates for employment in GSD.

When Johnson arrived in St. Louis he arranged a meeting with Hill for the next evening. Hill picked up Johnson after work and, as they headed for the nightclub that had been agreed upon for the meeting, Hill related some of the difficulties he was having with the city bureaucracy. After a drink at the bar they went upstairs to a private room. Inside were twenty-seven people—nineteen men from Hill's Black Community House, four black women from the Distribution Center, two black salesmen from the St. Louis Branch, an aide from Representative Charmichael's office (a black congressman), and a reporter from the largest St. Louis newspaper. Johnson described the ensuing events:

> The first thing Nathan said when we got inside was, "The reason we're here is to talk about racism at BPC!" I said, "Wait a minute, why am I here? I thought it was to talk with you about a drug program." He went into the meeting he had with Brad Williams. After this went on for a while, I turned to Hannah and said, "Why are you here?" She said she had some complaints at the Distribution Center she wanted to talk about. Then I asked one of the salesmen, "Why are you here?" He started saying, "I don't know . . . ah . . . we were told there was a meeting. . ." and was pretty uncomfortable about the whole thing. Then I balked. I told them, "I'm only a functionary. I can only bring information back but can't make decisions on the spot." At this point Nathan put on his show . . . 300 years of slavery, how the black man was exploited, how "you bein' bought off by whitey . . ." There was a lot of strong language. Some of the girls were crying. I listened for a while and then I picked up my things and started for the door. Nathan said, "Where are you going?" I told him I was not going to talk about this kind of thing. If they wanted to talk about BPC, o.k., but not with that crowd of people there. With that, everybody leaves but the four girls and the salesmen.

Shirley Gaynor started in on Lake. She said he was a figurehead, that Schocken was the real power in the Distribution Center and he (Schocken) was a racist, a bigot and so forth. I said, "OK, but can you give me some facts?" They gave me a lot of incidents, and I wrote them down. Then I asked the salesmen to give me some facts, too. They began to talk about being assigned to ghetto sales districts where there was less money to be made, about thinking they got lower starting salaries and so on. But when they saw me starting to write them down, they said, "Stop. The sisters have more problems than we do. You work on them first."

It was 9:00 p.m. by this time. The others came back. I went out for a break and tried to call Cox but couldn't get him. Then I came back and we had another long discussion about the narcotics program and everything else again 'til 11:00 p.m. Finally, the meeting broke up. I said to Nathan, "You'll have an answer from BPC on the drug rehabilitation program in three weeks." Nathan said, "When are we going to hear about the sisters?" I told him next Wednesday or Thursday. He asked why that long; I said it would take some time to communicate with other people, get things typed, etc. Then one of his lieutenants said, "Where is Roman?* Why don't you find him and tell him *now?*" I replied that Roman was probably back at home for the weekend in Chicago. It wasn't that I couldn't, it was that I didn't *choose* to. Then he said, "I'll bet you would if it was a matter of getting your breath straight." I had to admit he was right. That really got me thinking. . .

Johnson immediately committed his notes on the meeting to paper in the following form:

MEMO TO MYSELF!

SUBJECT: Notes from Meeting with Black Employees/Black Community House, St. Louis

Sometime during the period between March and June 1972 four (4) black clericals in the Elmsford Distribution Center filed a Class Action Suit** claiming racial discrimination against BPC.

---

* It had come out earlier in the discussion that Roman had been in St. Louis for a sales meeting that day.

**In August no one in BPC was aware of any legal action involving the Elmsford facility other than the pending Susan Wilson case.

Those four (4) employees were
>
> Hannah Hill
> Wilma Green
> Shirley Gaynor
> Jennie Williams

The alleged Class Action Suit filed by the above four (4) employees listed among their indictments the following:
> — Discrimination in employment processing
> — Segregated facilities
> — Discrimination in promotion practices and performance appraisals.

SPECIFIC INDICTMENTS

A. *Discrimination in employment practices*
1. In the start-up of the Distribution Center all of the black clericals were tested; none of the whites were tested.
2. Joe Schocken hired Elise Rawlinson (referred by Aileen Lambert) because she was blonde and wore mini skirts—she was never tested. The statement made concerning Miss Rawlinson was as follows: "One day Joe Schocken came out of his office and said to Aileen Lambert that he needed a girl. Aileen said she had someone to refer. Joe asked Aileen if the girl was blonde. Aileen said yes. He asked her if the girl wore mini skirts. Aileen said yes. Joe told Aileen to have the girl come in as soon as possible. The girl, Elise Rawlinson, came in that day at 1:00. At 1:15 she came out of Joe's office saying that she was hired. Joe never tested her and sent her hire package to region, where it was denied processing by John Noyes, who sent it back to Schocken and insisted that the girl be tested.
3. Carolyn Moody was hired as a temporary on March 19. Carolyn (a black girl) was processed initially by Peter Lake and told that she would be hired. Before her papers could be processed, Joe Schocken found out about the offer, came into Pete Lake's office, and insisted that this girl not be hired as a permanent but put on as a temporary so that they would have a chance to observe her. Pete Lake agreed, Carolyn was hired as a temporary, and told that there were no allocations at the time.

B. *Segregated Facilities* — the sole content of this area of alleged discrimination refers to the physical setting when the Distribution Center was located in a series of trailers.

1. Wilma Green and Shirley Gaynor both allege that they were physically segregated from the white girls and placed in a remote corner of one of the trailers. This they included in their charge to the Missouri State Equal Employment Opportunity Commission. Since that time the physical facilities have been moved into a permanent situation and the alleged segregated facilities are said to no longer exist by Shirley and Wilma.

C. *Discrimination in Performance Appraisals and Promotions*

1. Shirley Gaynor alleges that she was discriminated against in terms of receiving a promotion to lead inventory control clerk. She says that she was told by Pete Lake and Fred Moseley* that she did more work than any of the other girls in her area. However, they would not promote her because she failed to "go one step further." Shirley says that later Fred Moseley indicated to her that he was sorry that she did not get the promotion, that he agreed that she should have, that he had tried but his hands were tied, that the promotion would go to one of Joe Schocken's favorites.

2. Aileen Lambert allegedly was promoted two times in three months while her attendance record in terms of absenteeism and tardiness was just as bad as a black girl, Susan Wilson, who was fired.

3. Wilma Green alleges that she was told "you are good at your work, however, you do not help the other girls; therefore, we cannot give you a high performance appraisal." She received a "4."

4. The comment was made by Hannah Hill that no black in the Distribution Center has ever received a rating higher than a "4."

5. The charge was made that Elinor Stewart (a white girl) had a performance appraisal which reflected that her attendance was good. After the appraisal was submitted to Hannah Hill for typing, she brought it to Pete Lake's attention saying that "this is a blatant lie, she has missed well over 80 hours." The performance appraisal was then returned to Joe Schocken. He changed the comment about her attendance being good, indicated that it was not so good, yet he did not change her performance appraisal.

---

*Warehouse Supervisor in the Elmsford Distribution Center.

D. *General Allegations*

1. Allegedly, Susan Wilson was "railroaded out of the Distribution Center because she was black and because she was not liked by Joe Schocken." Allegedly, Joe Schocken began harassing Susan Wilson when she missed four days from work because of the death of her father. Supposedly, when she returned to work she was called in by Schocken and told, "After all it was not your husband, it was only your father, we cannot put up with your missing time this way." Later, when Susan approached Schocken and Lake, requesting temporary disability leave to have an appendix removed, she was denied such leave and forced to resign. That afternoon she collapsed and had to have an appendectomy. The girls went on to compare the treatment of Susan with the inequitable treatment of Aileen Lambert, who, according to Hannah Hill, was allowed to take seven days off for temporary disability because she had to have a corn removed from her toe.

2. Allegedly, a representative from Matson Employment Agency was visiting the Distribution Center when she was shown into Schocken's office by Wilma Green; Wilma and Shirley alleged hearing the following dialogue: "The representative from Matson saying, 'Oh, I see you hire blacks.' Answer from Joe Schocken, 'Yes, we have to hire them whether we want to or not.'"

3. Statement made by Shirley Gaynor agreed upon by the other girls: "The racist situation is so bad out at the Distribution Center that the white girls feel absolutely free about coming up to reprimand blacks about petty and menial stuff when they have no supervisory powers. They feel as though all they have to do is go tell Joe Schocken and he'll get right on the black's case."

4. A meeting was held to discuss the abuse of overtime, and all employees were told if they came in late that they could not make it up through lunch. No black has been allowed to make up late time since then, yet whites have been allowed to make up that kind of time on numerous documented occasions.

E. *Allegations Made by Salesmen*

The following statements were made by the sales organization or relate to that organization in the branch.

1. There is apparent discrimination in the assignment of territories and team assignments which relate directly to

compensation. The city of St. Louis is split racially into the east and the west. The blacks are in the east, the whites are in the west—the money is in the west. The western team of the St. Louis branch has historically been and is now all white. Before when it was Dom Pisano's team it was all white. Greg Norfolk made application for that team assignment and it was denied. Since then Joe Graffelo* has gotten the team, it is now still all white. There is no reason for blacks to think that they will be able to get over on the west side where the moneys are.

2. The employment process for blacks is anywhere from a week to three weeks longer than it is for whites. Blacks have, according to Greg Norfolk, two to five more interviews than whites do. Blacks have reference checking run on them, when whites do not.

3. Statement was made by Greg Norfolk that Joe Graffelo is in his opinion racially prejudiced. He goes on to say that records show that Graffelo has not given any black that he has ever reviewed a positive rating. This goes for black applicants as well as existing black employees who have come in contact with Graffelo.

4. Blacks are told that it takes at least 18 months in a job before you can be promoted while Joe Graffelo was promoted to assistant sales manager in less than a year.

5. There are no black managers in the St. Louis branch, and there have never been. Blacks don't believe that there are going to be any.

6. Blacks were told that there is a policy that says relatives cannot work in the same location, while Hannah Hill reports that her nephew-in-law, Francis Douglas, was refused employment because he was a relative of hers. Further, Greg Norfolk indicates that his brother was refused employment at the St. Louis branch though he was given a positive recommendation in terms of his interviews and his testing. His brother was then referred to the Springfield branch because they could not hire him in the same location where he had a brother working. Springfield did not hire him—while Herb Wilson (white) and his wife allegedly are working in the same branch—while Jane Thompson and Roger Thompson work out of the same

*Area Sales Manager.

branch — while Bert Sanger and his first cousin work out of the same branch.

7. Blacks feel as though the quantity and quality of training they get as area reps is inequitable with that given to whites. That in some cases the trainer's heart is just not in it.

The Region's Response

On Sunday, August 13, Johnson called Cox to tell him briefly what had happened in St. Louis. The next day Cox informed Roman, and the latter asked Evans and Johnson to join them to discuss the situation as it was presented by Johnson and to determine what ought to be done. Roman pressed for answers to two questions. First, what is the problem at the Distribution Center, and, second, to the extent it related to Schocken, what should be done about him?

Johnson commented on the response to the first question:

Daryl [Roman] wanted to do something quickly. We concluded that there should be an investigation by Lake and Schocken into the allegations by looking into the personnel records at the Distribution Center. In the spirit of continuing a dialogue, Lake was to have the black girls conduct their own investigation. In other words, Lake was to meet with them and ask their help. Then the information would be pulled together and we'd move on to recommendations.

Thus, facts were to be gathered, initially at least, by Distribution Center management and a continuing dialogue maintained by Lake.

On the second question, Evans argued that Schocken should be pulled out and Hannah Hill transferred to a less sensitive job where she would not have free access to personnel records and all communication in and out of Lake's office. Evans reasoned that, whether the allegations were justified or not, the best way to turn the situation around was to remove the primary irritant before matters became worse. His position was strengthened when Schocken's job history was reviewed and it was recalled that Lake had requested his transfer previously. In Evans' view, Schocken had the potential for being valuable elsewhere in GSD. He had done an outstanding job, for instance, in implementing a computer system for processing customer supply orders—better than anyone else in the company, according to Evans. His record suggested that he might well turn in a fine performance in staff work. Moreover, his dedication to BPC was enormous; he worked long hours and followed company rules to the letter. However, his lack of understanding and tact in a supervisory role were again causing difficulties. Evans also suggested as his replacement Jim Atkins, a black manager working in the other Midwest distribution center who had been requested by Lake earlier. Evans said he was the "best man available."

While Roman agreed that Schocken should be moved, he also wanted to determine if there was substance to the charges of discrimination. Consequently, the investigation was to proceed while Indianapolis was sounded out on the possibility of a transfer. In the meantime, both Schocken and Hill were to remain in place.

During the week of August 13 Lake was in Indianapolis attending a distribution center managers' meeting and had no knowledge of Johnson's get-together the previous Friday. Cox called him there and advised him to fly to Chicago to discuss the situation and the region's program for resolving it. On Wednesday, August 16, Lake met with Cox, Evans, and Johnson, and they thrashed out a course of action in more detail. Cox notified the black women that the region was investigating their concerns as Johnson had promised and would like them to meet with Lake as soon as he returned from Indianapolis. The purpose of that meeting, Cox said, was "to further communicate to him the nature of the problem and for them to set up, along with the manager, the guidelines for conducting an internal investigation of their own." That afternoon Lake flew back to Indianapolis for the remainder of the week.

Division and corporate headquarters were advised of the problem in conference calls on August 15, 17, and 18. The principal contact at the division was Robert Phillips, a personnel manager whose responsibilities included minority relations, and at the corporate level, Frank Wesley and one of his subordinates, Charles Smith, both of whom were in Personnel and holding responsibility for minority affairs.* Cox asked Wesley about corporate policy on meeting with outside representatives such as Nathan Hill. Wesley answered that BPC did not as a matter of principle deal with parties who were not

---

*Of these three, Smith was black.

either duly elected union representatives or legal counsel. This position confirmed a similar one taken earlier by Roman and subsequently concurred in by John Marlin, the division manager of GSD. Cox also mentioned Hill's drug rehabilitation program and a further comment that Hill had made about the design of a minority training program for BPC. Response to this type of issue fell most nearly in Smith's area, and he agreed to follow up on it with Hill.

When Smith learned of the pending investigation into the Susan Wilson case by the Missouri Equal Employment Opportunity Commission, he recommended that, if possible, it be advanced to coincide with BPC's in-house investigation so that all parties might proceed in a more formal conciliation process. Johnson then called a man he had met and Smith knew at the state EEOC to request that the investigation be moved up. The EEOC official replied that there was an eight-month case backlog and, as a matter of procedure, investigations were not accelerated. He also declined to be present at the meeting to be held when the results of the Distribution Center's findings were presented. Smith also talked with him that week and received similar responses.

The following Monday, August 21, Lake met with the four black women for seven hours in his office. He had the feeling that the women viewed this meeting as an obligation to local management and a necessary step prior to taking their charges to higher levels of management. Lake said, "They felt they had received no satisfaction from me in the past. They accused me not of discrimination but of condoning it." The women made a number of allegations which Lake noted, but no formal demands were articulated, and Lake recalled no mention of the possible intervention of Nathan Hill on their behalf. They also presented Lake with a written summary, dated August 16, of the areas in which they said discrimination existed (Exhibit IX-3). Lake relayed the outcome of this meeting to the regional offices in Chicago.

On Wednesday afternoon, August 23, Cox, Evans, and Johnson flew to St. Louis. Cox called Hannah Hill and asked if she would meet with him alone. She agreed. Cox commented on their conversation: "She said the situation was serious. 'I doubt if we'll meet with you without Nathan.' I asked her why she didn't stay inside the company. She said it was no use—Distribution Center management was not responsive."

EXHIBIT IX-3

BUSINESS PRODUCTS CORPORATION

Employee Summary of Allegations

August 16, 1972

We the black employees of the St. Louis Regional Distribution Center feel that we are being discriminated against by Pete Lake, Joe Schocken, Fred Holden, and Fred Moseley, Managers of this facility, in the following areas:

Performance Appraisals

Impartiality [sic] on performance appraisals is exhibited openly here. Not one black employee has been given a performance rating above "consistently met" regardless of job performance. Whites receive higher ratings.

Wages

Because blacks receive lower performance appraisal ratings our wages are not as high as some whites even though our job performance is equal to or better than white employees.

Promotions

Performance appraisals also play the major role in this area. If performance appraisals are low, promotional opportunities are impossible.

Absences & Lateness

We are harassed about absences and lateness and the whites are allowed to (be) absent or late without any repercussion.

We feel that Business Products Corporation must be investigated immediately. We will no longer tolerate the open and blatant discriminatory policies practiced by Business Products Corporation.

/S/
Hannah Hill
/S/
Shirley Gaynor
/S/
Wilma Green
/S/
Jennie Williams

NOTE
The above information can be documented if proof is required.

That evening and for ten hours the next day, the three regional managers met with Lake, Schocken, and Moseley to review the results obtained thus far in their investigation and to formulate a course of action. They also went over, point by point, the charges and incidents enumerated by the black women. Lake admitted that there were a lot of inconsistencies in administrative procedures, especially with regard to testing, promotions, and absences, often affecting whites as well as blacks, and a degree of insensitivity to minority relations that he had not been aware of before. He maintained that they were not overt but in large measure a function of the Distribution Center's difficult history.

On the other hand, the regional managers all felt that Schocken either evaded the questions or insisted that he did not see how those actions ascribed to him could have been misinterpreted. One incident included in Lake's notes from his meeting earlier in the week was cited as an example. Schocken, in response to some morale problems he was having, asked his people to think about how the situation might be improved. One by one he called them into his office to elicit their suggestions. One black woman, Wilma Green, a quiet, thoughtful person, had given the matter quite a bit of thought and was looking forward to talking with Schocken. At five o'clock, however, he closed up shop, and no further interviews were conducted or reference made to them thereafter. Green was hurt and felt she had intentionally been left out. Schocken's explanation was simply that he had obtained all the information he needed that afternoon by the normal closing time and saw no need for proceeding further. Moreover, he said another (white) woman had not been interviewed either.

By Thursday evening a plan was put together which included specific responses to the problems identified by the black women (Exhibit IX-4). Some of the corrective actions, such as changes in performance appraisal weightings and specifications, applied to the whole Distribution Center. Others related to redressing individual grievances. Evans raised a question about what the white employees should be told. He was discouraged by the group from saying anything at that time. The feeling was that the problems would be settled in a few days—there was no use stirring up the matter any further.

Early Friday morning, a "surprise" meeting was called with the

EXHIBIT IX-4

BUSINESS PRODUCTS CORPORATION

Midwestern Action Plan

The following is a compiled listing of problem areas as communicated to four black female employees of the St. Louis Distribution Center, along with Management's current corrective action steps in response to the management's understanding of the nature and origin of those problem areas.

The sources of problem communication included the following:

1. A meeting held August 11 in St. Louis between Sam Johnson, the Regional Minority Relations Manager, and the four minority employees involved.

2. A "Position Paper" from the above-mentioned employees submitted to Pete Lake, Manager of the Distribution Center on August 16, in which the employees cited what their concerns are in writing.

3. Verbal communications during the August 16 meeting of the employees with Pete Lake.

PROBLEMS AND CORRECTIVE ACTIONS

Problem	Corrective action
A. Discrimination in performance appraising.	1. Apply newly-developed percentage weightings of factors listed on the performance appraisal forms to gain greater uniformity in applying evaluation of performance standards:

	Percentage
Quality	30
Quantity	25
Reliability	10
Dependability	20
Effectiveness	15
TOTAL	100

2. Provide more exacting definition of dependability as it applies on the performance appraisal form in relation to attendance: i.e.,

EXHIBIT IX - 4 (cont.)

Problem	Corrective Action

Rating	Value code	Hours lost
1 unique performer	6	0-10
2 frequently exceeds	5	11-24
3 consistently meets	4	25-34
4 usually meets	3	35-45
5 sometimes meets	2	46-56
6 never meets	1	57 +

3. Review all appraisal ratings and correct, retroactively, any inconsistencies in light of the aforementioned new standards and make pay adjustments if justified to correct inequities where they exist. *Note:* only those appraisal factors reviewed under new standards which resulted in an increase in either rating or pay will be effected — those resulting in decreased ratings or pay under the new standards will not be put into effect.

4. Adjust Shirley Gaynor's evaluation for dependability on her performance appraisal to accurately reflect her attendance record.

5. Promote Shirley Gaynor to Inventory Clerk, Grade 5, retroactive to June 28 (date when similar promotion of Elise Rawlinson took place). Review of Miss Gaynor's attendance and overall performance appraisal under new standards justify and advise this move.

B. Lack of promotional opportunity into peripheral job responsibilities.

1. Establish a program of cross-training employees into various Distribution Center departments — preferably through promotions, if possible. This

EXHIBIT IX - 4 (cont.)

Problem	Corrective Action
	could also establish training ground for future promotion of female employees into non-clerical positions if other qualifications are met.
C. Lack of sufficient on-site dialogue between Management and employees, especially black employees.	1. Monthly meetings will be held by each supervisor/manager with their subordinates and with the location Manager every 2 months. Each supervisor/manager is to submit a report of the meeting including date, time, topics discussed, and general summary of meeting along with action plans to resolve problems that are identified.
D. Racial attitudes at Distribution Center are alleged to foster discrimination.	1. An attitude survey to be taken at the appropriate time in the future (hopefully mid-November) to provide insight into human relations problems existing in the Distribution Center.
	2. To deliver to the supervisory and management as well as lead staff of the Distribution Center the minority awareness training education session early in October.
	3. A communication meeting to be held with black employees (in addition to white employees) to communicate our position as a Distribution Center and Corporation in the area of Equal Employment Opportunity and mutual respect.
E. Wilma Green was not rewarded for best attendance.	1. To award Wilma the prize established for her accomplishment — a dinner for two at a restaurant of her choice. *Note*: computer report error 6/4/72 erroneously charged Miss Green with time lost.

EXHIBIT IX - 4 (cont.)

Problem	Corrective Action
F. Lack of effective and equitable methods of monitoring absence and lateness performance of all employees.	1. Institution of a new policy on an experimental basis for 45 days, based on an honor system of reporting time—all employees will be allowed to voluntarily make up lost time during their lunch period. Note: the four black employees feel they are being harassed on absence and lateness performance which is indicated on their reviews, while whites are not. Blacks would like to see a time clock utilized to eliminate time-reporting inequities. It is a feeling of management at this time that we would like to try an honor system for 45 days. If, after that period, the honor system is not working to the satisfaction of all people involved, we will consider the time clock.

black women, attended by Cox, Evans, Johnson, and Lake, to review the results of the investigation and present the remedial program. The women then said they would not discuss substantive matters unless Nathan Hill were allowed to represent them. Their argument was more or less as follows: "We are four poor little girls without training or experience in the matters that should be discussed. You people have your experts whenever you need help. How can we possibly get a fair deal when the odds against us are so high? Therefore, we need our expert, Nathan Hill, to represent us. He can make you understand our problems." For two and a half hours the discussion revolved around the women's insistence and the manager's intransigence on outside representation. The women's argument was received with some sympathy, however, and at one point, the managers caucused to review whether or not they ought to agree to meet with Hill. In view of the specific instructions they had to the contrary, however, they decided against it.

Finally, at 11:30 Cox said, "Will you listen to our corrective action plan?" The women agreed but said they would not approve or disapprove it until Hill was permitted to intervene. As Cox reviewed the plan, he felt for the first time a glimmer of rapport. The women, he felt, were surprised that management was willing to agree to changes; they weren't accepting anything, but there seemed to him to be a positive atmosphere in the meeting. On an optimistic note the group then adjourned for lunch. Cox described the subsequent events:

> Over lunch, they (the black employees) told us they had called Nathan Hill. He said we hadn't met their needs. "Here are nine points that they didn't even mention, which is proof they don't understand your problems," he told them. We had another hour of discussion and then quit, disappointed as hell. At one point, Shirley Gaynor, who was sort of uncontrolled, said, "We'll take our problems to the streets. We'll take them to the public."

As the meeting ended, the employees told the managers not to implement their program because Nathan Hill had not seen it and might not feel it appropriate.

At the airport a short while later, Cox called Wesley in New York to advise him that the employees had not agreed to the region's approach and in fact had even threatened to take the dispute "to the streets." Cox tested corporate opinion again on the strength of the policy ruling out negotiations with third parties. He also raised a further point, "If there is publicity, is the corporation going to bend? If so, let's do it now." Wesley reaffirmed the policy on third parties. He further assured Cox that the corporation would do what it felt was right and would not be dissuaded by the prospect of adverse public comment.

Week of August 28

The following week in Chicago, Roman was apprised of the events at the Distribution Center. Word was also received from Smith that he had succeeded in persuading the Missouri EEOC to advance its investigation to the week after Labor Day. With this bit of encouraging news, the matter remained in limbo in Chicago for the remainder of the week.

Meanwhile, at the Distribution Center, Lake was informed by the black women that there was an increasing amount of animosity between blacks and whites, in sharp contrast to the harmony that had prevailed before. In an effort to allay the tension, Lake decided to make himself available after work on Wednesday, August 30, to discuss, in general terms, what had been happening between the black employees and management. Most of the white employees stayed for a two-hour meeting which Lake described in these terms:

> I told the white employees about some of the problems brought up in the black allegations. I tried to defend the blacks' complaints and to explain what affirmative action means and what their rights are with EEOC. The whites didn't buy it. They felt there was a bigger design here. "What are their complaints? They've gotten promotions haven't they?" And so forth. There was a real lack of understanding on their part of what was going on. I was also under instructions not to say anything specific to them about the charges or the corrective action. I wasn't successful in getting the point across. They perceived that there had been equal treatment in the past and couldn't understand what the problem was. There was a lot of tension.

The next day Lake had a second meeting with the white employees at lunch time. This time the dialogue was subdued. Lake, however, felt that he had been mildly successful in establishing an atmosphere more conducive to open discussion. He was particularly encouraged to find white and black employees talking about problems at the Distribution Center during their afternoon break. As the week drew to a close, Lake felt better about the way events were progressing. With the employees talking more openly to one another again, perhaps local management could resolve its difficulties with the black women.

Some Public Exposure

On Labor Day afternoon, Monday, September 4, the public relations director of GSD received a call at his home in Indianapolis from a reporter from one of the network television stations in St. Louis, who indicated that some charges had been leveled at BPC in a story to be aired on the 6:00 P.M. news that evening. The GSD official, knowing nothing of the preceding events, refused to comment until he had further information. He immediately telephoned Scott Parsons, the GSD manager of Personnel, who, having just returned from vacation, had heard nothing about the problem since shortly after Johnson's meeting with Hill in August. Parsons then called Cox and warned him of what was coming, receiving in exchange a briefing on the intervening events in St. Louis. After trying without success to reach John Marlin, General Manager of GSD, Parsons next talked with Philip Adler, Corporate Vice President of Personnel. He indicated the reason for the call in these terms: "The corporate office has been involved in important minority issues in the past. They have not always faced this sort of thing in the decentralized mode. I considered what was happening to be important." Adler had been in Europe, and his only previous contact with the situation was a brief telephone conversation with Wesley in which the latter mentioned the Johnson meeting with Hill and indicated that the region appeared to be on top of the matter. Parsons' call now took the form of a briefing. Adler, in turn, reached Wesley, and they agreed to keep in touch as necessary with Brian Macauley, the Group Vice President and Howard Morgan, the President of BPC, both located in New York.

Meanwhile, Marlin had returned Parsons' call. Marlin's previous exposure to the problem had been a brief discussion with Parsons on a plane trip in mid-August, in which he was told of a "situation" involving some black employees in the Elmsford Distribution Center. He had not pursued it, simply telling Parsons to keep him informed. Now he became aware of an eight-year supervisor with a spotty employment record named Schocken, who, from what Parsons knew at the time, seemed to be at the heart of the difficulty. Marlin recalled getting the impression in either this conversation or a subsequent one with Roman that Schocken was poorly thought of by *all* employees, not just the blacks. In any event, he told Parsons that, should it appear appropriate to transfer Schocken to Indianapolis, he (Marlin) would "make it happen" and gave Parsons permission to arrange it.

Concurrently, Cox was also on the telephone to spread the news to Roman and Evans. Roman had Cox get back to the GSD public relations director to confer on an appropriate response to the press. He called Marlin himself to indicate that the region was prepared to deal with the problem. Meanwhile, Evans talked with Lake, who in turn called Schocken and Holden. The three managers in St. Louis each agreed to monitor one of the network television stations and record the story with dictaphones quickly procured from the office.

The story, in somewhat different versions, ran on both the 6:00 and 11:00 P.M. news programs. A transcript of the earlier broadcast follows:

Announcer: Four black BPC employees held a news conference today at the Westview Plaza Mall. They were accompanied by Nathan Hill, a local resident who has been quite active on a number of racial fronts. A spokeswoman for the group today explained what action they'll be taking if BPC does not respond to the charges by this coming Thursday.

S. Gaynor: #1 Obtain letter of suit from EEOC to take Federal Action against BPC in forms of an individual and class action suits for punitive and civil damages.

                #2 Request Congressman Carmichael's office to investigate the gross violation adhering to Federal Compliance as it relates to advertising.

                Due to improper management an otherwise affable relationship of white co-workers was jeopardized and caused a near racial clash.

                We have a series of nine local and six national demands which we will make public if BPC refuses to meet with and discuss the existing problems.

Announcer: A company spokesman who was reached in his home in Indianapolis today said that BPC could not possibly have a comment until the group's charges had been investigated.

The upshot of the news conference was that BPC faced a series of unspecified local and national demands and an ultimatum to respond by Thursday.

Tuesday, September 5

At the Distribution Center Tuesday morning the atmosphere was described by Lake:

I don't think any of the white girls had seen the TV news program but they had heard about it from friends and relatives. One of the lead girls came in with a real disgusted manner. She couldn't believe it. They thought they had a great situation here, and I had them believing we were #1. They couldn't see how things could be interpreted this way. Black and white employees weren't speaking. The atmosphere was "rock bottom."

In midmorning, Cox, Evans, and Johnson arrived unannounced at the Distribution Center and immediately held a meeting with the black employees. In particular, the regional managers wanted to learn the nature of the demands referred to in the broadcast and whatever further evidence there might be for accusing Schocken of racism. The employees again refused to talk unless Nathan Hill were allowed to represent them. The meeting was perfunctory. Cox reported to both Parsons and Roman that their latest efforts had been unsuccessful. Evans remained in St. Louis, and Cox and Johnson then flew back to Chicago.

As the wording of the broadcast became available in Indianapolis, tension mounted. At Marlin's request, Parsons began to arrange interviews for Schocken at GSD headquarters for the following Monday. Parsons also summarized the situation, as he understood it after receiving word from Cox about the meeting in St. Louis, in a memorandum to Macauley, the group vice president.

Meanwhile in New York, Smith telephoned Hill at Johnson's request, ostensibly to discuss minority training. Excerpts from his report of that conversation sent to Johnson (with copies to Wesley, Cox and Phillips) follow:

> . . . Mr. Hill did not discuss training programs, but expressed his concerns for the employees of our Distribution Center who had requested he act as their negotiator. . . He took a strong stand that without his involvement we would have incomplete information as to our employees' grievances. I advised that we would have to handle our employees' problems internally, and, hopefully, they would share with us, their concerns. . .
>
> Two observations, not previously perceived by this office, resulted from Mr. Hill's input. First: the grieved employees feel they are being put in the middle and forced to confront management when they are the victims of unacceptable practices. . . Such discussions might adversely affect their subsequent employment relationships when current corporate attention no longer exists. Second: it was pointed out that one of the most serious issues, beyond the specific individual performance, attendance and benefits aspects, was an attitudinal problem. The black female employees expressed considerable concern for being approached, communicated with and managed in a very disrespectful and demeaning manner. Subsequently, this attitude is transmitted to their peers and they are held in very low regard by all about them. . .

As indicated by you, the management meeting with them on 8/25/72 tended to confirm the employees' concern for their visibility. Our successful involvement of EEOC, who have agreed to expedite their investigation, should resolve this issue. *We should assure that all actions taken to resolve inequities be incorporated into a conciliation agreement with EEOC!*

Mr. Hill agreed that the commitment of Corporate Headquarters contacting him was fulfilled with my telephone call. He further accepted the requirement that his organization establish some reasonable time frame for evaluation of the steps taken by this facility. . . Mr. Hill would not agree on any time frame for evaluation or discussion on this point. He simply stated that he would establish a time frame and allow consideration for actions to be taken and evaluated. He cautioned on his impatience! He ceased demanding representation, *though remaining adamant that we could not secure all the facts without his involvement.*

Wednesday, September 6

At the regional office on Wednesday morning, Cox received word from St. Louis that the story had been given prominent space in both morning newspapers. After receiving copies of the articles, Cox wrote a four-page report that he teletyped to Parsons, noting three specific allegations (involving segregated facilities, the provocation of a "near racial clash," and the release of Susan Wilson) and the region's explanation for each.

At corporate headquarters Adler had become increasingly concerned about the apparent scope of Hill's charges and the implied threat to other BPC locations. The newspaper coverage devoted to the incident did not serve to allay his concern. Adler and Wesley met for lunch with Macauley. The group vice president took the position that the problem was GSD's and that Marlin and his regional organization were responsible for resolving it. The corporate staff was to provide counsel as needed. He also wanted the facts on Schocken before countenancing his transfer; he did not want GSD simply to put Schocken somewhere else rather than face up to the charges against him. "If Schocken is guilty, he should be fired or at least suspended, because if powerful steps aren't taken, why will operating management take the minority relations policy seriously?" It was further agreed that Wesley, William Roberts from public relations, and someone from the legal staff would go to St. Louis that evening.

Following the luncheon, Wesley met with Adler and wrote down the following specific instructions for his visit to St. Louis.

1. If any wrongs to girls—right them.
2. If no wrongs—don't right them.
3. Open question to be reexamined, whether Schocken to be fired. Should put facts down and carefully and objectively examine whether he should be fired, and Brian Macauley wants to see facts and recommendations before decision.
4. Roman will go to St. Louis.
5. Wesley and Roberts also go. Also lawyer.
6. Wesley, a non-ops guy, contact Hill (alone) to tell him unequivocally that we cannot and will not accept him as a third party negotiator—we'll talk to him in general terms if he's got minority relations matters to discuss.
7. Examine question of whether we'd fire any employees who picket.
8. Examine legal position re picketing—can we get injunction and tactically should we?
9. We've got uncooperative employees—examine, can we fire or discipline them?
10. Any other BPC offices in St. Louis.
11. Any press release should be reviewed by lawyers and not refer to any "third party intermediary."

Wesley, Roberts, and Clark Hanson, the lawyer nominated to go, put their affairs in order and went to the airport to catch the corporate jet for St. Louis.

While Adler talked with Wesley, Macauley telephoned Marlin and, after affirming GSD's responsibilities, argued that if Schocken were guilty of the charges leveled against him, he should be fired and not transferred. Marlin retorted that given what he knew then, a transfer was all he could justify. The sense of the conversation, as Marlin perceived it, was that cause had to be shown to Macauley for *not* terminating Schocken.

In a subsequent call to Roman, Marlin indicated that the investigation as it related to Schocken was to document why he should or should not be terminated. Plans to pull Schocken off the job were also discussed, and it was agreed that interviews could be arranged for him in Indianapolis the next day (rather than the following Monday). It was also agreed that the employees would now be met at a higher level; Roman himself would take charge, supported by staff from division and corporate offices as well as the region.

Meanwhile, Parsons sought to advance the interview date for Schocken. In doing so, he informed the managers he contacted in general terms about Schocken's record (and Marlin's interest in the transfer) but not specifically about the current Elmsford episode. Soon he was able to report to Cox that there was definite interest in both division and national distribution functions in interviewing Schocken the following day. By midafternoon, this information had been relayed to Evans in Elmsford.

In midafternoon Evans received word from Cox that on instructions from Roman, Schocken was to be pulled out and sent to Indianapolis the following day for interviews. After clearing it with Cox, Evans communicated with Atkins and offered him the Elmsford customer service manager job, which he accepted.

Late that afternoon in New York, Macauley and Adler briefed Morgan on the situation in St. Louis and presented him with a suggested press release drafted by the Public Relations Department. Morgan recalled his reaction to the proposed course of action.

> I objected to the press announcement—if you can believe it—that they were going to issue in answer to Hill and put a stop to it. It was bad public relations but beyond that it was just bad business judgment. They also said that it was to be announced to everybody that Schocken was being removed. While this was being said, I began to have some doubts about the information we were basing our decision on. I also objected to the timing of Schocken's removal; it shouldn't be on the deadline set by Hill. I don't think we were necessarily in full agreement, but we finally did agree that Schocken should not be pulled out until we had more information.

As events unfolded, Morgan's directive on Schocken was not implemented.

At the Distribution Center, Evans proceeded with plans to remove Schocken. He had Lake hold Schocken until about 7:00 P.M. to work on assembling records pertinent to the Susan Wilson case soon to be investigated by EEOC. Evans recalled his impressions of the ensuing meeting:

> Earlier I had been for removing Schocken, but now I felt all we

were doing was reacting to the press—it was going to blow the lid off. But the decision on the timing of his removal had been taken out of my hands.

I told Schocken that "for operational reasons" we were pulling him off the job. A lot of evidence pointed to his area, and in our judgment, I said, all we could do was make a change in management. Schocken objected to being pulled out but said, "I've been expecting it." He was very concerned about going to Indianapolis for the interviews—said he didn't want to go, couldn't arrange a babysitter in time, and so forth. We spent an hour discussing it. He said, "Maybe I'll resign but how will that make the company look?" I told him, "That doesn't matter." He kept on, however: "I've got to make a stand, to clear my name. Maybe I should sue the blacks." I argued that the best thing for him to do was to go to Indianapolis the next day and try like hell to sell himself. Finally, he agreed to go.

After the meeting Evans went to a nearby motel where a crowd of BPC managers had assembled. The corporate jet had arrived with Wesley, Roberts, and Hanson from New York and Roman and Johnson from Chicago. Cox and Gregory Butler, the Regional Manager of Branch Operations, had also come from Chicago. There, too, was Brad Williams, the St. Louis branch manager who reported to Butler. Parsons appeared from Indianapolis.

Roman was recognized in the ensuing meeting as the manager in charge. He summarized the discussion:

We started mapping out a strategy for the Distribution Center for the next day. We asked a lot of "what if . . ." questions. What do we do if there is a strike? If no one shows up? If there is another press conference? If the sales branch is picketed? And so forth. The multifunction group was a good idea—we were ready for just about any contingency.

I had instructions from Marlin that I should meet with the black employees. We decided that night to do it unannounced the next day so as not to alert Nathen Hill and increase the possibility of a demonstration. As far as Schocken was concerned, I was told to prepare a case if he was not to be dismissed by the end of the week. So in the worst case fire him; in the best case, transfer him. Parsons had talked with Marlin before he left and said he was being pulled out. Everyone was 100% sure that he was coming out of Elmsford; the only question was sooner or later.

We were then in a position that no matter what we did, we lost. If Schocken is removed, we have caved in; if he is not, Nathan Hill may make it worse. I felt that the sooner he was pulled out the better. Who knows what the situation might be like in the event he remained until the following week?

The decision was made during the meeting that Schocken, who had expected to return to the Distribution Center on Friday, was to remain at home until he got further instructions.

Also discussed that evening was Wesley's proposed visit with Hill. It was affirmed that Wesley should talk with him about "national issues" and whatever ideas for training programs might be forthcoming, but that he should also reiterate BPC's position on third party negotiations.

Thursday, September 7

The BPC team split up on Thursday morning. Roman, Parsons, Cox, Johnson, and Evans were joined by Lake at the Distribution Center; Roberts, Hanson, and Butler remained at the motel to be available for whatever crisis might develop at the Distribution Center or the sales branch; Wesley arranged for a meeting with Nathan Hill at lunch time, staying with the second group until that time.

At the Distribution Center, Roman, Parsons, Cox, and Johnson called the black women into the conference room. The initial response from the employees was the same as it had been in the past; they would not talk with management unless Hill were present to represent them. Gradually, however, a rapport was established, helped along by Roman's announcement that Schocken had been removed to be replaced by Atkins. Johnson recalled acting as a mediator at one point:

> I finally said, almost in an aside to the girls, "You're afraid of losing your jobs and scared of being misrepresented if Nathan isn't here, right?" They said, "Right." Then I told them some of management's fears about having an outsider represent a group of employees; it would be a precedent which could be picked up by other special interest groups, it could be used to hold the company up to public criticism, and so forth. They said, "Oh, why didn't you say so before . . ." and to Roman, "Is that right?" He said, "Yes." The girls said that wasn't Nathan's intention. Roman said, "We believe you . . . but it's still a precedent." Then we

started to talk about how we could communicate. This was the first productive meeting because they felt that now they were talking with someone who could make some decisions.

At about noon, after what seemed to the managers to be an increasingly positive discussion, the women agreed to reconsider. They left the room and tried to call Nathan Hill, but he had already left for his meeting with Wesley. The session then adjourned for lunch, Johnson leaving with the black employees and Roman, Parsons, and Cox, in a hopeful mood, joining up with Evans and Lake.

The morning had been considerably less pleasant for their associates. Evans and Lake called the white employees together for a brief "stand-up" meeting to bring them up to date on what was taking place. Aside from Lake's earlier attempts in August, this was the first occasion anyone had talked with them about it. Evans described the event.

> I announced that Joe Schocken was in Indianapolis and was to be transferred and that Jim Atkins was taking his place. There were murmurs, "Those four blacks did that . . . ." and one girl whispered loudly, "Jim Atkins is a black," which was followed by a number of gasps. Someone asked me, "Is this related to the newspaper article?" I said, "No, for operational reasons only." Another asked, "Is Atkins being moved here to pacify the blacks?" I said, "No. He's the most qualified for the job." The answers really got them mad.

As the meeting closed, the white employees were told that Roman would have a response for them by the end of the day. Evans called Schocken in Indianapolis and told him that his transfer had been announced at the Distribution Center that day and he was to remain at home until given further instructions.

Downtown, Wesley was lunching with Hill. Wesley recalled that the conversation opened with Hill saying, "I know who you are. I checked you out on the grapevine." After Wesley replied, "And?" Hill continued, "You're O.K. I can talk with you." A three-hour discussion followed, described by Wesley below:

> I started by saying that the meeting was not to discuss local issues, that BPC did not negotiate with third parties, that there was to be no publicity from the luncheon and that if there were

national issues, let's talk about them. He harangued for a time. I got a lesson in black history, how the economic system is exploitive, why blacks can't make it in the U.S. "America, America, you've never been America to me."

He was having a hassle with the city about drug addicts, and we talked about his rehabilitation center. He's a fascinating person; very sincere and committed. He also claimed he had gotten concessions from (a very large company) and had put pressure on a local TV station to broadcast a program devoted to black issues. I tried to learn the tactics he used. One time he took over a government office, another time he put on a demonstration with 20 of his people. This was the kind of action he inferred might be taken with BPC. At one point he said, "We have a list of your customers. Unless you meet with me, we'll go to them and say you discriminate." I suspected he probably did have such a list.

After hearing this, I told him, "It's still my opinion that we won't meet with you." Then he seemed to soften. "You're almost there. I want to put it all in perspective. Just let me come in and make my presentation — that's all."

I began to feel he was looking for a way to save face in view of the representations he had made to the girls. So I said, "Let's assume we could arrange a meeting with top management people in St. Louis without the employees. You don't talk about local issues but present the larger picture." He agreed. I said I'd run it by local management.

During the luncheon, Wesley also learned that the black salesmen in the eastern half of the region were getting together the next day in Detroit to discuss some minority relations grievances. Wesley felt that Hill was implying he had called the meeting.

At about 3:00 P.M. the black employees at the Distribution Center reached Hill. Immediately thereafter, their meeting with Roman Parsons, Cox, and Johnson reconvened. The women announced that they had talked with Hill and were again convinced that only through his intervention would the issues be properly identified and resolved. The meeting continued unproductively for another hour and then disbanded.

Roman spent the next few minutes with the other managers composing the remarks he was to make to the employees. When he emerged from the conference room to make the following statement, the temperature was described as "below zero."

Recently there have been articles in the press and items on TV about complaints of four black employees that we discriminate against black employees. This statement is to apprise you of the facts and our position.

You are all aware that we have been working very hard throughout BPC to provide the kind of atmosphere that will continually attract minority employees to our ranks. It is the company's policy that all members of management view minority hiring, development and promotion as vital to BPC objectives and success, as well as exceedingly important to the individual manager's career.

This is simply an extension and amplification of our basic personnel philosophy of treating all employees fairly and with dignity and respect.

Consequently, the allegations made by these four black employees in the Distribution Center three weeks ago are viewed with great concern and are being looked into by a team from Regional, Division and Corporate management.

As a consequence of our investigation, thus far, we reached a decision yesterday to make a change in management at the Distribution Center. This follows a number of other actions recently taken and communicated to the employees involved.

Our investigation and conversation with the people involved will continue. Yesterday we met with these four employees, and we believe we have made some progress toward a further resolution of this problem.

After Roman had finished there were some rumblings, and a number of people posed questions similar to those raised earlier with Evans and Lake. He indicated that he did not want to discuss the problem or answer questions at that time. However, he said an investigation was under way and he would be back to review it with them no later than the following Friday. The reaction to this comment was negative. One manager commented, "I'll bet this was the most hostile meeting ever conducted by a BPC vice president."

After the meeting, Roman got together briefly with the black women again. They asked him how he felt the session had gone. He said, "Poorly." They agreed.

The BPC managers then met again at the motel. Wesley raised the proposition he had made to Hill related to a presentation to management. The response continued to be "no"; such an interchange would still be interpreted as negotiations with an employee representative. Wesley relayed this message to Hill, receiving the comment, "If that's the decision, we'll see you on the battlefield."

Calls to Marlin and Adler brought Division and Corporate management up to date on the day's events. Marlin asked Parsons and Butler to stay in St. Louis for another day. He agreed, however, that Roman should return to Chicago for an important conference the next morning with an unhappy customer. Johnson, who by this time had received an invitation to the black salesmen's meeting in Detroit, also prepared to leave, catching a ride as far as Chicago with Roman on a corporate jet. Johnson learned in passing that Hill had not set the meeting and in fact had been denied an invitation by the salesmen, who felt they could resolve their problems more effectively themselves.

On the plane, Roman asked Johnson what he thought of the situation. Johnson proceeded to lay his frustrations on the line. He indicated that there was no operating machinery to back up minority affairs; he was out in the field with no authority to get policy implemented. Moreover, his function was buried in the personnel department and had little visibility. There was really nothing different about the Elmsford Distribution Center except that Nathan and Hannah Hill were involved. Johnson said that he and Cox had been trying to get the minority relations job done but the priorities given to it in relation to salesman's quotas, for instance, reduced their efforts mostly to talk.

Friday, September 8

Evans and Lake arrived at the Distribution Center before starting time on Friday. Soon the white employees, one after another, began to call in sick, and within a few minutes it was clear that BPC now had a boycott on its hands. The black employees were shaken and asked for a meeting with Lake in which they indicated that they had not intended such a thing to happen, that they had no quarrel with the other employees.

Hannah Hill also exhibited a piece of "hate" mail that her husband had received which included a threat to his life. She was understandably upset. Later in the morning, Parsons, Evans, Hanson, and Hannah Hill took the letter to the police, requesting at the same time increased surveillance for the Distribution Center. The remainder of the day in Elmsford was spent scrambling around answering telephones and trying to keep customers happy (the backlog had been accumulating all week).

In Chicago, Roman spent most of the day at a large customer's office, trying, without success as it turned out, to resolve some major difficulties; the account was lost. Roman also received word from Johnson on the salesmen's meeting in Detroit (attended by 17), followed the next day by a letter from them outlining problems and requests (Exhibit IX-5). Johnson felt their approach was businesslike and their complaints similar to the ones he had picked up earlier in St. Louis.

Elsewhere the day was devoted, in part at least, to report writing. At the motel in Elmsford the previous evening and most of Friday, Parsons and Cox assembled the study requested earlier in the week by Macauley, Marlin, and Roman, summarizing the problem and justifying, if possible, Schocken's transfer. Johnson's initial description of his August 11 meeting continued to be the primary source of problem identification. The tentative conclusion from their work was that some of the allegations could not be attributed directly to Schocken, others were unfounded, and still others he denied. On this basis, they faulted him for poor management but could not, with confidence, accuse him of discrimination.

Contingency plans were also made for Monday. Parsons, Cox, and Wesley decided that Friday's absences should be laid to emotion, and no disciplinary action taken, even though it was clearly a concerted and deliberate violation of company procedures. However, if they called in sick on Monday, they would be told to bring in a doctor's slip if pay was expected and, if they were absent without one for four days, they would be dismissed in accordance with established policy. If the black employees picketed, they would be asked to return to work or face disciplinary action also.

Meanwhile, in New York Adler wrote a memorandum to Graham Moore, Chairman of BPC, bringing him up to date with the events at Elmsford and the corporation's response to them and including the blacks' original press release. "As of now (Friday noon), there have been no demonstrations or any other public disturbances in St. Louis. Something may yet happen today or next week. If anything happens over the weekend, it will likely be a press story, as there'd be no point in demonstrating before an empty building."

EXHIBIT IX-5

BUSINESS PRODUCTS CORPORATION

September 9, 1972

Mr. Daryl Roman
Vice President and Regional General Manager
Mid-Western Region
Chicago, Illinois

Dear Mr. Roman:

After several weeks of preparation, the Black Sales Force of the Eastern* Operations Group met to discuss problems that are of Regional significance. After many uninterrupted hours of discussion, it became apparent that many of the problems have "solutions" written into "BPC law." We believe that implementation of these written solutions is not adequately fulfilling the corporate desires as it relates to Blacks.

Accordingly, the problems and recommendations for suggested *realistic* solutions are as follows:

The Minority Relations Program is suffering because it does not enjoy the priority that Corporate obviously intended.

Recommended Solution: The importance of this area must be emphasized to first-line management in terms of career evaluation and progression.

There is a lack of viable and relevant resources with internal problems.

Recommended Solution: A Regional level Advisory Board, reflective of the Black population within the Region.

Job opportunity information is not properly disseminated.

Recommended Solution: Timely public listings of all open positions pending or available.

There are vague and ambiguous performance evaluations.

Recommended Solution: This problem is so complex that further study in this area must be expedited.

There is a distinct absence of Black representation in policy-making management and supervisory levels. Further, there is an absence of programs directed at developing Blacks for promotion.

Recommended Solution: Immediate review of existing Black personnel for immediate promotion, and the establishment of accelerated programs for the preparation of Blacks for upward mobility.

*The Midwestern Region was divided into Eastern and Western Operations Groups.

The employment process, as it relates to Blacks, is irrelevant, totally inadequate, and fails to meet Corporate direction.

Recommended Solution: The institution of a "White Awareness Course."

The absence of aggressive programming and sufficient resources for productive community involvement at the local level.

Recommended Solution: Sizable increases in financial and manpower resources made available at Region and Branch levels.

The orientation program for new employees, as it currently exists, is totally inadequate.

Recommended Solution: Reevaluate and establish specific guidelines.

We perceive degrees of inequitable and racist patterns in job assignments.

Saturday, September 9

A number of the white employees met on Friday and prepared a press release. They approached the same newspaper reporter who had covered the story earlier in the week and held an interview with him. The next morning the following article was carried in the paper:

10 BPC AIDES DENY BIAS BY BOSS

Ten white office workers at BPC's regional Distribution Center in Elmsford, rose to the defense yesterday of their customer service manager who has been accused by four blacks of racial discrimination.

The ten white women denied that discrimination had existed in the office and said the black workers, rather than the manager, had created tension by taking grievances to management without discussing them with white workers.

High-level BPC executives from New York, Indianapolis, and Chicago were in St. Louis yesterday and Thursday to work out the problems and to meet with Nathan Hill, spokesman for disgruntled black BPC employees in St. Louis and other states. It was learned that the customer service manager, Joseph Schocken, was abruptly transferred out of town during the talks. Both white and black employees described Schocken's removal as an attempt to placate the black workers.

Hill said the removal of Schocken, whom the blacks had described as a "racist" during a Labor Day news conference, would not satisfy the black workers' demands for changes in working conditions, employment, and promotion policies.

The white workers noted in a prepared statement that Schocken's removal was announced Thursday, the deadline Hill had set for settlement of the black grievances before starting legal action. "The white customer service manager is being replaced by a black BPC employee without prior notice to any of the white customer service managers or white fellow workers," the statement read.

The white women said that when they asked the reason for Schocken's removal, "A BPC spokesman replied that it was not due to the black situation," but that "several other BPC spokesmen would give no justifiable comment to the relocation of the white customer service manager."

The white women contended that whites and blacks worked under the same conditions in the BPC office. They said Schocken's departure was so abrupt that his replacement is not expected to arrive here for two or three weeks.

Willard Roberts of New York, head of public relations for BPC, confirmed that Schocken had been reassigned during investigations into racial problems at the Distribution Center. Roberts said a number of other actions were also taken besides the transfer of Schocken. He declined to discuss them. Roberts reiterated that the service manager was not transferred because of the racial situation. He added that it was a coincidence that the transfer was made on the day the deadline had been set by Hill. Roberts did, however, say that Schocken had not asked for his transfer.

The 10 white employees who declined to name a spokesman and issued their statement jointly . . . all work for the customer service manager. They denied any racial motive and insisted they would not have issued their statement if they had any suspicion of racial discrimination in their office.

On Saturday, information was shared by managers in New York, Indianapolis, and Chicago. A further complication was unearthed. The white employees had approached the union which represented most of the BPC factory workers in Indianapolis and elsewhere. They reasoned that, with their greater numbers, they would be able to outvote their black co-workers on matters affecting employment through the democratic process of the union. In view of its good record in minority relations in Indianapolis, Parsons doubted if the International would permit an organization attempt under these circumstances, but he could not be sure. It was generally agreed, however, that the white employees had gone further than anyone had anticipated.

Sunday, September 10

Wesley was aware, after a long discussion with Adler on Sunday, that top management was becoming increasingly concerned about the St. Louis situation. Although he had been involved in some of the events of the previous week, Wesley did not feel that he had a particularly good handle on the facts. He reviewed with Adler the possibility of conducting an "impartial" investigation, and Adler said he would raise the issue with Morgan on Monday.

In Chicago, Roman, Butler, Cox, Evans, and Johnson met in a motel room to determine a strategy for Monday. Roman put Butler in charge of the region's forces. Evans was to go to the Distribution Center by himself, while Butler waited at the motel. Roman, Cox, and Johnson would remain in Chicago to deal with the minority relations issues that had cropped up toward the end of the previous week among the salesmen.

Monday, September 11

Lake was sitting in his office early Monday morning watching the entrance to the parking lot. At 7:50 the white employees arrived en masse. As he watched them walk toward the building, Lake called Evans at the motel and the latter said, "Get it straightened out." Later in the day Lake described to Wesley the comments made by the white women at the ensuing meeting. Wesley wrote them down in the following terms:

> Girls up tight — "Roman blew it." He did not answer questions truthfully. "We found out more from the newspaper reporter than we did from our own management." Newspaper man "knew" that Joe was going to be fired. The handling of Joe was poorly done. He didn't even have a chance to say goodbye. Evans lied to us by telling us it was not related to the racial thing. They mentioned going to a union for representation because "no one is

representing us and with Joe gone, no one will protect us. If it could happen to Joe, it could happen to us." The black girls never tried to talk to Joe—he would have listened to them just as he listens to us. The removal of Joe won't satisfy Nathan Hill and where does it stop? If 4 black girls can get Joe, then they could get us. Do we (BPC) have to hire a black manager? BPC will suffer a great loss with Joe gone—knowledge etc. Knows his job, tells us when we're wrong and why we're wrong. Tough, but doing the job for BPC. Blacks have banded together and with a black supervisor coming in, what chance do we have. *Bringing in a black will make the situation worse.* Even the blacks agree to this. How could 4 black girls do this to the Distribution Center? Black girls did not go to Joe first. Jim is black and is one of them. Therefore, a union is needed to protect the rights and jobs of white workers. After this trouble, will whites ever be able to go in to their black supervisor to discuss their problems? Why was Joe pulled out so abruptly? You're moving people based on allegations. How can you do that? Everything was equal, but not any more. Joe was not racist; "he overlooked a lot of things the black girls did that we would have been reprimanded for." Shirley Gaynor threatened "not to take this lying down" after she wasn't promoted. Also, she has no respect for the American flag—"does not represent equality." Hannah Hill was "planted" by her husband two years ago to further his cause. How could the press get all this information if our personnel clerk wasn't passing it out? We're tired of being puppets and lied to. Management doesn't care since they refuse to answer our questions—we find out more through newspapers. What do you expect us to do with treatment like that? Black girls got Schocken out of here, white girls will get him back in. We are not convinced that *our* jobs aren't on the line, therefore, we need union protection. Management acts abruptly to react. Photo commissions with Wilma—Joe was nice to her—how could he be a racist. All the blacks are laughing at BPC, why doesn't BPC stand up to them? Whites will have to "keep on giving" to blacks after this "victory." Where does it stop? Could legal action be taken against Hannah based on information on the white girls getting out. Newspaper told gals that white girls do not mark their time cards properly. Shirley complained she wasn't trained properly—if she stayed at her desk long enough, she might learn her job. Blacks made the comment, "You'll never get rid of us now that we're here." *"Anyone can be removed based on allegations."*

At 10:00 Evans arrived, and the meeting was moved to the conference room. The white employees then delivered an ultimatum: either Schocken is reinstated in his old job at the Distribution Center by Thursday or they would (a) join a union, (b) retain a lawyer, or (c) quit.

As if to emphasize their point, the union representatives arrived. Evans "hid," telling Lake to be cordial but to say that he would have to contact Indianapolis before doing anything further. The union people talked briefly with the shop steward in the warehouse, which was already organized, brought up one minor grievance and told Lake that they would probably make an organizing attempt later. The discussion was amicable and, after a brief meeting with the white employees, they left.

At noon Evans and Lake concluded their session with the white employees and went to the motel to join Wesley and Butler. After they had heard the news, Wesley and Butler retired to another room, caucused and concluded that any further action at this point would only be the subject of increased criticism. However, after a further investigation by people not already involved (neither Wesley nor Butler had been to the Distribution Center at the time), the employees might calm down and subsequent decisions could be related to this new study. They called New York, Indianapolis, and Chicago to find that others were also reaching similar conclusions. It was quickly cleared with Adler, Roman, and Marlin that Wesley would represent corporate and Butler the region.

That afternoon Evans and Lake returned to the Distribution Center, called the employees together, and Evans read the following statement:

> All of us are concerned about the events of the past few days, and we want to resolve any differences which exist here. Senior management has asked two people who are not connected with the Center to examine all of the questions that have been raised.
>
> Frank Wesley from the Corporate Staff and Greg Butler representing GSD management will be here tomorrow to talk with many of us. Their conversations will be private and impartial. Their purpose will be to arrive at a full report and recommendations to management. Let's all cooperate with them fully.

The atmosphere continued to be very tense. The husband of one of the white employees called and said he felt it was too dangerous for his wife to work there. Evans managed to convince him otherwise.

During these hours, Wesley and Butler developed the procedure to be followed in their forthcoming investigation. The study was to include a thorough review of all documentation and interviews with all management and clerical personnel in the Distribution Center.

While these events were occurring, the Parsons-Cox report, which had been completed the previous Friday, was working its way up the line. In his covering memorandum to Marlin, Roman summarized his position as follows:

> I believe for an eight-year employee, as in our judicial system, I must only be able to make a decision on intentional racial discrimination when I have little or no doubt in my mind that that is what has taken place. In this case, I do have some doubt and therefore feel I cannot take that position, at this time. As more complete information develops over the next few months, I may change my present recommendation. However, to keep this case open for a prolonged period of time will prevent the establishment of required trust with white employees, and necessary harmony in employee working relationships. By the same token, it is equally clear that Mr. Schocken cannot continue in his former assignment, as demanded by the white employees. For both of these reasons, an immediate decision is required on his transfer.

The covering memorandum from Marlin to Macauley (Exhibit IX-6) recommended — based on a similar reading of the evidence — that "Schocken be offered a position in Indianapolis with the understanding that if the current or any subsequent investigations demonstrate that he, in fact, is a racist, he will be immediately terminated." The memoranda were written more or less concurrently after the two managers had conversed by telephone. Both stated that the future organizational health of the Distribution Center would depend on a "timely resolution of the Schocken issue."

That evening, Atkins arrived in St. Louis and had dinner with Wesley, Cox, and Butler at the motel. They apprised Atkins of the dimensions of the backlash. Roman, Cox, and Evans were convinced that the transfer under the circumstances was not in his or anyone's best interests. Atkins now began to come to the same conclusion, and the next day told Roman that he had reconsidered and did not want to accept the Elmsford position.

EXHIBIT IX-6

M E M O R A N D U M

DATE: September 11, 1972

TO: Brian Macauley
FROM: John Marlin
SUBJECT: Joseph Schocken
           — St. Louis Distribution Center

Joseph Schocken has been employed by BPC since June 23, 1964. Schocken's last two performance appraisals have been standards frequently exceeded (4 on a scale of 5). From the third quarter of 1970 until September 6, 1972, he was the Customer Service Manager in the St. Louis Distribution Center. On September 6, 1972, Joe Schocken was advised that

> In view of the seriousness of the discrimination allegations made against him by four Black employees in a press conference on September 4, which were subsequently reported on two local TV stations and in the two major St. Louis newspapers,

his credibility as a manager in that location was seriously jeopardized, and that he would have to be reassigned to Indianapolis. If this option was not acceptable, Schocken was advised that he would have to resign because there were no alternative job opportunities for him in St. Louis. Joseph Schocken was interviewed in Indianapolis on September 7th. No job offer has been made to Schocken pending Corporate's review of the circumstances resulting in the allegations of discrimination made against him by four black employees in the Distribution Center.

The attachment* lists the allegations directed against Schocken and the Mid-western Region's response to those allegations. It must be noted that these allegations are based on comments from the black employees during the first two of four recent meetings (one of these meetings was held at night in a downtown nightclub) with them. During the last two meetings, the blacks have refused to comment further on their allegations indicating that they want a non-BPC employee, Nathan Hill, to speak for them.

Of the fourteen identified allegations, only five can be directly attributable to Schocken. The other allegations must include the Region Distribution Manager because he either participated in the decision or approved the action taken by Schocken. Of the five allegations that are directly attributable to Schocken, three appear to be without foundation, based on the explanation offered. The remaining two allegations are a matter of credibility. In these two cases, Schocken claims he cannot

*Not included.

EXHIBIT IX-6 Cont.

September 11, 1972

recall meeting with the employment representative (we have not hired anyone from that agency since 1970), and he cannot recall not advising Jennie Williams of the proper starting time.

Therefore, in view of these circumstances, coupled with the intense and public denial of discrimination allegations against Schocken by all ten of Schocken's white employees, we recommend that

SCHOCKEN BE OFFERED A POSITION IN INDIANAPOLIS WITH THE UNDER-STANDING THAT IF THE CURRENT AND ANY SUBSEQUENT INVESTIGATIONS DEMONSTRATE THAT HE, IN FACT, IS A RACIST, HE WILL BE IMMEDI-ATELY TERMINATED.

Timely resolvement of the Schocken issue is key to restoring order to the Customer Service section in that the ten white employees in this area failed to report for work Friday, September 8, and on Monday, September 11, demanded that Schocken be reinstated or they would exercise one of the following options:

(1) JOIN A UNION (they have already contacted the International)
(2) RETAIN A LAWYER
(3) QUIT

We recommended that you approve our recommendation if the Wesley/Butler individual interviews of employees, black and white, today fail to establish any new evidence that bears on this issue.

If you approve our recommendation, Schocken will be assigned a non-supervisory job. Schocken was on probation in late 1968 and early 1969 for marginal supervisory practices. The job offered would be a lateral move with a 7% relocation adjustment. This is standard practice for all employees who are transferred into Indianapolis on a lateral basis.

Finally, an examination of the management practices clearly suggests that we must question the management ability of the St. Louis Distribution Manager, Pete Lake. Upon completion of the current investigation, we will have to decide whether or not to remove Pete Lake from his assignment.

Attachment

c: S. Parsons
      P. Adler

Tuesday, September 12

On Tuesday morning Wesley and Butler began their investigation. They divided the work force and interviewed each employee individually, including the warehousemen who had not previously been involved (and had little to say about the matter now). Butler reflected on his experience:

> The white girls were generally clear and consistent in what they said. They were concerned about job security and unaware of the blacks' complaints or the specific instances they brought up. All they had seen was what was in the paper, they said. They felt Schocken as a manager was rigid and inflexible but totally fair — *everyone* had to be there on time and so forth. A large percentage said they didn't particularly like him but respected his dedication to the company. One or two said they liked him. They were deathly afraid of having a black manager and were concerned that the black girls had involved them personally. And they were concerned that the company would take this quick, cruel action in response to an ultimatum. For Schocken, they said, BPC came before his family.
>
> I was fortunate among the blacks to talk early that morning with Wilma Green. She had been away for a few days — a death in the family, I think — and had not been around for a lot of the tense times. She's quiet and sincere. I caught her without warning or instructions and she opened up with me. Most of her thoughts on discrimination, she said, were Shirley Gaynor's. She had been involved in only two incidents. The one that was key in her thinking was an occasion in which Schocken failed to interview her when he was soliciting employee reactions to a morale problem.

Wesley conducted the interview with Rosyln O'Neil, the lead operator, and also among the prominent Schocken supporters. His notes on her comments follow:

> Joe is a neat supervisor — feelings for people — treated all equally — listened — tried to help blacks as well as whites; all included in meetings and consultations.
>
> Girls can't understand why blacks chose the route they did. Local management would have listened and investigated.
>
> Management lied to us. Pete Lake, after a 6-hour meeting with blacks, talked to whites to "reassure us" between 5-7 P.M. (one week before black press conference). He said, "No one has to be afraid of losing their jobs" — one week later Schocken is gone.
>
> Regardless of who comes in here as Joe's replacement, whites

will be unhappy. Joe was mother and father to *us*. We built the Distribution Center together and had no problems until blacks came in with their attitudes. Where will it end? Is Pete Lake next?

During the previous week, unfinished work had accumulated in the Distribution Center. In an effort to get the backlog under control, two women were flown in from Chicago Tuesday morning. Their appearance apparently pricked the unit's pride because Lake felt the work pace picked up somewhat. However, at noon, Nathan Hill appeared with a friend to have lunch with the black women and for a time the place was in an uproar. Some further allegations were made against Schocken in the midst of some obscene language. One young white employee began to cry. Evans, who was observing the scene, felt Hannah Hill was embarrassed.

While Nathan Hill was there, Wesley and Butler were interviewing Lake. He again acknowledged numerous inconsistencies in the treatment of employees, but indicated that they were both unintentional and often more general than simply black-white.

That evening at the motel Wesley and Butler spent more than four hours with Schocken, the first time he had been contacted since the previous Thursday. The investigators discussed with him both the allegations first collected by Johnson and a few others that surfaced later. Butler summarized Schocken's reaction:

> As an operating manager he was in concurrence with his initial removal. He was told it was for "operational reasons," and he agreed that if he was a hindrance he had to go. But he had no understanding at all of his lack of sensitivity. He just could not see racial bias in what he had done, and he categorically denied making the statements attributed to him.

On one occasion, Schocken said that a phone call from a customer was taken by Wilma Green. She made an $11,000 sale. Schocken indicated that he had worked very hard to get her a commission on the order, concluding with the comment, "Would I have done that if I were discriminating?"

Elsewhere the organization waited for the results of the investigation.

Wednesday, September 13

On Wednesday, Cox arrived in Elmsford to be with the EEOC investigator who also came that morning to begin his study of the

Susan Wilson case. During the day Wesley and Butler finished their interviews and began to formulate conclusions. Before five o'clock, when Wesley left to catch a plane to New York, they agreed in general terms on the findings, conclusions, and recommendations, and the format for the report. They collaborated in writing up the findings and that portion of the report dealing specifically with Schocken shown below:

Schocken Issue
1. Hardworking, dedicated, bright, but inflexible manager who lacked awareness of and sensitivity to minority issues, as well as the degree of BPC commitment in this area.
2. The action removing Joe Schocken was hastily taken in the heat of defensive emotion, with insufficient investigation and knowledge of the real issues, without hard factual data, and based on an inadequate assessment of the situation.
3. Although the allegations made against Schocken occurred over a one and one-half year period, they were only brought to management's attention, by the employees involved, within the last three months. In fact, many of the specific incidents were communicated only within the past several weeks.
4. Of the specific allegations made against Schocken:
   A. Some questionable practices were equally applied to blacks and whites.
   B. Some alleged Schocken statements were denied by him and may never be resolved.
   C. Some Schocken admitted to, but claimed his actions were taken without racial motivation.

Conclusions
Schocken was singled out for his ineptness in dealing with minority relations matters. Responsibility for the disparate treatment that did occur to minority employees should be shared by the Distribution Center manager—who, in fact, was the one to whom problems were pointed out. In most cases, he delayed or took inadequate action.

Ample consideration was not given to Joe Schocken as an individual or as an employee in this matter. He was abruptly removed without adequate explanation or investigation (under the demand of management and the pressure group's deadline).

Recommendations
Schocken should be admonished for his people-handling in general and his minority awareness in particular. He should be

transferred, laterally, to a non-line position in Indianapolis, because:
1. He was untrained and poorly counseled to handle the problem.
2. Because of the emotionalism of the minority issue, his continued effectiveness at the Distribution Center is questionable.

Upon completion of this portion of the report, Wesley said goodbye, while Butler was on the telephone to Roman bringing him up to date on the outcome.

After Wesley had gone, Butler dictated the remainder of the report to one of the secretaries from the St. Louis branch. Cox, Evans, and another lawyer from corporate headquarters reviewed the draft and offered a few comments, but they expressed no major "hang-ups." After covering the background, methodology, and findings, Butler wrote the following relative to recommendations for the Distribution Center.

Black:
1. Make payroll and appraisal changes immediately and retroactively.
2. Transfer Schocken.
3. Re-emphasize to all employees (blacks present) our EEO commitment.
4. Promote James Atkins to Distribution Center but into Traffic.
5. Train Distribution Center management and people on white awareness and corporate attitude and actions as they relate to minority relations.

White:
1. Move Fred Holden from Traffic to Customer Service Manager (to offset fear that exists within this group about their jobs and careers).
2. Communicate that Schocken is:
   A. Not hurt—lateral transfer.
   B. Happy with change and accepts it (injustice).
3. Make Joe visible—bring him back to spend two days with Fred Holden.
4. Communication meeting explaining problems and actions, to be conducted by Region General Manager as soon as possible, preferably 9/15 latest.

Management
1. Pete [Lake] admonished and placed on probation (removal at this time would be disastrous).

2. Minority awareness training. Region is preparing decisive action plan to implement promptly.

Clerical:

Internal changes will be necessary soon by Distribution Center management.

Union:

We believe above actions will diminish interest of employees in this as an alternative.

Hill:

Do not engage with him as a representative of our employees, continue to evaluate his sincerity in training of minorities and potential assistance from BPC.

ACTION TIMETABLE

1. Secure management approval of action plan by 9/15 A.M. or 9/18 A.M. at the very latest.
2. Confront Schocken with job offer and summary of the case.
3. Confront Pete Lake with summary.
4. Offer job to Holden and Atkins.
5. Schedule employee meeting, or small group meetings, with clericals.
6. Advise blacks of changes to appraisals and compensation.
7. Conduct communications meetings to announce findings, changes and future plans, as well as answer questions (relative to Point 5 above).

By the time the report was finished, Roman, Parsons, and Marlin had been apprised and were in basic agreement with its contents.

Thursday, September 14

Regional management had two concerns as the week progressed: securing a replacement for Schocken as rapidly as possible, and explaining the results of the investigation to the employees. The Wesley-Butler report was received in Chicago late Thursday morning. Roman made a few minor changes and forwarded them to Indianapolis and New York. There seemed to be general agreement among Marlin, Parsons, and Macauley on the report. Evans and Lake were anxious to get the management question settled and the Distribution Center back in production. Furthermore, Roman had made a personal commitment to the employees to advise them of the outcome by the end of the week and, under the circumstances, felt it particularly important to honor that deadline.

The need felt in Elmsford to proceed expeditiously was reinforced Thursday morning when the white employees approached Lake and requested a meeting. They feared a return of Nathan Hill and again indicated that they would only be satisfied with Schocken's reinstatement. Finally, they apparently sensed that the decision was now out of Roman's hands; Roslyn O'Neil asked, "When is Howie Morgan coming down?"

Evans then called Roman at about noon and asked for permission to approach Atkins under strict secrecy and give him the alternative of the traffic job in Elmsford or a probable promotion where he was in several months' time. Evans also requested authority to approach Holden in confidence about a transfer to the customer service manager position. Roman acceded to both requests.

Early that same morning in New York, Adler advised Wesley that he was attempting to arrange a meeting with Morgan and Macauley to discuss the Elmsford investigation. Wesley sent copies of the findings and the "Schocken issue" portions of the report (he had not at this point received the remainder of the report dictated by Butler the previous evening) to the three managers, indicating that they could provide a basis for discussion.

At noon, Macauley, Adler, and Wesley met for two hours with Morgan. Wesley presented the findings and recommendations, the latter supported by both Macauley and Adler. No decision was reached on Schocken, however, and Morgan indicated that he wanted to discuss the matter with them again the next day before *he* decided what to do. At about 2:00 P.M. Wesley called Roman in Chicago to tell him that Morgan was going to make the decision on Schocken and, in the meantime, the region was not to initiate any moves. He also advised Roman that it was impossible to say whether or not a decision would be available in time for him to hold the meeting with the employees before Friday, as Roman had promised them the previous Wednesday.

Subsequent Events at the Distribution Center

Wesley's call was a couple of minutes late. Evans had already talked with Lake about the Holden transfer, and at 2:00 P.M. Lake began his interview with Holden. At 2:03 P.M., Butler burst into Lake's office, having just received the call from Roman advising him of Morgan's instructions. Butler stopped the meeting and after apologizing to Holden, told him, "All bets are off. No commitments can be made. Turn the clock back five minutes. You are subject to dismissal if one word of this leaks out!"

By this time Roman began to sense that the Friday meeting was in jeopardy. He called Marlin, who was in Miami at a sales convention, and said that, from his point of view, a delay was "unacceptable." Marlin discussed it with Macauley but to no avail. When no further word was received from New York by late afternoon, Butler concluded the meeting was out for the time being and returned to Chicago, leaving Evans and Cox (who was still working on the EEOC investigation) in St. Louis. Word was received during this time from Atkins, who decided that he would rather not accept any opening in Elmsford.

Subsequent Events at Corporate Headquarters

After his meeting with Macauley, Adler, and Wesley, Morgan called Moore and indicated that he was contemplating offering Schocken the alternative of returning to his old job at the Elmsford Distribution Center or of a transfer to Indianapolis. He reasoned as follows:

> I was mad when I found out that Schocken's removal had already been announced the previous week after we had decided here to wait. After the investigation, what bothered me was that there was no way to make the transfer without also making Schocken guilty. I also learned of the white backlash and the fact that we had acted too hastily. Everyone would be mad at us — both blacks and whites — and the factual basis on which Schocken was removed was questionable, if not wrong.
>
> The region's judgment had been to sacrifice the person and not the company. But Elmsford is probably just the first in a long series of problems we'll have like this. So we might as well start by doing what is right. We should not make a bad decision and then try to rationalize it afterwards.

Moore agreed.

Friday, September 15

On Friday morning Macauley, Adler, and Wesley met again with Morgan, this time for four hours. Wesley reported on some of the discussion:

> After a time Howie [Morgan] said, "What if we put him

[Schocken] back in Elmsford?" The others of us said that would be an impossible situation from a management standpoint. Finally, [Morgan] asked me, "We've just had an inquisition and now you're telling me we have no hard facts to justify the result. What is the right thing to do?" I said, "Put him back in Elmsford — but why take that risk when it's not in the best interest of the company?"

Macauley stated his position:

My position was that we haven't proved the blacks wrong either. They would see putting Schocken back as a whitewash. In my judgment, such an action wouldn't be right in the larger sense of over-all black-white relations. Howie felt it was morally wrong to have relieved Schocken. In the long run he argued that doing what was right for Schocken would be in the best interests of the company. I thought in this case that was debatable.

Adler indicated the eventual resolution:

Finally, Howie made the decision on the basis of what was equitable for the employee. It was a moral decision, not a business decision. If it costs the company, that's a cost we have to bear. In addition, he made the decision that the employees should be told about the offer whether it was accepted or not. The white employees had some gripes, and in the interests of full honesty we should tell them we made a mistake. Pragmatically we had the feeling they would probably find out anyway because of the close relationship between Schocken and Holden.

Morgan reflected on the group's reaction to his decision:

Everyone agreed that offering him his job back was the right thing for Schocken. But there was great argument about what was right for the company. I think they finally came to see that these eventually were the same. No one really liked the decision, but I really believe they felt better after it had been made in the way it was.

At about 1:30 Friday afternoon, the second Morgan-Macauley-Adler-Wesley meeting broke up. Wesley called Parsons and Roman to say (a) Schocken is to be offered his old job or an equivalent one in Indianapolis; (b) those alternatives would be announced to the employees; and (c) the meeting would probably be the next week, but Morgan wanted to review an outline of what was to be covered beforehand.

Wesley's first call was to Parsons, whose initial response, as

Wesley recalled it, was "That's the worst business decision I've ever heard." Wesley said he agreed but indicated that it wasn't just a business decision. From Roman, the initial response, again as Wesley remembered it, was "That's insanity — I can't believe it."

Roman again pulled Marlin out of the meeting he was attending in Miami and told him the decision, saying, "It's not acceptable. We've reversed ourselves. I've been told it's a personal decision, not a business one. I won't fight the decision of offering Schocken the job, but I will fight telling the employees about it. It's a no-win situation if we do that." Marlin agreed, first called Adler, tried to reach Macauley, but could not, and then talked with Morgan. Marlin reported on that conversation and a subsequent one with Roman:

> After discussing the decision with Howie [Morgan], I was satisfied that he had thought it through and it was *his* decision. He logically went through his reasoning. We used the same facts and came to different conclusions.
>
> When I called Daryl [Roman] back, he said Howie might not have been told all of the region's previous attempts to transfer Schocken but he wasn't sure. I said I wouldn't go back to Morgan and hold it up to find out.
>
> There was one other bone of contention: delaying the meeting. I didn't like doing it either, but I couldn't be terribly supportive given how fast we had moved before.

Marlin talked with Adler again and indicated that he understood the decision and would have it implemented.

Meanwhile, Parsons confirmed two job opportunities in Indianapolis and sent the descriptions to Wesley, who then called Roman and indicated that Schocken was to come to New York the next day and be advised of the alternatives available to him. Roman said, "That emasculated the region." Once more he called Marlin, who this time was successful in reaching Macauley. Macauley vetoed the suggested procedure for advising Schocken and had the primary responsibility placed with the region. Butler subsequently called Schocken and asked him to come to Chicago for a meeting at 11:00 the following morning.

At the Distribution Center, Cox was told by Roman at about 2:00 o'clock that the meeting with the employees was to be delayed until the next week. Cox then made a brief "bear with us" speech and returned to Chicago on the company plane. It was not until he got back, however, that he learned of the alternatives to be given to Schocken.

In Chicago, Roman and Butler were making plans for the forthcoming meeting with the employees. The format selected included three sessions. In the opener, to be attended by everyone, Roman would simply describe the next two: first, a session with the black women to discuss "individual situations," and second, a general meeting to review the "entire situation," including corrective measures to be taken and the announcement of Schocken's decision. There would then be time for questions.

Weekend, September 16 and 17

An hour before Schocken was scheduled to arrive at the Chicago motel room arranged for the meeting, Roman, Butler, and Wesley convened to discuss strategy. It was agreed that the latter two would present to Schocken the results of the investigation, saying he was not "clean" but that the company handled the situation badly. Then Roman would make the job offers.

Later, after he had heard these statements, Schocken "opened up." Wesley at the time wrote down some of the highlights of the meeting:

Ran through the script.
Alternatives discussed and why decision is his and should be made on the basis of what's best for him.
Company will support him regardless of what decision he makes.
Schocken: "What does company want me to do?"
Answer: "Do what's best for Joe Schocken."
I can't believe the company would put me back in Elmsford.
Is it a setup? What's my performance review going to look like?
You've given me two alternatives. Indianapolis is desirable, Elmsford is undesirable. I've got a third alternative—quit and sue Hill.
Answer: Joe, you've decided that Elmsford is undesirable. We aren't forcing you but merely laying out the pros and cons. Quitting would be a poor decision.
NEW WRINKLES
Schocken—never had a performance review in 3 years except
        about 6 months ago when he insisted on seeing it.*

*Cox reported later that Schocken had been given performance reviews but had refused to sign the appraisal form because he disagreed with the contents of the reviews.

—move down here (to Elmsford) was financially dis-
advantageous.

—ordered to go, over his objections, to training school
in Virginia and when he came back, he found he lost
his wife.

—told by Lake last week he had two alternatives, to go
to Indianapolis or resign.

Later, Wesley added to his impressions:

He said he worked 18 hours a day, drove himself and his
people. He mentioned one time coming in at 5:00 A.M. Saturday
morning to clear up some of the backlog himself. In effect, he was
telling us, "I get clobbered and no one helps. What do you want
of me?" There was a great deal of mistrust. In essence Schocken
was saying, "I don't believe the corporation is making the decision
to offer me reinstatement in Elmsford." He felt he had only two
alternatives: to move to Indianapolis or to resign.

Schocken, however, continued to feel that his removal was a good
business decision; at several points Roman recalled him saying, "I
would have done it myself." The allegations made by the black
employees were again brought up, with much the same results as
before; they either did not involve him, were not in his judgment
discriminatory, or never happened.

After lunch, the discussion focused on Schocken's specific job
alternatives. He said he was really being given only two, and for
once in his life he wanted to take a stand by resigning and filing suit
against the black employees, Nathan Hill, and the St. Louis press.
The other managers tried to counsel him otherwise by saying that he
did not have the money to invest in lawyers' and court costs, that the
blacks had no money to pay off if he won, and his case probably
was not much good anyway.

In midafternoon the meeting was summarized by Roman.
If Schocken wanted to return to Elmsford, Roman said he needed to
know by Monday evening because he was anxious to get the Distribution Center straightened out. If his decision were to go to
Indianapolis, GSD wanted the answer within two weeks. Schocken
asked if he would be eligible for profit-sharing in 1972 if he resigned; Roman said he would find out.

On Sunday, Schocken called Roman and resigned. Roman replied that he would not accept that as an answer and asked him to

reconsider within the guidelines set earlier. Schocken said he would but that he doubted there was much the company could do to change his mind. Roman reported this conversation to Marlin, Wesley, Butler, and Cox.

Monday, September 18

On Monday, attention focused on the forthcoming meeting with the employees at the Distribution Center. Wesley had returned to Chicago to participate in the detailed planning with regional executives. Meanwhile in New York, Morgan read the region's outline for the meeting, made a number of comments on it, and concluded that he wanted to talk about it further. This precipitated an afternoon session attended by Roman, Wesley, and Butler, who all flew in from Chicago, and Macauley.

This session provided an opportunity for Roman to discuss the events of the past several days with Morgan directly. Roman went through the presentation and secured basic agreement for the region's plan and the participation of his managers in the program. However, only the general session was to be held; the separate discussion with the black employees was eliminated. Finally, Wednesday was agreed upon as the date for the meeting.

Regarding Schocken, Morgan indicated that if he submitted his resignation, Roman, having done all he could, should accept it and provide Schocken with a letter exonerating him and stating the separation benefits. Roman received permission to go a bit further and "order" Schocken to Indianapolis, thinking that he might react to this stimulus in view of his "military" attitude.

Tuesday, September 19

Roman called Schocken on Tuesday for a discussion, which he summarized as follows:

> I went one step beyond Howie [Morgan] and put Elmsford back on the table. He [Schocken] didn't react to it. Then I said I had to close out Elmsford but reiterated the offer of two weeks to decide on the transfer to Indianapolis. It was the warmest discussion I had with Schocken. He said he appreciated the time and understood the region's problem. I told him to think about his kids and take the transfer.

After relaying this information to Indianapolis and New York,

Roman authorized Lake to approach Holden once more about the customer service manager's job. Holden accepted.

Wednesday, September 20

Roman, Butler, and Wesley flew to St. Louis early Wednesday morning, met with Evans, and at 9:30 summoned Lake to the motel. Lake said, "I was told we were going to take a bit of a public whipping but that I was to be candid in discussing our problems." At 1:30, the out-of-town group arrived unannounced at the Distribution Center and called the employees together for a meeting that lasted nearly two hours. At the end of it, Roman promised the employees that he would return in 30 days to discuss the situation with them again.

Butler described parts of the meeting:

One objective of the meeting was to give the whites a feeling for what the blacks were saying. For the first time they were made aware of the details—the testing, stray comments, and so forth. We stressed that no employees were involved in the discrimination charges. Then Daryl made the announcement about Schocken, and Pete made the announcement about Holden.

The meeting went better than we expected. The blacks had nothing to say. The whites were surprised we'd level with them and admit our mistakes. They were turned off by the decision to give Shirley Gaynor a retroactive promotion, thinking that the white girl's promotion was being taken away, but I clarified this later in the meeting.

Roman commented on some impressions:

There was a good feeling—some joking and laughing for a change. We talked about action plans and how not to make the mistakes again. I said that our goal was to be the number one region in minority relations, just as we were on top in meeting our sales targets. Everyone seemed to have the feeling that one of our main responsibilities was to learn how to work together. We left the meeting feeling pretty good about it.

As soon as the meeting was over, several of the white women, led by Roslyn O'Neil, rushed to a phone and called Schocken. In effect they told him, "We worked to get your job back, and now what are you doing by refusing it?" At that point Schocken would not acknowledge that he had ever been given the alternative of remaining in Elmsford. The employees then asked to meet with him. Schocken told them he would think about it.

In a few minutes, Schocken telephoned Lake to seek advice on what he should do then. Roman was alerted and immediately called Schocken to find out why he had not confirmed the existence of the Elmsford offer. In a lengthy conversation, Schocken would not admit that he had ever received a real offer, and Roman's efforts to convince him otherwise were to no avail. Perplexed but unable to stay, Roman asked Butler and Evans to meet with Schocken "to find out what's going on in his head."

For three hours that evening, Butler, Evans, and Lake talked with Schocken but could make little sense of the discussion. Butler commented:

> I went over the whole story with him, including Morgan's involvement. Apparently what he heard was, "I could go back to Elmsford, but I would be on probation and out of the business in two months." He was concerned about who would review his record. I told him he would get the fairest treatment of anyone in the company. I went over all the political aspects of it.
>
> Then he asked me, "Did you offer the job to anyone else?" I said, "Yes. It was frankly not our recommendation to put you back but we were overruled." I told him that the job had been offered to Holden and then withdrawn. It finally dawned on me that he must have gotten some information about the Holden offer before the meeting with Roman the previous Saturday.

Schocken also indicated that he was very concerned about the economics of a move to Indianapolis. In particular, he felt his house might take longer to sell than the three months allowed by BPC, that he would have to incur considerable baby-sitting expenses, and that the standard 7 percent relocation increase would not be sufficient. He also said, "I just can't live with this any longer. Give me an answer on these points and I'll decide."

Schocken left about 10:00 P.M., and Butler, Evans, and Lake had dinner and talked for another two hours. After pressing Lake on whether he had told Schocken about the Holden offer (which Lake found upsetting), Butler concluded that if there was a leak, it most likely came from Holden himself. His hunch was strengthened when he learned that Holden, as Schocken's best friend in the Distribution Center, delivered Schocken's paycheck the previous Friday evening.

Thursday, September 21

The next morning Butler confronted Holden:

> I asked him, "When did you tell Schocken about your job offer?" I had him trapped, and he said, "Friday night." Evans and Lake were incredulous that this could have happened. I think Holden would have been fired on the spot if that wouldn't have loused matters up further. Daryl was at a regional managers' meeting in Indianapolis and I contacted him there. Parsons was with him, and within a few minutes everyone knew about it. Then the witch hunt started at Corporate.

Prior to this, it was not known in the Corporate offices that Holden had been offered the job before Morgan's decision on Schocken had been communicated. Consequently it appeared that Morgan's directive about withholding action had clearly been violated. One corporate executive commented: "It really made us look like asses." Adler, on instructions from Morgan, asked Marlin to investigate this breach.

By midafternoon, following some intensive research by Roman, a memorandum from Marlin to Adler described the events surrounding the Holden affair and the nature of the financial relief recommended for Schocken. Morgan accepted the report.

At the Distribution Center that morning the employees were not entirely satisfied with the way the episode had been resolved. A number of the white women approached Lake asking, "If Joe's job had been offered to Holden, he must have had time to think about it. When was he told?" The black employees maintained that, since Schocken had been offered reinstatement, management's response had been a "whitewash" after all. However, the emotion appeared to have subsided. Evans reflected on the future in human terms: "My hope is that the employees will have confidence in Pete Lake. Without him there I don't know if we can pull it out. His job won't be easy but maybe his ability to get along with people and his willingness not to hold a grudge will do it. I'm banking on him saying, "Damn, look at all these comments. Here are some things I can do.'"

Subsequent Events

The implications of the Elmsford incident for the management of the minority relations program at corporate and division levels have been discussed in the preceding chapter. In a narrower sense, however, managers in the region had to contend with the aftermath. Marlin indicated to Roman at one point: "The Midwest Region is number one in sales. Now I want you to be number one in minority relations."

Not suprisingly during the next months there was a good deal of activity on the minority relations front in both the Distribution Center and the regional offices.

Distribution Center

After several weeks of further hesitation, Schocken finally decided to accept a lateral transfer to a staff position in the GSD offices in Indianapolis. (Incidentally, a year later he was reportedly receiving good performance reviews.) Otherwise, the work force in the Distribution Center remained essentially unchanged. Tension did not dissipate immediately; in fact, at the end of October the same charges of racism were aired in the press following their presentation by Nathan Hill at a congressional hearing on discrimination in industry. This time, however, there was no direct response from the company.

Lake immediately began to draft plans to address the complaints and charges made by the minority employees. The program ultimately agreed upon by Evans and others at the regional office provided for new performance appraisals for the four black women and some salary and pay grade adjustments. More important, greater objectivity was introduced into the measurement system for nonexempt employees by quantifying the ratings applied to latenesses, absences, and so forth. Parsons greeted this development with some misgivings, feeling that it tended to remove an element of judgment and adaptability from personnel administration, but he did not interfere. Assurance was also given that "merit ratings for performance appraisal will have a similar bell curve distribution for whites and blacks." In addition, Lake's plan called for sensitivity and job training, as well as more frequent meetings between supervisors and their staffs.

Region

The region's response to Elmsford and the concurrent meeting of the minority salesmen began to take shape on October 9 at a special meeting of branch managers and senior staff called by Roman. He left little doubt during this 10-hour session that the priority given to minority relations had to increase and that he intended to hold his management group personally accountable for meeting the targets in the Affirmative Action Plan. Officially, 15 percent of the performance appraisal among managers in the region was to be allocated to this end. Special attention was to be given to the identification of promotable minorities for "gateway jobs." Roman recognized the pressure he was placing on his organization:

> Very few of our DSM's* are minority right now. It's hard to get the branch managers to take the risk and time to change that. The expectation is that he will risk putting in a black DSM before he's really sure that the candidate is ready for the job. Then, if I say to the branch manager "You're in deep trouble if you don't make 100% of plan, he says, 'What's going to happen to me if that DSM doesn't work out?' " There is a high turnover among DSM's — it's a tough job, and the failure rate is high. Performance is expected instantly. In six months if a DSM is at 50% of plan, he has trouble not only with his manager but with me. At the same time the branch manager has to depend on him to make plan.

"Making plan" was of more than passing interest to the sales organization because it clearly influenced performance appraisals. Bonuses were a significant factor in the manager's income, and, more important, promotion rates had been rapid for those on a "fast track." Roman's message created apprehension over the way it would affect appraisals, and a degree of resentment over the burden added to already heavy workloads.

At the same time, Roman announced an expansion in the responsibilities of the minority relations managers. He told his staff: "I am immediately delegating authority to Sam Johnson to speak for me throughout the region with respect to minority relations programs." Another person was added to the personnel staff to specialize in minority recruitment, a step Roman hoped would permit Johnson to concentrate on advancement, counseling, training, and trouble shooting.

Among the first programs considered was the minority awareness seminar then being completed on a crash basis at GSD. Even though early reports suggested that it fell far short of the region's needs, Roman pressed for an accelerated introduction. He also engaged a

---

*District sales managers, perhaps the most critical gateway job in GSD.

consulting firm to design a more operational program, slanted specifically to the difficulties his organization was encountering. This program was to be paid for with funds that had been ear-marked for salesman training. A third program related to community affairs, an area the black employees said was being neglected or left to corporate management. The region had a small amount in the budget for this purpose, which, as of October 1972, had not been touched. Roman then put some pressure on the branch managers to develop ideas for community involvement, and soon a variety of requests were flowing in for baseball bats and second-hand pianos.

Only one regional initiative required extensive discussion with GSD and corporate management. In October, when Moore visited Chicago for a sales force awards dinner, Roman approached him with a proposal for an advisory council to be composed of one minority employee from each location. During the next several weeks, while this proposal was being considered, the region staff became increasingly concerned about the effect such a council might have on relations with nonminority employees. They concluded that, although the idea was sound, the committee should be composed of a representative cross section of all employees and should delve into broader personnel issues than just minority relations. A new request to this effect was turned down, however, because of potential union connotations. The original proposal was then approved on an experimental basis and Roman elected to implement it.

As a result of these and other programs, Roman sensed that solid progress had been made in minority relations by the spring of 1973. On the other hand, the cost, especially in terms of the time that he and others had devoted to the problem, had been considerable. At least for the near term, however, there seemed to be little prospect of relief.

Reflections

In the course of gathering information related to the events described above, the researcher probed for reflections on some broader questions raised by this incident. Why did the Elmsford problem arise? What implications did it have for the organization? What was likely to happen next, and who would be involved? And so forth. Some of the impressions expressed by managers at region, division, and corporate levels about the situation that had very recently engulfed them are provided in the comments below:

Evans (Region Manager, Logistics and Distribution)

The company can't *just* commit itself to affirmative action — "quotas" aren't enough. We must make managers aware of the deeper problems and allow them to cope with them. Going further, is the company willing to change the criteria used for promotions? Are we willing to sacrifice some performance-oriented people, when selections are made, in favor of managers who can deal effectively with minority relations? The company must spend the bucks to train managers, but it may also have to allow them to manage their organizations differently . . .

This has hurt careers for Lake, me, and, of course, Schocken. But I told my wife I wouldn't leave now even if a hell of a promotion came along somewhere else. I feel responsible and ashamed of letting BPC down. I've prided myself on having a good organization, and I've got to see this through.

Johnson (Region Minority Relations Manager)

Until recently, equal employment at BPC meant Moore's 1968 letter — it was a moral issue. Managers would see me coming and say, "Here's Johnson again to ask us how many blacks we've hired!" But the issue is bigger than minority relations — it's really employee relations, and that's what makes it so important. For instance, in performance appraisals, a manager tells an employee he's great and then comes through with a low salary increase. 90% of the problem is this — only 10% is bigotry.

Roman (Region General Manager)

BPC has minority objectives, but they are all expressed in numerical terms — the number of hires and so forth. We also have some strong letters from Moore. Now we've built a significant minority population but we're ill-informed and insensitive as managers. I've talked with managers in the region and there is a reluctance to get involved — it's seen as easier and safer to stay on the fringes. We have got to make the transition from meeting hiring quotas in entry-level jobs to acting as managers in training and promoting blacks.

Are the white managers really interested in the advancement of blacks in the organization? Probably not. But they are interested in targets. Is there prejudice in BPC? I don't know. Certainly if it exists in the country, we must have some of it here.

Parsons (GSD Personnel Manager)

One has to question the efficiency of the decision process when six levels of line management get involved in it. The local manager was quickly voided of responsibility. It created a situation which could have been explosive internally. However, while some of us took exception to specific actions, we could at least talk about it together. . .

Morgan's decision on Schocken was key. BPC makes comments about respect for the individual. Some of us who work long hours sometimes question management's sincerity, but this incident told us that top management does care. It was not a popular decision. It ran against previous decisions made at lower levels and was dangerous in terms of potential publicity. But he said we had not treated Schocken fairly, and we were going to correct it. This gives me renewed confidence and a willingness to investigate employees complaints as I look back on it.

Marlin (GSD General Manager)

The Distribution Center is a remote location and the guy's boss is in Chicago. To run a distribution center is one thing, minority relations is another. I'm sure we can teach people to handle minority relations better, but the competence to deal with the sort of incident we've had here is far greater than we can expect to teach. As a result that manager has to have support available quickly, and it should be made so that he doesn't feel like he's failing in the job by calling for help too much. . .

I'm a little schizophrenic about having top management jump in. In the Baltimore incident I thought it had a positive effect.* In this situation I'm not so sure it has. Roman's frustrations were pretty high. He felt he wasn't being supported, though he felt better after he saw Morgan face-to-face. But he felt that too many orders were coming down on him and that he got criticized for making some "modest" decisions.

Morgan (President)

This incident was one that very few of our managers had experienced before, especially with a subject as complex as this one. Ultimately, however, it gets down to how a supervisor handles his people. Every once in a while a situation comes along which constitutes an example for the organization—really an example of

---

*See Chapter VIII for an elaboration of the circumstances surrounding the Baltimore incident.

what can happen to this company and will, I'm sure, happen again in the future. . .

To understand why the Elmsford decision was handled as it was, the first thing to look at is the Baltimore incident last year. The blacks contacted us [Moore and Morgan] directly. We sent some people out there to investigate. What they came back with made us want to go further, so I went to Baltimore with Marlin. He ran all the meetings but I sat in. I wanted Marlin, as the operating manager, to handle it, but my presence lent emphasis to the corporation's concern. We learned a lot from that experience. Everyone was involved. We learned that we had to think differently about minority affairs, that we had to audit our performance differently.

The fact that I went back there was considered traumatic, as overkill by some people. So with Elmsford there was a strong incentive to handle it themselves, to do it quickly and with local management and keep goddamn Morgan out of it. Decisions were made without enough information; had they taken an extra week, the results probably would have come out differently.

ANALYSIS

The Elmsford Distribution Center incident contributed in an identifiable way to the significant transition in the approach to minority relations that occurred in the operating units of BPC during 1972. As in the case of the Dolton Plant incident in Weston Industries described in Chapter VIII, the decisive events covered a period of six weeks. Once again, however, an understanding of the antecedents is essential in order to obtain a grasp of a situation which permitted a seemingly local demand to develop into an episode of crisis proportions. Consequently, the commentary below deals with these points: (a) the context in which the incident arose, (b) the dynamics of crisis, and (c) the response to trauma.

The Context: May 1969 - August 1972

In early August 1972, the forces which were to be unleashed at the Elmsford facility were not readily visible to managers in the Midwestern Region. Indeed they seemed implausible. After all, the Distribution Center was viewed with some pride; at the time, performance had been improving rapidly and the difficulties encountered during its start-up had been successfully surmounted. The traditional indicators of employee discontent, such as turnover and absenteeism, were remarkably low, and informal observation tended to confirm the presence of a happy, industrious work force. Lake had managed the facility without much help from the region staff, and nothing thus far suggested that he needed increased coaching. Moreover, he had gone to some lengths to insure that minorities were adequately represented, probably further than was customary at the time. And finally, a small service unit accounting for less than 1 percent of the region's employees seemed an unlikely spot for a corporate crisis.

What caused the incident to spin out of control? Part of the explanation, of course, was in the mix of factors which prompted and sustained the protest. An employee's charge of discrimination was in itself not a rare occurrence. In this case, however, the situation happened to involve some complicating elements. One of the protesters was the facility manager's secretary who was privy to the personnel records. Her husband, an activist of unknown (to BPC managers) persuasion, was also involved, and succeeded in securing the attention of the media. Then there was a supervisor who had a record of insensitivity toward his subordinates but was frozen in his job because a transfer could not be arranged and the company's seven-year tenure policy inhibited his release. The original hiring procedures, conditions in the temporary quarters, and operating priorities produced a variety of aberrations that — whether intentional or not — could be ascribed to discrimination. The list may be expanded at length.

One expects protest to be built on some such convergence of factors which in concert dramatize the underlying grievance. The situation itself is an historical accident that will probably never be repeated. Yet future incidents, if they occur, will undoubtedly be fired by circumstances which at the time appear to be equally improbable. For our purposes, the importance of the incident is not in the specifics of the problem or the proposed remedies but in the effect that it had on the organization's response to subsequent incidents and more generally to the conditions under attack. The context in which managers in the Midwestern Region operated during the summer of 1972 influenced how they approached the events in Elmsford.

Roman was straining his organization to achieve a difficult business plan. Some indication of the "stretch" expected is suggested by the region's first-place finish in sales through June of 1972 at 91 percent of budget. Lake also felt the weight of budgetary constraints during his two years in Elmsford, as, for example, the hiring freeze in 1970, the delay in approval for the new facility, and the increased work load. Controls were tight, measurement frequent, and the personal stakes high; not surprisingly, management was geared to meeting targets for the remainder of the year.

The reader will recall from Chapter VIII that increased minority hiring and advancement targets had also been levied on operating management by corporate personnel earlier in the summer. There is little doubt that the commitments were being taken seriously. In fact, the purpose of Johnson's trip to St. Louis was to wind up a recruiting campaign for minority customer service people, and Cox was anxious to see if Nathan Hill might be of help. However, the emphasis in equal employment was on increasing the intake numbers in exempt categories (e.g., what was being measured), and for the most part the personnel function was assigned this task. In contrast, personnel allocated far less attention to management training and counseling on minority affairs and minority employee needs and grievances. Either the funds and time for such activities were directed elsewhere or responsibility was perceived to rest with management at division level or above.

Finally, region management was fully aware of the precedents for corporate intervention in the affairs of operating units on minority-related problems. If a situation arose which was in any way out of the ordinary, such as the presence of an outside activist, the region was confronted by a dilemma. How much should corporate headquarters be involved? Obviously, if no information were forwarded up the line and the situation exploded, region management would be in trouble. On the other hand, by engaging corporate specialists the region might appear indecisive and invite second guessing.

From the operating manager's perspective, the summer of 1972 was a distinctly poor time to have a minority relations confrontation. Moore's letter in July, stating that performance evaluations were at stake (though it did not say just how), further raised the level of anxiety. In short, the organization was edgy and prone to over-reaction.

The Anatomy of Trauma—August-September 1972

Although the BPC organization was increasingly sensitive to the problems of implementing a policy of equal employment for minorities by August 1972, it was peculiarly unprepared to deal with the Elmsford incident. Morgan's intervention was traumatic. The elements of trauma appear to be contained in three interrelated problems which at the time lacked appropriate remedies:
  —an uncertain balance between action and investigation;
  —an inability to fix responsibility; and
  —the absence of an accepted due process.

I suspect that these problems are evident in most instances of trauma in large scale institutions. Each will be discussed in turn.

Action and Investigation

Regional management was plagued by poor information. The formal systems that were supposed to reflect employee performance and attitudes were quickly found to be irrelevant or suspect. Attendance reports and employee appraisals were in some cases misleading and, from the black employees' viewpoint, used in a discriminatory fashion. The personnel records were of limited value, and employment procedures had been abrogated on occasion for operational reasons. There was no simple and objective means of determining whether the charges of racial bias were justified. Then when regional management attempted to tap informal sources of information, chiefly commentary from the parties involved, their efforts were either frustrated or inconclusive.

Despite weakness in the information, it was soon felt that corrective measures of some sort were warranted. By responding decisively to the problem, even though it was only partially understood, region management hoped to demonstrate good faith to the minority employees and to defuse the issue. Similar reasoning was applied to the decision to remove Schocken. Faced with an increasingly anxious organization above him and a deteriorating situation at the Distribution Center, Roman elected to administer some stiff medicine based on the fragmentary August investigation and the signals he was getting from his division manager. On a third occasion, the decision to approach Holden about Schocken's job, this cycle was repeated. Now supported by the Wesley-Butler study and with his subordinates pleading for action, Roman once again decided to act before the final (and presumably confirming) decision had been made by Morgan.

Ironically, decisiveness might have paid off were it not for subsequent unexpected events. For instance, the region's initial action plan might have served as a basis for resolution had Nathan Hill not succeeded in airing the dispute on television. Roman might have kept the lid on after removing Schocken had there been no white backlash. And the facility might have recovered sooner had Morgan agreed with the recommendations on Schocken in the report. In each instance, the sequel was unanticipated by the decision-maker and decisiveness came to be labeled overreaction.

In a general sense, the issue is not that Roman should have foreseen these possibilities and therefore have done something else. He was applying his best judgment to the facts he had available; while others might have reached different conclusions, he was the one under pressure to make a decision. More interesting is the question, should he have gathered more intelligence before doing anything at all? The answer is unclear. Region management had not been overly successful in securing information from the protesting employees and were prohibited from meeting with Nathan Hill. On the other hand, they were thoroughly familiar with Schocken's supervisory record. By the time Roman had Schocken removed, the amount of new information likely to be obtained from further investigation by his organization appeared limited. The subsequent Wesley-Butler study seemed to confirm this notion. Although this study was considerably more detailed and served a variety of other useful purposes, it did not materially change the basic findings to which the region had been responding from the outset.

Thus a traumatic incident poses serious judgmental issues for the manager who seeks to assert authority over it. The response has to be weighed against the severity of the problem. Measured by the effort expended in the past on employee grievances in a minute service unit rather than by the demands of the eventual, unanticipated outcome, the Elmsford situation may initially have received more than its share of attention. The cost of *anticipating* dire consequences in every such incident would be enormous. Exercising judgment under these circumstances involves a recognition of the tension between action and investigation and the limitations and pitfalls of each.

Responsibility

A second characteristic of the Elmsford incident was an inability to fix responsibility for managing the company's affairs. The employee accusations raised problems that fell in the province of managers at different levels in the organization. The Distribution Center immediately fell prey to declines in productivity and morale. For Lake a timely resolution was literally a matter of survival. Roman and others on his staff were held accountable for providing guidance and support to the field units and for personnel administration in the region. Moreover, the Elmsford protest appeared to be spreading to the sales force, a development that conceivably could have serious budgetary implications. Marlin was in the middle. Macauley had specifically indicated that GSD was responsible for resolving the problem, yet Marlin was also familiar with corporate management's proclivity for intervention. At the corporate level, concerns first centered on the "national demands" mentioned by the employees and the extensive publicity being given to the event. Later, Morgan's attention was drawn to the white backlash and the possible injustice to Schocken, both matters he took to be of company-wide significance.

In the midst of events which appeared to be swirling out of control, the diffusion in responsibility had several unfortunate consequences.

First, with each momentary setback, the level in the organization from which response was directed drifted upward, and, as it did, the capability of those below to discharge their responsibilities was compromised. Lake's control over the Distribution Center waned with the arrival of Evans, Cox, and Johnson for a meeting with the four black women in August. Evans was largely voided of influence as Roman took charge following the decision to remove Schocken. Roman's position in turn was compromised by the white protest. For a short time the buck was passed to Morgan.

Second, as the point of decision was progressively removed from managers in the field, the chances of misunderstanding and contradictory behavior increased. Those at the top were inevitably less familiar with the intricacies of the situation and constrained by a lack of up-to-date information. Communication downward was also a major problem, a point illustrated by the two situations in which Morgan's directives were not implemented.

Third, top management intervention produced a good deal of anxiety in the organization. Morgan's concerns for the individual, for example, were considerably different from those of Lake and Evans, who had an overriding interest in getting the Distribution Center under control and back into production. Responsibility for resolving the Elmsford incident may have been difficult to pin down, but accountability for performance had not changed. Lake (rather than Morgan) would be criticized if the facility did not meet its targets. Not surprisingly, operating managers favored decisions which they felt were likely to protect their ability to secure results in the future. Frustration mounted in this instance when Morgan elected to risk a short-term penalty for a principle that he believed was morally correct and in the long run beneficial to BPC.

Due Process

A final characteristic of the Elmsford incident was the absence of a generally accepted due process for resolving the questions raised by it. In addition to poor information and unclear responsibilities, BPC managers had few guidelines to help them sort through the decisions that had to be made. Two types of decisions were called for, the first hinging on questions of equity and the second on the decision process itself. The organization, as a decision-making entity, had not been confronted by situations of this sort with any frequency in the past. Almost from the outset, regional management treated the problem as something different from a normal employee grievance. Abandoning the established grievance procedure with its recognized limits of appeal and its grounding in personnel policy left the organization without an accepted means of responding to the protest.

Equity was a very important issue in this case. For instance, what were Schocken's rights? Morgan was concerned that he was being tacitly convicted of a charge that could not be substantiated because his transfer was seen as being in the best interests of the company. How was equity best served for the employees and other managers caught up in the incident? What disclosure, reprimands, and reparations were appropriate? As long as the feeling persisted that equity was not being served, the suggested remedies were disputed, ignored, or resented.

Similarly, a process for resolving such controversy did not exist.

What were the limits of appeal? Under normal circumstances, one would expect a manager as close to the situation as possible to function as the company's spokesman, albeit acting at times on orders and advice from those above. Despite its obvious efficiency, such a procedure becomes ineffective if the concerns of higher management or the aggrieved cannot be accommodated. However, the right of appeal in this instance was unbounded, in part because the employees doubted that an acceptable response would be forthcoming from the next level of management, and in part because Morgan sensed that the underlying issues of equity were unresolved.

In a sense, the Elmsford incident provided an opportunity to formulate a due process for responding to the organizational problems accompanying a pledge of equal opportunity. On a broader plane, it also broached issues of governance that involved the rights and responsibilities of employees and managers generally. As perhaps is typical of the response to social demands, the lessons to be learned extended beyond the immediate demands to the more consequential problems of managing a purposive organization.

The Aftermath

It was significant that Roman, the middle-level general manager, took the initiative in defining the subsequent approach to minority relations in the region. He did this by exercising the leadership and providing the emphasis that had previously been left for the most part to staff specialists both in his organization and at corporate and division levels. His lever, the performance evaluation and career system, was the one he used to encourage performance in sales, service, and other facets of the business. He also presided over the development of programs designed to support his managers in the accomplishment of the commitments assumed in the minority area. The fact that scarce resources were allocated from the region's budget for these purposes was an indication of the impetus being given to the effort. Moreover, rather than tolerating or postponing GSD training programs and other such assistance, regional management now actively requested them.

In essence, responsibility for managing the implementation of the minority relations program had been clarified. Just as Bush, the Division manager in Weston Industries, took the responsibility for pollution control expenditures in his unit, so now Roman assumed this burden for equal employment in the Midwestern Region of GSD. The burden was tangible, for it translated into a diversion of time and funds from other programs such as sales force training, and placed new demands on already pressed managers. On the other hand, the episode appeared to have its rewards, for as the region demonstrated a willingness to take charge of the issue, direct corporate involvement receded. Learning had indeed taken place. As the organization settled down after the episode, the outlines of a modified due process had taken shape that held the promise of forestalling trauma in the future.

X
Managing the Response Process

The preceding chapters have reflected the close and continuing interaction between the corporation and the social forces in its environment. The experience is not always greeted with enthusiasm by managers on the firing line. As one division manager commented, "Business used to be fun. But now there are so damn many people around demanding this and that, I just don't enjoy it any more." Nevertheless underlying the seeming confusion and conflict both within the organization and in its negotiations with external agencies, a process has evolved in large corporations through which they attempt to respond to social challenges.

My contention now is that the process can be *managed* by chief executives and their staffs. This is not to say that there are single or best answers to the thorny administrative issues that inevitably arise along the way. Case studies based on the Business Products Corporation incident in Chapter IX have been discussed in repeated sessions of the Advanced Management Program at the Harvard Business School; consensus emerges on only one point — "It's a hell of a problem." Nevertheless, there appear to be a relatively small number of critical decisions that have a dominant influence in shaping how a corporation adapts to its changing environment. Recognizing and analyzing these decisions should result in significant benefits to the firm.

One may ask the following question at this point: Does the process for responding to social demands differ in any fundamental way from that normally observed in the management of strategic issues in divisionalized corporations? The answer requires an important distinction to be drawn between issues of significance to the corporation as a whole and those having a primary impact on the activities of a single operating unit.

As described in the preceding chapters, the response to social demands tended to be a "top down" affair in terms of initiative, analysis, and commitment. This condition was particularly noticeable when the decision had been made to engage an issue early in its life cycle. Although problem definition may first have been broached in isolated divisions, the bulk of the analysis appeared to be performed, or at least directed, from the corporate level. Moreover, it was the chief executive who accepted the burden of securing the organization's commitment to responsive action. Program and persuasive efforts in Phases I and II were projected *downward*. Not until responsiveness had been effectively assimilated in Phase III was the initiative taken by division-level managers and a decentralized pattern of decision-making to emerge.

In contrast, the formulation and implementation of product-market strategy for established and continuing operating units normally reflects "bottoms up" initiatives in the divisionalized firm. For instance, Bower,[1] in his research on resource allocation, found that project definition was performed by functional managers in the operating unit based on their detailed familiarity with both market needs and technical requirements. The impetus for funding was provided by their superiors, middle-level general managers, who integrated the performance targets that they had negotiated with corporate managers with the needs of the business and agreed to commit themselves to the project. Rarely were projects or plans from managers with good records rejected in subsequent reviews by corporate managers (though they might have been delayed or recycled for further study). The corporate level guided the allocation process indirectly by setting the contextual framework of goals, measures, and incentives within which middle-level general managers made their commitments. Consequently, one thrust of the divisionalized organization has been to shelter the chief executive's office from operating detail and often from close contact with operating managers.

There is, however, another class of strategic issues which affects the corporation more generally. The resolution of issues of this type tends to reflect the "top down" characteristic ascribed to the social issue response process. The most common examples are changes in the composition of the business portfolio in the divisionalized firm, either through major new commitments beyond the scope of existing divisions or through divestments. In these instances, corporate management appears to exercise authority over product-market decisions rather than permit them to percolate up through the organization. Examples include the huge investments made by General Electric in nuclear power, computers, and commercial jet engines in the 1960s;[2] the company's program to reallocate resources among businesses in the 1970s;[3] and the decision at IBM to launch the series 360 computer.[4] Unfortunately, comparatively little systematic research is available on such decisions to determine the extent of the detailed correspondence to the response to social demands.[5]

In the past, divisionalized firms have confronted corporate-wide strategic issues infrequently. It is unlikely that a procedure has developed, or at least been explicitly recognized, for routinely approaching them. In view of the increasing evidence of resource constraints in the U.S. economy — in terms of energy, raw materials, and funds for investment — the incidence of centrally directed resource allocation programs is likely to increase in the future. Thus, to the extent that the organizational implications of social demands bear similarity to those accompanying other corporate-level initiatives, the process described here may have wider application. At the same time, the process runs counter to the "bottoms-up" strategic planning familiar to most operating managers on matters pertaining to their divisions.

The social issue response process passed through three phases enroute to implementation at operating levels, each phase serving the function broadly defined in Exhibit X-1.[6] The questions to be addressed now are, first, what is to be learned from the experience of these companies, and, second, what price is paid for upsetting the accustomed decision-making format in the divisionalized firm? I will take up each phase in turn.

Enriching Corporate Purpose

The chief executive has the ultimate responsibility for the definition and "institutionalization" of corporate purpose. Selznick, in his provocative book, *Leadership in Administration*, wrote:[7]

> Institutionalization is a *process*. It is something that happens to an organization over time, reflecting the organization's own distinctive history, the people who have been in it, the group it embodied and the vested interests they have created, and the way it has adapted to its environment. . . The degree of institutionalization depends on how much leeway there is for personal and group interaction. The more precise an organization's goals and the more specialized its operations, the less opportunity will there be for social forces to affect its development.
>
> . . . In what is perhaps its most significant meaning, "to institu-

Exhibit X-1
The Social Issue Response Process

	Organizational level	Phase in response process		
		I	II	III
Emerging social demand →	Chief executive	Enriching purpose		
	Staff specialist		Learning	
	Division management			Obtaining commitment → Institutionalized response

tionalize" is *to infuse with value* beyond the technical requirements of the task at hand.

Decentralization and stress on internal financial performance measures tend to make the institutionalization of purpose in terms other than simply economic performance difficult for the chief executive of the divisionalized firm to achieve. The annual financial plan is a simple but powerful organizing device that, with a nod to longer-range concerns, may naturally become a surrogate for corporate purpose. The plan may be viewed as the only common denominator on which general agreement can be reached in the absence of close working relationships. Yet, the chief executive must formulate and sustain a more complex statement of purpose if the firm is voluntarily to embrace the dictates of social change.

Corporate response to a social demand hinged initially on the chief executive's interest in pursuing it. Policy decisions rarely proceeded from formal analysis. Nor did their implementation appear to be significantly influenced by attempts to communicate economic justification. The limitations of environmental analysis will be reviewed first before turning to the consequences of alternative approaches for justifying involvement.

Limitations of Analysis
When William Fredericks of Weston Industries proposed $4 million worth of pollution control equipment for a new facility in 1964 (described in Chapter VI above), he did so formally on the grounds that the expenditure in the long run would be beneficial to the firm. He did not, however, attempt to demonstrate that the net present

value of expected future benefits to the company exceeded the investment or, more narrowly, the amount that might be saved by postponing it. Approval was forthcoming but not necessarily because his argument was persuasive. Rather, division management trusted the judgment of an experienced manager who was prepared to take personal responsibility for the results, corporate management was committed to the facility and appeared supportive of the expenditure, and so forth.

Had Fredericks possessed a crystal ball, he might have predicted some beneficial second-order consequences of the investment. For instance, as ecology became popular in 1970, the plant received widespread praise as an example of responsible corporate action. Weston used the recognition to demonstrate a record of good faith that contributed to generally cooperative relationships with regulators and ecologists. In practical terms, this meant an absence of onerous consent decrees and greater latitude to experiment with new control technologies. More specifically, in 1972, comparable control equipment was prescribed throughout the industry. Not only did Weston avoid the expensive necessity of reconditioning an existing plant, but also this facility appeared to be an important factor in the determination by EPA of industry standards. In the meantime, the division had continued to upgrade its other plants with the same technology, spreading the cost over a number of years in line with engineering availability and complementary refurbishing projects.

It is conceivable that reasonable estimates of the economic return on social responsiveness may some day be used in evaluating investment opportunities. The technique would be similar to that now evolving from environmental impact statements — one might term it a social impact analysis. Efforts to be precise may, of course, produce odd results. For instance, one bank attempted to calculate the "true cost" of its social programs. Among the major items listed were the salaries of security guards and the damage caused by vandalism to a branch office! Nevertheless, the accounting profession and others are making progress in developing social information and measurements systems, though few see the conversion of these data into economic terms as practical in the near term.[8] Despite numerous shortcomings, forcing the explicit consideration of second-order social consequences in investment decisions may be a matter of good business judgment for two reasons.

First, careful analysis may ferret out additional sources of future costs and benefits accruing to projects normally considered on narrowly economic grounds. The analysis may reveal pleasant surprises. For example, one large bank was approached by an association of senior citizens who demanded less restrictive loan policies and free checking accounts.[9] The bank's first reaction was to duck the matter. The association effectively pressed it, however, and forced the bank to study the implications of acquiescing. Further analysis revealed that elderly persons had higher savings account balances and wrote far fewer checks than the average customer. Consequently, even though a reduction in service fees and a loss in interest income was likely on existing accounts, top management became intrigued with the opportunity of securing profitable new accounts. The plan was approved, and market share among that age group increased dramatically. Competitive retaliation may, of course, limit these gains in the future. Nonetheless, a policy that was at first viewed as an expensive burden became, on reflection, an effective competitive weapon.

Second, analysis may police socially directed expenditures. As one environmental control director put it: "Productivity used to be the buzz word around here on capital requests. Then it was product quality. Now it's ecology. If you really want something but can't make a convincing argument on a rate of return basis, you put these words on the request. One of my problems is to sort out what's environmental from what just says so."

Assessing the second-order consequences of a *project* is a far less demanding proposition than forecasting the economic or operational implications of a *policy* early in the life cycle of a social issue. The environmental uncertainties in this case are far more substantial. Although a more sophisticated capability for predicting the impact of social change may be developing, it is interesting that futurist organizations frequently cite the failure of client firms to act on their findings as a major weakness in their work.[10] The president of the Institute for the Future commented: "The Institute has not, on the whole, been sufficiently resourceful in coupling the results of its research to on-going planning and decision-making processes within its sponsoring organizations. This shortcoming has often reduced considerably both the utility and potential impact of the Institute's research output."[11]

The tendency in large corporations has been to pursue analysis piecemeal, if at all, as social policy is defined. Invariably, however, the chief executive buttressed his personal convictions with the belief that the long-term interests of the firm would in the long run be served by aggressive involvement. The reasoning provided is familiar. For instance:

> Clear evidence of social awareness increases the attractiveness of the corporation as a place to work for younger, presumably more concerned managers.
>
> An "enlightened" corporate posture contributes to market acceptance, employee morale, community receptivity, and so on.
>
> It is better to respond before regulatory or social agencies force *their* standards and timetables. Evidence of corporate activity may forestall or mollify subsequent strictures.
>
> It is less costly in the long run to "get on the learning curve" before an issue has congealed and while social advocates are also groping to understand it.

The promise of such anticipated benefits is not necessarily compelling to operating managers who absorb the immediate burden, financial or otherwise, of responsiveness. Were he permitted the luxury of free access to his organization, the chief executive would find widespread skepticism. Yet, given the current status of environmental forecasting, it is probable that he will have little more to offer initially as inducements to gain internal support for a social policy.

Institutionalizing the Response Process

In the absence of conclusive economic argument, the chief executive has the difficult task of creating a climate in which the assumed benefits to the firm of involvement are viewed as credible and ultimately worthwhile. Using Selznick's language, this task implies institutionalizing the response to social change. Two elements in doing so should be noted.

First, consistency in arguing the merits of aggressive involvement is of great importance. Although policy statements, by themselves, were seen to be largely ineffective, they were nonetheless essential features of the process. Operating managers monitored the signals received at management meetings and on corporate reviews of capital requests and business plans for changes in the firm's posture. Of particular significance to them were perceived differences in viewpoint between the chief executive and the individual(s) thought to be in line for succession. The hint of a divergence, particularly near the end of a chief executive's tenure, was cause for a "wait and see" attitude in the organization. While the manifestations of this perception were not immediately apparent, the specialist introduced during Phase II often found his efforts severely impeded by it.

Consequently, the decision to embrace a social policy should not be viewed as the chief executive's alone. The time may not be his to see the response process through to conclusion. He is well advised to test beforehand the support that would be given to the policy, at least by the likely candidates for his office. If apathy or resistance is encountered, the prognosis for implementation is decidedly less favorable. One reason for the success in introducing change at both BPC and Weston was that in each case the chief executive and his heir apparent were perceived to be in close agreement on the issue involved, an impression that no doubt had some impact on the managers directly beneath them as well. Going one step further, it is possible that the most powerful endorsement for corporate responsiveness is an impression that it plays a part in the selection of the next chief executive.

Second, corporate-level efforts to communicate commitment may produce a degree of anxiety at middle levels in the organization that should be understood and, where possible, abated. It is, of course, difficult to hedge commitment and still present a convincing picture of aggressive forward progress. By the same token, it is easy to overestimate the current state of knowledge and the organization's amenability to change. Policy does, and should, run ahead of implementation, but too large a gap in time and achievement may create unfulfilled expectations among activist groups that result in unproductive pressure on the firm. Activists have often directed attention to companies with reputations for social responsiveness. In fact, one can fairly argue that the more a chief executive talks about the corporation's intentions, the more likely he is to draw fire from those anxious to hold him to this word.

While absorbing increased (and seemingly inevitable) demands may be the price of leadership, the risks of forcing response to external threats in a Phase I posture may be high. There is a serious danger of undercutting the authority of operating managers before they have acquired the skills to manage the process. The chief executive, faced with a public complaint, may swoop into the divisions to redress the grievance himself. Activist groups are then naturally encouraged to press for continued action from the chief executive rather than from the managers who must ultimately respond to their demands. Corporate intervention may be productive later on, after the issue is reasonably well understood and systems have been designed to manage it. But at this early stage, the operating units are ill-equipped to reassert their initiative once it has been upset.

The managers experiencing the highest anxiety in the beginning frequently appeared to be in functional departments at division levels and below, such as personnel, engineering, and product development, which related directly to the issue. These managers felt the need to develop programs that would lend substance to the policy but had little success in securing a place for it in the unit's budget or in gaining the attention of line management. Nonetheless, criticism for insufficient adherence to the spirit of the corporate commitment was likely to fall on them. One division personnel manager in this position commented:

> Top management statements can really hurt. There is a gap between what they [top management] say we are and the way it is, our black employees tell me, and it's vast. There aren't enough resources to fulfill our public commitments. We have intense pressure for performance. I had to cut $5,000 from the travel budget that my industrial relations manager was going to use to recruit minorities. . . Without a doubt, this is the most unrewarding assignment I've ever had — the emotional cost is terrific.

A remedy, aside from simply delaying the expression of corporate intentions, may not be fully attainable. However, acknowledging that the definition of policy is only the first of a sequence of planned steps in corporate adaptation may reduce frustration at operating levels and hasten the infusion of corporate resources. The anticipation of subsequent phases may also serve to moderate corporate public pronouncements and internal criticism. In short, to the extent the chief executive is able to communicate how the process for responding to social change is to be institutionalized he may increase the organization's tolerance for adaptation.

Organizational Learning and the Specialist

If responding to social expectations were accomplished solely by changing management attitudes and reordering the priorities governing operating decisions, the process would no doubt be substantially different from the one described here. Adaptation, however, requires the assimilation of new skills, relationships, and information as well. Since the requisite time and experience are typically lacking in existing functions, new positions are created to acquire and distribute specialized knowledge. The corporate-level specialist plays a particularly important part in drawing together external demands, corporate policy, and operating decisions. He is in a very real sense an agent of change through whom the organization learns to negotiate with an unfamiliar and sometimes threatening environment. He is also in a highly vulnerable position from which to launch an assault on the indifference or resistance that often awaits in the operating divisions.

The question raised by the specialist is one of increasing importance for the management of the large corporation: how should specialized skills be introduced in organizations dominated by generalists? I have argued that a forceful response to social demands requires strong direction from the corporate level. The specialist is the cutting edge used by the chief executive to narrow the gap between his expectations and operating realities. To the extent this edge is blunted, the chief executive loses a critical source of influence in managing the response process. In fact, without the prior efforts of the specialist, the chief executive would be hard-pressed to insist on implementation. On the other hand, permitting the specialist to direct implementation at operating levels himself tends to subvert an otherwise useful general management focus. Were powerful specialist roles created for numerous social issues, the impact on the organization could be dramatic.

In most corporations, this question has not been satisfactorily answered. There is a pronounced tendency among specialists dealing with social issues to fail or at least to experience severe frustration. The cause of failure is typically ascribed by the specialist to an intransigent organization that is unwilling to grasp the severity of

the social demand and possibly a chief executive who is not sufficiently supportive. Further investigation may reveal incidents that
precipitated sharp reversals for the specialist in confrontations with
operating management. Feeling let down and convinced that meaningful change is not soon forthcoming, he either leaves the firm or
retreats to the safety of the headquarters offices and busies himself
with administrative matters and external affairs.

The frustrations encountered by the specialist are in part endemic
to corporate staff in the divisionalized organization.[12] Yet because of
the dynamics of an evolving social issue, the degree of learning
required, and the probable resistance among operating managers,
the social issue specialist may be in a more tenuous position than his
staff counterparts. To manage this phase of the response process in
a manner that permits a meaningful specialist role to survive calls
attention to three sensitive areas: (1) introducing the specialist; (2)
managing the specialist's job; and (3) designing a corporate specialist capability.

Introducing the Specialist
In Chapter V three critical choices were identified in creating the
specialist position having to do with (a) the characteristics of the
individual selected, (b) his assignment to an existing department or
the establishment of a new one, and (c) his relationship to the chief
executive. A satisfactory resolution of these issues at Weston and
BPC evolved only gradually.

At Weston, the specialist had little formal standing at the outset.
The environmental control section remained nestled in the large
central engineering organization. Moreover, the position was given
to an engineer who had no experience in ecology and little visibility
in the company. Although he was supported by clear corporate
intentions, he did not enjoy close contact with top management. On
all three counts the specialist's position was underplayed; it is not
surprising that he encountered difficulty from time to time in securing access and cooperation from the operating divisions.

The initial design at BPC was different, although the results were
similar. In this case, the first minority relations specialist was a man
familiar with the aims of the civil rights movement but unfamiliar
with the workings of a large corporation. Although his office reported through the personnel organization, his job was designed to

permit an independent expression of minority issues. The personal attention given to these matters by the chief executive held the prospect of frequent contact between the specialist and top management. In contrast to Weston, the specialist was provided with high visibility and some implied degree of influence. Implementation lagged, however, in part because the specialist was unable to relate his efforts to the needs of operating managers; both the specialist and his position may have been overly differentiated from the remainder of the organization.[13]

After several years the specialist's position was redesigned in each corporation through changes in structure and personnel. At Weston a top-rated young manufacturing manager was promoted to the new position of Vice President of Environmental Affairs. Under this umbrella, the effectiveness of the original specialist increased rapidly. At BPC, equal employment figured prominently in the selection of a Corporate Vice President of Personnel, and he in turn appointed a high-performing personnel manager from an operating unit to assume responsibility for this area.

The revisions in each company augmented the specialist's importance and relevance to the operating divisions in a number of ways:

  (a) The new "specialists" had strong backgrounds in traditional functions and were consequently familiar with the concerns of managers in the operating units.

  (b) The positions were given status and credibility because they were occupied by individuals assumed, on the basis of past records, to be progressing along accelerated career trajectories.

  (c) The relationship between specialist and chief executive was strengthened by elevating the specialist's position in the organization (Weston) or giving the issue top priority with a key corporate executive (BPC).

Thus the design of the specialist's position requires careful attention to personal considerations. The incumbent must be acceptable to both operating managers and social activists, including government regulators and technical experts. The prognosis for a new department staffed by outsiders with backgrounds and skills related to the issue is generally not very good. Nor is the prognosis much better if junior managers without prior relevant experience are assigned to specialists' jobs in an established corporate staff group.

Ironically, skills as a manager may be a more accurate predictor of the specialist's performance than technical excellence or issue-related reputation. Locating an individual with both qualities is clearly not always feasible. However, some companies have had success through pairing individuals with complementary skills, backgrounds, and cognitive or problem-solving styles.

Managing the Specialist's Role

A source of frustration among specialists is the quest for a clarity and stability in their assignments that in fact may not be attainable. The specialist role is highly ambiguous, a characteristic that in this case may be a benefit to those who can tolerate and utilize it. While they may prefer to view themselves as experts and facilitators, they may in fact need to be equally politicians and negotiators. Implications for the specialist are found in a diagnosis of the relationships to be managed and the tasks to be performed.

The corporate specialist operates in a web of relationships—depicted in simplified form in Exhibit X-2—which link external agencies, corporate management, and division management. These relationships should be carefully understood for they are typically multidimensional. On the other hand, external demands and corporate commitment provide the initial impetus for change. The stronger they are, the more influence the specialist is likely to have in pressing the operating units to apply resources to lifting the constraints limiting responsiveness. But, on the other hand, the specialist is implicitly held responsible for keeping social expectations, corporate policy, and operating realities in some sort of balance in a dynamic environment. Although he has little or no authority over any of the parties involved, he has a vital concern in their relationships with one another.

Consequently, the specialist must be a politician; he must manage relationships he cannot directly control. For instance, the environmental control director may want more (or less) attention given to the issue in business plan reviews or in speeches before the Chamber of Commerce. He may attempt to stage the negotiations between social agencies and operating managers. In one instance, an equal

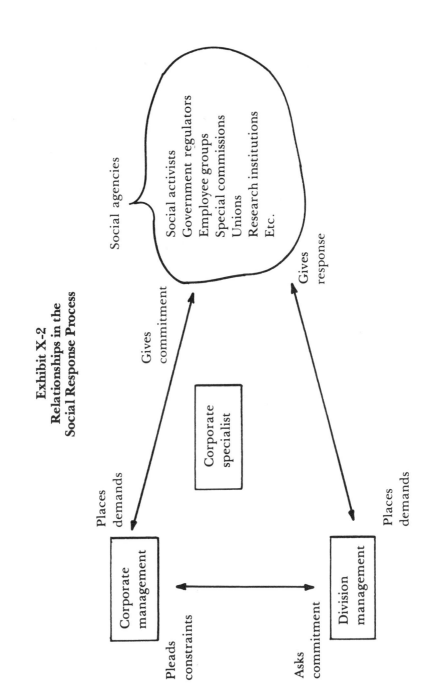

Exhibit X-2
Relationships in the
Social Response Process

employment director even advised the government compliance agency that an audit of one unit would be helpful! To perform this function, the specialist needs an intimate knowledge of the motivations, concerns, and goals of each party to this network. He must know the depth of the chief executive's commitment, the budget problems and career concerns of operating managers, and the political pressures on the representatives of social agencies (employee leaders, regulators, activists, and so forth).

The specialist must also be a skilled negotiator. For if he totes up the mandate given to his office, it generally does not put him in a position to force response on anyone. At this stage in the process, neither corporate policy nor social demands carry overbearing sanctions for noncompliance—he cannot say to operating managers, "Do it!" As a result, the specialist bargains for support and responsiveness. With social agencies he argues the company's case and promises compliance in return for favorable treatment; with operating managers he uses the results of outside negotiations plus technical help to obtain information and personal assistance for the support of his office. The relationships in Exhibit X-3 are highly interdependent; if one breaks down, all are likely to suffer. In each relationship the role assumed by the specialist may be cooperative or combative; to the extent the latter is chosen, however, he confronts a new set of complexities. Although friends may be difficult to win, enemies can be ill-afforded. As one wise specialist commented: "The point you have to remember is that if you are serious about winning the war, you can't afford to get killed in a skirmish."

The specialist may well ask, "Whom do I represent? The community? The operating managers? The president?" The answer may well be all of them. Hence, the role is ambiguous, a characteristic that the resourceful specialist may use to establish a measure of independence that prevents him from being typed as captive to one set of pressures. Perhaps more than any other manager in the firm, he needs an explicit strategy for the conduct of his department that encompasses both the dictates of the environment and the constraints cast up by the organization.

Designing a Corporate Specialist Capacity

The role of the specialist changes as the social issue and the corporation's response to it mature. The initiative for action quite

Exhibit X-3
Corporate Social Issue Specialist
Transactions

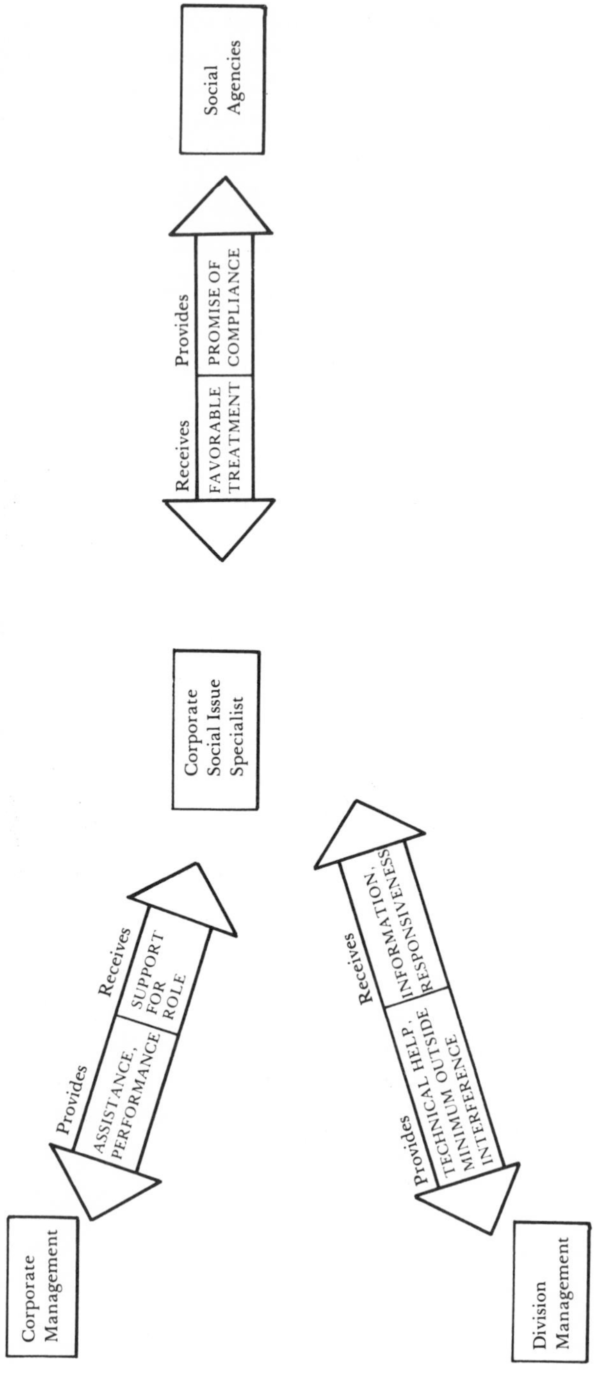

rightly passes from his hands to those of operating managers who often employ their own specialists. The corporate specialist, if successful, plays a major part in making this transition possible by two process-related achievements:

Sensitizing operating managers to the social demand and providing them with the technical capability to manage it at their level.

Designing the administrative systems that permit corporate managers to set standards, controls and performance measures.

In effect, these contributions prepare the issue for implementation in a form that is familiar to both operating and corporate managers.

The transition to Phase III raises an interesting question: What is the function of a corporate specialist as response becomes institutionalized? There is clearly the danger, both for the corporation and the specialist, that he will cling too long to a role that was appropriate in Phase II. Such behavior will almost certainly result in confusion and conflict that will probably not long be tolerated. In broad terms, there are two plausible alternatives: (a) the residual tasks of coordinating and managing the reporting system, providing legal and technical counsel, and so on, may be reassigned to existing staff units and the specialist's position discontinued; or (b) the specialist may retain these residual duties and be assigned other social issues that are entering Phase II.

The choice determines the configuration of the response mechanism the corporation is to maintain at the corporate level. Adopting the first alternative points toward a succession of specialists in temporary positions which exist for perhaps three to six years and are then folded into the traditional organization. The second envisages a multipurpose corporate specialist whose job is to process issues one after another. Both Weston and BPC exhibited signs of adopting the second approach; the environmental control director at Weston was becoming involved in product safety, and the minority relations specialist at BPC was quickly embroiled in female employment problems as concern for that issue developed. Yet, spreading the specialist's responsibility over a variety of issues may dilute his efforts and over-extend his capability to deal with substantively different responses. There are obvious implications in this decision for the chief executive as he considers the career aspirations and skills appropriate to those selected as specialists.

Obtaining Organizational Commitment

The number of companies with corporate social issue specialists almost certainly exceeds by a wide margin the number in which operating management will be committed to responsiveness before action is mandated or generally accepted in practice. The transition to Phase III in the response process is difficult and in some respects costly. If achieved, however, the results are of considerable significance for the large corporation for two reasons.

First, a corporate purpose that is more complex than simply growth in earnings has been institutionalized. The chief executive has succeeded in converting a social concern into a factor influencing business decisions throughout the organization.

Second, the process for implementing social policy which heretofore had been driven by corporate initiative, is transformed into one characterized by problem definition and resolution at lower levels, with ratification and measurement at the top. Decisions are then made in a fashion that is customary to the divisionalized corporation. In effect, the critical assessments involving the balance between social and economic purposes are eventually decentralized after an interlude during which a social issue has been lifted up for examination and emphasis by the chief executive.

Implications for management are found both in the transition to Phase III and the administration of responsiveness once that stage in evolution has been attained.

The Implications of Trauma

In my observation the transition to Phase III was consistently accompanied by one or more incidents that traumatized portions of the organization. Trauma may seem to some readers too strong a term to describe the events reported in Chapters VII and IX. I invite the skeptic to return to those incidents and place himself or herself in the position of Daryl Roman, Regional Vice President of BPC, or Jim Bush, the Division Manager in Weston, and consider the situation through his eyes. From the perspective of an outside observer, the problems may seem of no particular or lasting consequence. However, for the operating manager confronted with protesting employees or technological and political uncertainties, the dangers loom far larger. Most significantly, the shock of being enmeshed in a highly visible situation that could have unpleasant consequences sparked the realization that the social demand and the corporation's reaction to it was of direct and immediate significance to him. It could not be avoided or left to others. Yet, these findings raise a number of important questions. First, is trauma inevitable? It is readily acknowledged that more peaceful means of effecting change may be available; in time, managers may know enough about how to employ them effectively in the large corporation. But, I suggest that under current circumstances, trauma is highly probable. In particular, this assertion is made with respect to corporations that have elected to respond aggressively to social demands. They do so when immediate action is largely voluntary and before general consensus has developed on the social issue, let alone on how to deal with it. Social change is forced on the organization, and differences in perceptions and values among managers are virtually assured. Moreover, pressure for performance as historically measured is likely to continue unabated. As operating managers cast about for ways of reconciling conflicting demands, they find no precedents that point to acceptable compromises or remedies. Their response is almost certain to be disputed by some of the parties involved. Trauma results from the absence of an accepted means of containing the dispute and the eventual participation in it of their superiors.

Second, is trauma useful? The answer, on balance, is again yes. In a practical sense, behavior following the incident was demonstrably different from what it had been before; operating managers were observed to assign a higher priority to the corporate social policy and to take direct steps to insure that it was considered in the affairs of their units. In short, they took responsibility for its implementation. Two less tangible benefits were also noted:

> News of the incident was informally and widely communicated in the organization. An appreciation of top management intentions may be more forcefully acquired through tangible events than through statements of policy.

> Resolution of the problem constituted valuable precedents on (a) the standards and compromises acceptable to corporate management, and (b) the due process to be observed in resolving future incidents. Ambiguities in responsibility were appreciably reduced.

Third, is trauma costly? Once again the answer is likely to be yes. There is the ever-present danger that operating managers caught up in the incident will be harshly sanctioned for behavior that up to that point had been tacitly condoned. Although the chairman in BPC had alerted management some months earlier that performance appraisals would reflect progress in minority affairs, there was no interpretation of this statement that his subordinates could consult. Some incident had to serve as an example. The President of BPC was clearly aware of that implication when he noted that the Elmsford Distribution Center problem would probably not be the last of its kind.

Traumatic episodes are perilous for the specialists as well. They are liable to be caught in a crossfire between division and corporate management that can destroy the effectiveness of their working relationships with both parties. Suffice it to say that the level of anxiety created by strong corporate intervention is high for all concerned.

There are a number of implications in this discussion for the management of the response process. First, traumas should not be a common indulgence. Indeed, the impression created by the experience is magnified by its rarity. Both the chief executive and the specialist should think beyond their immediate actions in the event that a situation tempts top management involvement. It should be clear from the earlier analysis that intervention in Phase I or the early days of Phase II will not have the same impact on the organization as intervention later, after the systems and response capability is available to sustain full responsibility at middle levels.

Second, clear indications that performance expectations have changed should be communicated to the organization when top management is prepared to move to Phase III. This suggestion is more easily written here than implemented. A policy statement relating social responsiveness to performance appraisals will almost certainly seem ambiguous to those affected by it. For instance, managers in BPC could not determine, from the Chairman's letter of July 1972, just how important minority relations activities were to be in their performance reviews. Indeed, at the time, no one had a precise position on that issue. Moreover, there are obvious risks associated with attempts to reduce this ambiguity. The response in the Graphic Systems Division was to allocate 15 percent of the manager's bonus calculation to equal employment opportunity efforts. Was this percentage too much or too little? Was precision in evaluation likely to force a quantification in the basis for measurement? If so, employment figures, the logical yardstick in this case, may not really reflect the quality of opportunity offered. Despite these problems, the personal stakes for managers must be raised to secure the implementation of corporate policy. Making this point explicit and acknowledging that truly appropriate yardsticks will only emerge through experience will alert the organization and may serve to reduce the anxiety encountered in responding to social demands.

Third, the management of test cases offers important opportunities for learning in the organization. Seldom, however, are the events replayed for the benefit of both the participants in the incident and their interested, but inevitably partially informed, colleagues. A willingness to be open about what happened, how such situations might be handled when they arise again, and so forth, would be of great value in fashioning the ground rules that are to guide the organization's behavior in the future. Moreover, explicitly recognizing the incident as a test case may provide a means for easing the personal costs levied on those unfortunate enough to have been enmeshed in it.

Finally, the passing of a crisis at this point in the response process is cause for taking stock of how the corporation is organized to deal with the social demand. Ironically, the opportunity may well be at hand to reinforce the responsibility of operating managers for implementing the social policy. Are they able and willing now to assume that posture? If so, the roles of corporate management and the specialist are also due for revision. The objective at this point should be to prevent future incidents from causing trauma, and to move rapidly toward a systematic approach to managing responsiveness which fully utilizes the resources and energy of the operating units.

Toward a Steady State

I have argued that crisis, although perhaps appearing at the time to be costly and unproductive, may in fact be an opportunity to develop a long-term solution to the problems of incorporating social responsiveness in operating decisions. Sculpturing a process which places responsibility for implementation at operating levels implies the need for changes in role and perspective for both corporate and operating management.

The most obvious implication for corporate management of moving to Phase III is the need for restraint and trust. The operating units are almost certain to devise programs which miscarry or appear stupid to the corporate specialist; employee councils may backfire, new technologies may prove unproductive, and so forth. At the same time, they may also develop highly effective innovations which are beyond the capability of a central staff department to implement, such as detailed employment audits, manufacturing process changes, and the like. This is not to say that the corporate specialist should disengage from the social issue entirely. Matters demanding uniform treatment in the firm or having potential firm-wide ramifications should, of course, receive the continued attention of corporate managers. In the long run, however, they should exercise the same degree of involvement here that they do in other facets of the business. As environmental uncertainties are reduced, the judgments necessary to manage the response to specific social issues are probably no more complex than those accompanying new product or process developments.

Despite a more restrained posture, corporate management has the opportunity to negotiate performance standards and evaluate the results of operating unit implementation efforts. The critical need of developing systematic bases for assessing performance has been dwelt on at length. But there is another dimension to this issue that has not yet been addressed. For perhaps the first time, the chief executive is able to ask, "Are we spending or doing too much?" without sounding a death knell for social involvement. As this question is raised, an important step is taken toward blending the social demand into the fabric of business strategy. An example may clarify the point.

Some months after the events at Weston described in Chapters VI and VII, the corporate plan for 1973 was completed and approved. The President observed that a sizable proportion of capital expenditures for the corporation — over 20 percent in some divisions — was consumed by pollution control projects, and the near future boded still further increases. He requested a study from the planning staff (not the environmental specialist) of the implications of this trend on the profitability necessary in the remainder of the capital budget to sustain the over-all yield he considered necessary for the corporation. The results were sufficiently disquieting that he asked his staff to repeat the presentation for each of the operating divisions. He did so in the belief that the environmental policy had become institutionalized to the point that his managers would not immediately set out to dismantle it.

For the middle-level general manager, the transition to Phase III is perhaps more demanding. In particular three actions are suggested by these findings.

The first is a comparatively easy one: Skills requisite for response to the social issue must be brought to bear on the specific situation in the unit. This probably implies hiring or developing specialists. Designing and filling those slots is not likely to involve the complexities described earlier with installing the corporate specialist. The assignments are very different. The division specialists report (perhaps indirectly) to a general manager who integrates operating functions and is directly responsible for the achievement of a business plan. The specialists may not always win their arguments, but at least they are officially members of the team that decides on implementation. If they lose in spite of sound analysis, responsibility for the outcome clearly lies with their general manager. Relationships are enormously simplified, and loyalties are less subject to conflicting pressures. Consequently, the general manager may have more latitude to choose specialists with technical excellence without as much concern for their facility in handling organizational conflict.

Second, the middle level general manager has the enormously difficult task of revising the method of measuring and rewarding the performance of his subordinates. The task may seem both painful and risky. One newly appointed division manager who had recently heard of a minority relations dispute in one of his plants, reflected on his dilemma in these terms:

> To be honest, I haven't been too successful in getting the organization interested in the problem. If you took a poll among my managers in this division, most of them would say, "I'd rather not be bothered with it." It hasn't helped that we've had some tough experiences in the past. For instance, we had two black salesmen in other divisions who left for better opportunities elsewhere. . . . It's easy to point to that as an example. . . . How can I rip

into my best branch manager for not meeting a minority hiring quota? He's liable to say, "The hell with it," and go over to the competition. With his sales record, he'd probably have no trouble making the switch either.

　. . . Changing the attitudes of management people is tough. If you insist on naming their employees, you've given them a built-in excuse for poor performance. These are emotional issues that conflict with their view of their jobs, which is pretty simlistic—targets, profits, and so forth. . . I have to figure out a way to say to the organization, "This is in both your interest and the company's interest." If I knew how to do it, I would. . . The way to solve the equal employment problem is to set quotas. But if you ask, "Have you set them?" I'd have to say, "No." If you ask, "When are you going to?" I'd have to say, "I don't know."

The step the division manager refers to above is not an easy one to take. It is at this point that the process is most likely to break down. Although the manager may have adequate systems available to track and audit performance and clear justification for doing so from the chief executive, implementation ultimately rests on his willingness to add this burden to those already borne by his subordinates.

Finally, the general manager assumes responsibility for integrating social and economic goals. The equation used to gauge his effectiveness has been enlarged, as well as the fields in which he is to exercise judgment. In most large corporations, middle-level general managers have heretofore been protected from external forces— aside from those of the marketplace—by corporate staff departments and a public which has woefully underestimated the significance of the organization. Often, chief executives have attained their positions by performing admirably in assignments which have been effectively insulated from social demands. Careers sheltered from public view are less likely to be encountered in the future. The intrusion of social concerns will have a cumulative impact on the complexity of the middle manager's job. There is a tremendous need to instill attitudes and develop skills in middle managers that will enable them to cope with the administrative consequences of social responsiveness. It is not at all clear that traditional executive development programs and business school curricula have as yet taken full cognizance of this need.

XI
Toward a Strategy for Social Responsiveness

Thus far I have conveniently ignored the problems created by the multiplicity of social issues simultaneously impinging on the typical large corporation. A chief executive, however, does not often have the privilege of disposing of issues one at a time; they break over the firm willy-nilly as the product of a complex and highly diverse society. Moreover, the firm's posture on individual issues is likely to vary considerably.

For instance, Weston Industries, in addition to pollution control, was grappling with product safety, occupational health and safety, equal employment, and solid wastes as near-term concerns. Although no formal decision had been communicated with respect to their relative importance, some enjoyed a higher priority in the minds of operating managers than others. In some instances, Weston appeared to be following the pattern observed in Chapters VI and VII in pollution control. In others the chief executive had identified the issue as a target for aggressive response, but had, as yet, been unsuccessful in obtaining the necessary commitment from his operating managers for implementing action. And in still others, corporate management had taken the position that the issue was essentially a "local problem," which meant that a concerted effort to manage response from the top was not forthcoming.

Variability in the speed and scope of response to different social issues is probably inevitable and even desirable. The corporation must be alert to shifting priorities among its numerous constituencies and, as I will illustrate later, has a limited capacity to impel the implementation of leadership positions. Yet a weakness observable in many instances is the absence of a thorough assessment of just where the corporation stands on the social demands of relevance to it. The result is often a "cookbook" of very general corporate policies and isolated programs that are imperfectly understood (or disregarded) by the operating units and poorly monitored by the central office.

Ultimately, I believe the corporation should develop a strategy to govern social responsiveness. A useful model would encompass the answer to two questions: (a) Which social demands are of sufficient importance to warrant a corporate-wide implementation effort? (b) Should this effort have as its goal above-average or higher than currently required performance? The strategy should also be sufficiently detailed that the chief executive can determine if the response to individual demands is progressing as intended.

The reader should hold no illusions that such a strategy can be precisely developed or easily managed. Nonetheless, careful study would reveal that some semblance of a strategy has already evolved in most large corporations, in part through intention and in part by default. For instance, a profile such as the one in Exhibit XI-1 would not be atypical, though of course specific issues and assessments would vary widely from company to company. The task for the chief executive and his staff may initially be one of evaluating and possibly redirecting what already exists. The analysis required to construct a profile of this sort bears elaboration, for it constitutes a form of social audit that is highly relevant for measuring the strategic response to social change.

The Process Audit

Bauer and Fenn, after describing the difficulty of accurately determining social costs and benefits, suggested the development of a "process audit" to reflect performance in areas which present severe measurement problems. Such an audit would reflect "the reason for undertaking a particular program, the rationale for action, a description of what is actually being done and intermediate measures of performance if they are available."[1] The procedure proposed here is a variant of this suggestion. For each social issue, performance indicators would be sought along two dimensions, one related to process and the other to results.

Process

The first type of information is intended to answer the question, "How is the firm's response to specific social issues being managed?" The answer for each issue may fall into one of three broad categories corresponding to the phases in the response process:

> (a) through corporate-level activities, perhaps supported by a policy but without a specialist group assigned to it;

Exhibit XI-1
Corporate Social Issue Profile

Social Issues	Phases in Response Process		
	I	II	III
Air & Water Pollution			▶
Equal Employment		■	
Solid Wastes		▶	
Occupational Health and Safety		◀	
Job Enrichment	■		
Product Safety	▶		

Relation to Standard Industry Practice

▶ Lead

■ Equal

◀ Lag

(b) through a specialist group operating more or less independently of normal operating functions;

(c) through the operating managers in charge of normal functions.

Variations in the status of response to different issues and among operating units on the same issue at the time of the audit should be expected. An adequate investigation may necessitate the construction of a history of the corporation's involvement, especially if the significance of transitions is to be recognized. The reasons for differential treatment among divisions should be carefully diagnosed for they may hold the key to more effective implementation. Why did one division pick up the issue before another? Was it the nature or location of the business? Or the inclinations and leadership skills of the general manager or someone on his staff? Or was it some action or program initiated by the corporate staff? The answers will provide an indication of the sources of resistance and innovation in the organization and preliminary approaches for dealing with them.

A number of more detailed questions should also be included. For instance, if response is generally in Phase II, the audit should indicate the personal profiles of the corporate specialists; the status of efforts to develop an information system; the breadth of research into potential technologies or other remedies; the method of identifying problems and responding to external demands; the relationship between the social issue and relevant operating decisions—for example, pollution control and capital budgeting; and the attitudes of corporate and division management with respect to the issue and the firm's posture on it.

The inquiry may then be extended by asking, "How well is the process being managed?" Again, for Phase II response status it would be useful to know how effectively the specialist is managing his relationships with the operating divisions, how useful the information system is for management control purposes, the degree of success experienced in resolving controversies with regulators or public interest groups, and the extent of concern for the issue in business decisions. On the basis of such an evaluation, the chief executive could begin to isolate problem areas and opportunities for improvement in the management process.

Results

The second type of information relates to the basic question, "What has the corporation done to respond to the social demand?" The results would, of course, be more extensive for issues in Phases II and III than for those just recently identified. For the former, records may be prescribed by law (e.g., equal employment, work safety, etc.), while for the latter a simple narrative of isolated activities may be all that is available. One must, of course, be wary of the validity of statistical measures. As in the case of employee demographics and absentee reports in the BPC Elmsford Distribution Center, the figures may be unreliable, even misleading, indices of social performance. If relied on too heavily, operating managers may produce the requisite numbers without commensurate attention to the quality of the over-all results achieved.

An historical perspective may also be useful as an indication of trends. Discontinuities are particularly interesting. Did the proportion of minorities in the work force decrease during the 1970 and 1975 recessions? Were spending plans for pollution control equipment affected by the energy shortage in 1974? On the other hand, trend lines do not, by themselves, reflect performance accurately. For instance, most large corporations have a greater proportion of minorities in skilled and managerial positions today than a decade ago, yet some are doing a far more effective job of promoting equal employment than others. More critical questions phrase the issue in relative terms. Was the increase more or less than might have been attained? Or than the firm sought to achieve?

An extension of these questions, then, is "How does the company's performance in each area compare with that of a suitable reference group?" The reference group may vary from issue to issue, in some cases defined by comparable company or industry experience and in others by more generalized data. The exercise may not always produce hard comparisons because evidence may be very sketchy or viewed by others as proprietary. Nevertheless, this exercise forces attention to be given explicitly to the development of standards and provides another basis, in addition to internal trends, for measuring the corporation's performance.

The reader will recall that the stated purpose of the process audit is to provide the chief executive with a snapshot of the firm's posture on a spectrum of social issues as a step in the formulation of a social responsiveness strategy. It would, of course, be beneficial to have the work done thoroughly and with the full cooperation of the operating units. However, the procedure is pragmatic and may also be performed "on the back of an envelope," so to speak. The audit has served its usefulness when the chief executive is satisfied. In subsequent years, the same device may be employed to evaluate progress in both process and results, and in all likelihood would gradually become more detailed and sophisticated.

Organizational Constraints on Strategy

Deciding which social demands are worth responding to on an aggressive, corporate-wide basis is an important managerial decision for the chief executive. The process described in this book places considerable strain on the organization. There are two points that are particularly susceptible to overload—the chief executive's attention and the performance appraisal system. Looked at the other way around, these are two resources that should be apportioned to social demands with great care.

There are several factors moderating the chief executive's pursuit of corporate social policy. Personal considerations, including background and affinity for varying issues and sheer physical energy, may constrain his willingness or ability to assume a role in leading social expectations. The time required to manage the response to even a single issue is considerable; the task of demonstrating interest in a number of different areas of social concern is enormous. Moreover, there are already signs that the chief executive's agenda is in danger of becoming overloaded.[2] The vast increase in legal action alone has added a significant burden to the office.[3] Complexity in the environment directly impinging on the corporate leader is unlikely to abate.

The number of social issues that can be raised simultaneously to prominent positions in the evaluation system is, I suspect, also limited. For instance, Graham Moore was keenly aware of the pressure he had placed on his operating managers to advance minorities in BPC. Although he was anxious to move with dispatch on opportunities for women, he was concerned about the capacity of the organization to absorb further change with the same intensity before the minority issue was well in hand.

The chief executive may also be presumed to have an interest in protecting the integrity of his office; to manage Phases I and II of the process in a leadership posture only to falter in executing Phase III can only serve to weaken the responsiveness of operating units to corporate policy.[4] A recognition of the dilemmas discussed at length in Chapter IV may consequently tend to limit corporate choice. The chief executive may intuitively shrink from announcing commitments he suspects will be difficult to implement. As a result, it is not unreasonable to expect moderation in the number of issues to be aggressively pursued.

This argument may be extended one step further. Earlier it was noted that some firms maintain a more receptive attitude toward social demands than others. Often these have been enterprises with above-average records of growth and profitability.

Two explanations are typically given for this association of riches and good works; first, wealth is available to support social policies, and second, profitability correlates highly with "good managers," who are presumably more sensitive to the business implications of social trends. While both arguments undoubtedly have merit, neither is wholly satisfying. It is certainly true that the firm in dire financial straits will exhibit little interest in pursuing social programs. However, it is naïve to contend that the spending latitude granted to operating managers in the growth company is necessarily more permissive than in a firm with a stagnant record. In fact, the profit center manager in the former may be under greater short-term financial pressure to meet a bloated growth target than his counterpart in the latter, who may be charged with simply holding market share. In the second instance, one wonders about the quality of management in highly profitable companies in which little attention is paid to social responsiveness. How is a "good manager" characterized to support the argument without reducing it to a tautology?

A third explanation is suggested by this research. It is bound up in the proposition that managers in large organizations differ in their receptivity to central direction, which in turn defines the capacity of the chief executive to manage the response to social change.

Accepting responsibility for implementing corporate social policy requires the operating manager to accept added burdens. In the companies we observed, financial expectations were rarely lowered. The operating manager was expected to score points on multiple scorecards with an imperfect understanding of how the points were aggregated. If requests that resulted in increased work load and ambiguity in measurement were to be taken seriously, the operating manager had to see that compliance was of importance to him personally. The earlier case studies illustrated that concern in the organization increased dramatically as soon as it became apparent that performance evaluation was at stake.

It follows now that responsiveness may vary directly with the chief executive's ability (and willingness) to extend rewards and levy sanctions on operating managers. In this regard, the chief executive of the profitable, fast-growing corporation enjoys an enormous natural advantage. The number of new positions and the steady enlargement of existing responsibilities create opportunities for the middle manager that motivate him to respond to *whatever* requirements his superiors place on him as long as he is convinced they are truly serious. The ultimate rewards for doing so appear both large and attainable; the bargain seems equitable. I do not imply that growing firms are necessarily more responsive to social trends. However, the leaders of such corporations have a greater variety of available choices, not simply because they have funds per se, but because corporate expectations are more likely to receive attention in the organization.

Contrast this situation with that of a large but stagnant firm. The upward movement of executives is likely to be more limited and the stakes resting on performance evaluation commensurately less. For instance, what can a plant manager under such circumstances be offered that will induce him to accept a stiff equal employment target that he feels will be unpopular with his organization? Corporate aggressiveness may be confined by the scope of the available rewards. To simply place penalties on noncompliance may create an imbalance in the plant manager's view of personal incentives that will prompt his resignation.[5]

There are other means of shaping the incentives in an organization to foster adherence to corporate expectations on social responsiveness (or anything else for that matter) that do not depend on an expanding pool of opportunity. They range from the magnetism of a charismatic leader to the harshness of a reward system that grants high benefits in terms of compensation and influence to those executives who comply with corporate expectations and casts out the remainder. One implication of reallocating a limited stock of incentives to the achievement of social policy is probably a drift toward centralization of the firm.

The argument in the last paragraph takes an intriguing twist by extending it one step further. For just as there are risks involved in overloading the evaluation and incentive systems, so too are there dangers in failing to extend them enough. Consider the following example:

In 1973 the Bank of California was charged by a consortium of advocacy groups with a widespread failure to provide opportunities for minorities and women in management. The bank was placed under a court order which, among other strictures, provided that at least 60 percent of the promotions in officer and manager categories would be granted to qualified minorities and women. By 1982 specific goals were set for each management level at 9 percent blacks, 14 percent Spanish-surnamed, and 37 percent women.

The threat of externally imposed compliance may be less in the financial burden it places on the corporation than on its impact on the corporate office. Imagine what the above action portends for the performance evaluation system and the distribution of incentives in the Bank of California! The effect of external incursions into operating decisions may be the erosion of the leadership role of the chief executive, a role that has at its core the discretion to set standards and allocate rewards in the firm.

Formulating a Strategy for Corporate Responsiveness

Students of business policy have long recognized a fundamental flaw in the economist's assumptions about the role of profits in the firm.[6] In theory, how the firm is organized and how it allocates resources should be the function of a strategy for maximizing profits which weighs environmental risks and opportunities and corporate resources. Apart from the implausibility of maximizing anything as complex as a corporate strategy, such a line of reasoning is generally not descriptive. In fact, in the large corporation it often has reality just backwards. Instead, the organization and the process for allocating resources frequently produces results which, over time, shape the firm's strategy.

The response to social demands appears from my observation to be particularly subject to the influence of incremental decisions and organizational arrangements. To a large extent this sequence is understandable. The chief executive and his staff nose their way through a murky environment that discourages long-range planning and analysis. Early statements of policy typically represent their efforts to summarize corporate intent and have little resemblance to a strategy which embodies a plan for the accomplishment of purpose. However, practicing the art of "muddling through"[7] tends to produce certain unfortunate results in this instance. Because in most cases activity on social issues is concentrated initially at corporate levels, it tends to be ignored in the formulation of business strategy in the divisions. Not until Phase III in the response process do division plans consistently include a serious consideration of these issues, and by then the corporation's posture may be difficult to change. Thus, the implicit strategy that evolves to govern social responsiveness tends to develop outside of the ongoing process for developing business strategy.

The suggestions below will not close the gap entirely between a concern for social performance and business planning in the large corporation. (In view of the organizational complexities involved, I would be skeptical of any scheme that promised this result.) Nor are they free from conceptual and practical difficulties. Nonetheless, they serve to summarize the prescriptive statements made in this and the preceding chapter and I hope will provide the reader with a basis for elaboration or dissent.

First, the definition of a strategy for social responsiveness should be a general management concern at the corporate level. The strategy should take the form of decisions on the portfolio of social issues identified as relevant to the firm with respect to (a) how aggressively each is to be engaged and (b) the organization level from which response is to be managed. If an issue affects numerous operating units, one would expect that the more aggressive the intended response, the more likely heavy corporate direction will be required. Conversely, if the intent is merely to avoid legal sanction and only a few units are involved, response will properly be left to division management with limited corporate assistance.

The corporation's posture on individual issues should be guided by the best assessment available of (a) the probable impact of the social demand on the business strategy of individual units, and (b) the availability of distinctive skills in the company to contribute innovative remedies. Of particular concern should be those demands which may have an important effect on overall corporate strategy. To accumulate the necessary data, it may be appropriate to assemble ad hoc investigation teams with representation from the operating units, or to devise some other means of securing inputs from these units. In effect, corporate management has a resource allocation problem that is considerably more subtle than dividing up capital budget allotments. It should be treated with at least the same care and attention to rigor.

Moreover, before electing to press the organization for response beyond that enforced through regulation, the chief executive has the responsibility to demonstrate that an effort has been made to understand the ramifications and potential tradeoffs involving near-term economic performance that may ensue. Operating managers are on the lookout for evidence related to corporate staying power. They may find the policy more credible if the problems of implementation are acknowledged in economic terms to the extent possible.

Second, the strategy for social responsiveness should take into account organizational constraints. The chief executive should ask, what is the firm's status on other social issues? What are the implications, several years hence, of asking operating management to assume yet another burden? Is there likely to be discord among key top management personnel over a social policy? Does corporate general management have the interest, energy, and credibility to commit to the issue?

Managing social programs has a definite "top-down" flavor to it. In many, probably most, cases middle managers work on equal employment or other social issues because in one way or another they are "encouraged" to do so. If their efforts are in direct response to government pressure, the burden may be viewed as an onerous but acceptable result of the political process. However, to the extent encouragement is perceived to be a corporate dictum, a governance issue is broached. What right have chief executives to insist on behavior they consider to be socially desirable before it has become generally accepted in public policy? The more familiar phrasing of the problem is posed by the obverse question: When should employees no longer quietly submit to or condone behavior that they feel to be morally reprehensible?[8] The former query invites "backlash"; the later suggests "whistle blowing." Although typically at opposite ends of the ideological spectrum, these phenomena share a common cause: a desire on the part of employees for a voice in shaping the policies governing their work. There is some evidence that concerns about corporate democracy and middle management discontent are growing in the United States.[9] Thus, before proceeding with an aggressive social policy, corporate management would be well advised to build support and a sense of participation among those who will ultimately be called upon to shoulder the burden of implementation.

Finally, implementation should be explicitly planned and managed. Critical decisions in managing the response process have been discussed at length in the preceding chapter and need not be repeated. The corporation's flexibility in responding creatively to social demands is fashioned to a large degree by the care and understanding with which the process is administered. Institutionalization of purpose occurs when the organization is prepared by its leaders to accept change. If a process for responding to social demands can be made a part of the firm's problem-solving repertoire, the organization's willingness and ability to embrace new issues will be enhanced.

Implications for the Multinational Enterprise

The scope of this study was expressly bounded by the domestic operations of American corporations. With the enormous growth of multinational business in recent years, however, it has become progressively more difficult to posit that the social concerns of the large firm can be limited to fulfilling the expectations of a single country. The spread of the multinational enterprise, led by the more diversified, rapidly growing, research-oriented companies, has been documented extensively.[10] For instance, by 1966 the *Fortune* 500 industrials contained 187 firms having manufacturing activities in six or more countries and an average of 22 percent of total revenues obtained abroad.[11] Both Weston and BPC became truly miltinational firms in the 1960s.

Of what relevance is the process described here to the multinational corporation, or, more narrowly, to the overseas activities of U.S.-based multinationals? The question must be approached very carefully, for before the practical problems of implementation can be addressed, a number of new complexities of a policy nature must be considered. The first is the desirability of extending policy adopted to respond to issues of social concern in the United States to overseas operations. It would be logical for, let's say, a chemical company which has attempted to incorporate ecological demands in its United States operations to evidence a high level of concern for the environmental impact of its offshore production facilities. A contrary position would be inconsistent and in some quarters viewed as irresponsible insofar as social costs are inflicted on other nations which are discouraged domestically.

The other side of this coin, however, presents us with a dilemma. The social agenda and the configuration of public policy vary from nation to nation. In much of the developing world the benefits of economic development may be viewed for years to come as far higher than those of controlling the pollution created by industrialization. Two examples that receive periodic attention are the application of U.S. labeling and safety standards to export or internationally manufactured products, especially drugs, and the extension of equal employment practices overseas, particularly to South Africa. Such issues raise two serious problems. Adopting U.S. standards may be viewed as a threat to national sovereignty, raising the possibility of reprisals. In some cases such as equality in South Africa, they may even run counter to the laws of the host country. Second, they may put the company at a long-term competitive disadvantage with respect to those firms which do not follow suit.

A further complexity involves the desirability of directing corporate attention to social concerns of importance in other nations that are, for one reason or another, not accorded such attention domestically. As in the first instance, the difficulties are likely to be more acute in the developing world where disparities in social agendas and ideologies governing the relationship between private enterprise and the state are often greater, and the perceived challenge to national sovereignty more acute. In fact, Raymond Vernon has indicated that the responsiveness of the multinational corporation to the social needs of host countries in these areas may have little impact on its exposure to political intervention relative to the dispensability and strategic importance of its business to that nation.[12] Nevertheless, by virtue of their size and scope, multinational corporations have an influence on the social milieux in which they operate, even though they choose to avoid leadership in fostering change. That fact has policy implications, whether or not it is explicitly acknowledged.

Success in unraveling these issues should not be expected from abstract or ideological debate. They demand careful scrutiny of the economic, political, and social impact of corporate behavior in specific instances. However, they do suggest that in multinational corporations, added burdens are placed on a response process that may be reasonably successful in implementing policies in areas of social concern in a single national environment. The chief executive who places value on social responsiveness may find (1) that global policy may have to be at a very high level of generality, acknowledging wide latitude for variations in standards or objectives from place to place; and (2) that specific policy differences may have to be countenanced in response to conditions in individual host countries. The role portrayed for him in Phase I may be untenable. He may not have the time, exposure, or experience to gauge which issues justify his personal involvement. Moreover, the value of the corporate staff specialist in Phase II who serves to acclimatize the corporation to social demands in the domestic setting may be limited on a worldwide basis. Finally, establishing systematic measures of performance in the implementation of a patchwork of policies that can be incorporated in a worldwide executive appraisal process is certain to be a formidable undertaking.

Under these circumstances, there may be only two practical alternatives for United States multinationals. The first is simply to encourage overseas subsidiaries to obey the law of host countries and provide them with assistance to cope with specific social demands calling for corporate involvement as they arise. One suspects that this is the pattern in most multinational firms to date. The second is to attempt the institutionalization of a process for responding to social demands similar to the one described here, but at some level below the corporate office.

This latter alternative poses two further administrative difficulties — where to locate responsibility for managing the process and how to determine whether it is being managed satisfactorily. The first difficulty is complicated by the cross-currents reported in the organizational development of the multinational enterprise. These firms are confronted by conflicting needs that have opposing organizational remedies. To rationalize and secure economies in production and logistics on a worldwide or regional basis begs for centralized direction. At the same time, the effective response to local markets and political contexts suggests a structure biased toward local autonomy.[13] As a result, a stable organization structure may not yet have evolved in many multinational corporations; innovations in the role of the corporate office and the design of measurement and control systems are required. It is probable that a systematic approach to managing corporate social responsiveness on a worldwide basis will have to await the clarification of this organization structure.

Implications for the Administration of the Large Corporation

Thus far, analysis has focused on the proposition that the manner in which a large corporation is managed has an important bearing on its response to social demands. In these final few pages, I propose to examine the other side of that relationship by addressing the broader question: What effects are social demands likely to have on the administration of the firm? To some degree the answer must be speculative. Generalizations about the behavior of systems as complex and heterogeneous as the large corporation cannot be drawn with precision from a limited number of in-depth studies. The general directions of change are nonetheless sufficiently clear to warrant explicit attention.

From an administration point of view, efforts to respond aggressively to social demands add to the complexity of managing the divisionalized corporation. Among the sources of complexity described at length in this research are the following:

> An increase in the scope and variety of social expectations calling for corporate policy, commitment and intervention.

> An augmented corporate staff capability intended to facilitate the response to social demands.

> A proliferation of reporting systems put in place to control and measure implementation efforts.

> A realignment of the bases for executive evaluation to give a heavier weighting to performance in areas of social concern.

These accommodations to social responsiveness are likely to foster three tendencies in the administration of the firm. The first is a greater corporate interest in and awareness of the social impact of business decisions made at middle levels in the organization. Confronted by a more demanding environment and more inquisitive superiors, operating managers may find their discretion diminished. If there is a drift in the location of effective authority over operating decisions prompted by these forces, it is certainly upward. Indeed, even the board of directors may feel compelled to assume an interest in social performance.[14]

Second, for operating managers the result is likely to be more ambiguous and difficult assignments. The relationships to be managed, both inside and outside the corporation, increase with each social demand. The number of functions general managers must comprehend grows as does the complexity of the task of coordinating and balancing diverse skills and concerns. Although official responsibilities may be unaltered, in practice, higher levels in the organization and others on the same level in sister units may have an interest in specific decisions. The opportunities for being wrong in somebody's eyes increase. Consequently the tension and pressure experienced among middle managers may be expected to intensify.

Third, it may be progressively more difficult and undesirable to rely on summary financial measures for assessing the performance of either operating units or managers. One can hardly argue on the basis of this research that in the near future financial controls will cease to be the dominant means for determining management effectiveness or allocating resources within the firm. Nor can it be said that the maintenance of good employee and customer relations, product and process research, and other such hard-to-quantify investments have not heretofore been recognized elements of forward-thinking business practice. Nevertheless, a greater portion of the operating manager's time may of necessity be consumed by social issues which have long-term, ill-defined payoffs. How well that job is done today may influence quite substantially the prospects for the business in the future. More sophisticated means of measuring performance may be expected that reflect the added complexity of the operating manager's assignment and the quality of the judgments he is called upon to make. Correspondingly, the dominance of financial controls may be moderated.

While tendencies such as these contribute to changes in the way the organization is managed, social demands will probably not provoke modifications in the basic product division structure of the diversified firm. Some activities may be centralized for a time, but the cumulative effect of assimilating social expectations is more likely to be blurred responsibilities rather than a new structural format. The extent of the blurring is very much dependent on the intensity of the pressure placed on the corporation and the time it is given to adapt.

If the firm elects or is impelled to respond to a large number of demands simultaneously, the outcome will probably be a pronounced diffusion of effective control over operating decisions. If the response process were to become so overloaded that it collapsed (i.e., programs mandated by government were not implemented or operating managers rebelled), fundamental structural change would certainly be more likely. Under these circumstances, the large corporation will become increasingly bureaucratized. The crispness in decision-making that accompanies clear responsibilities and simple performance measures will be eroded by numerous and often conflicting demands. Such a result may not, of course, be necessarily bad. What is lost in efficiency may be gained in more socially responsive behavior. Nevertheless, should bureaucratization become more pronounced than it already is, the outcomes will most likely be slower economic growth and the gradual encroachment of the public sector into private investment decisions.

Appendix
Notes
Index

Appendix

Case	Topic	Intercollegiate Case Clearing House Number
Xerox Corporation (A), (B)	Social Service Leave Program	9-372-294, 9-371-330
National Bank and Trust Co. (A)	Accounting for Social Costs	9-373-086
National Bank and Trust Co. (B)	Implementation of Student Loan Program	9-374-016
Parker Perry Systems	Social Auditing	9-373-176
Federal Insurance Company of America	Accounting for Social Costs	9-373-278
Borden, Inc.	Public Affairs Program Implementation	9-374-013
Avon Products, Inc.	Public Affairs Program Implementation	9-374-023
Illinois Investors Insurance Company (A), (B)	Social Auditing - Role of the Social Issue	9-375-177-178
Eastern Gas and Fuel Associates (A), (B), (C), (D)	Design, Implementation and Reporting of Social Audit	9-374-070,-071,-072-073
Omar Industries	Occupational Safety Program Implementation	9-373-344
Metropolitan Development Corporation (A), (B), (C), (D)	Community Development Corporation	9-375-262-263,-264,-265
The Golden Eagles (A), (B), (C), (D), (E)	Banking Services for the Elderly	9-375-266-267, -268, 269,-270
Genco, Inc. (A), (B)	Pollution Control Program Controversy	9-375-080,-081
FOODS, Inc. (A), (B)	Community Relations Audit	9-374-294, 9-375-103
Instar General, Inc.	Equal Employment Program Implementation	9-375-105
Affirmative Action at Aldrich	Minority Relations Controversy	9-373-355
DESCO, Inc.	Relationship of Performance Appraisals and Information Systems to Equal Employment	9-375-007
University of Pennsylvania (A), (B), (C)	Information Systems Implementation for Affirmative Action	9-375-211,-212,-213

Notes

Preface

1. Robert W. Ackerman, "Public Responsibility and The Businessman: A Review of the Literature," in *Top Management: Business Strategy and Planning,* Eds. B. Taylor and K. Macmillan (London, Longman Group Limited, 1973).

2. Jules Cohen, *The Conscience of the Corporations: Business and Urban Affairs, 1967-1970* (Baltimore, Johns Hopkins Press, 1971).

Robert L. Heilbroner et al., *In the Name of Profit: Profiles in Corporate Irresponsibility* (Garden City, Doubleday & Company, 1972).

S. Prakash Sethi, *Up Against the Corporate Wall* (Englewood Cliffs, Prentice-Hall, 1971).

G. William Trivoli, *Business Issues and the Environment,* University of Akron, 1972 (mimeo).

Patrick T. Jesaitis, "Corporate Strategies and the Urban Crisis," unpubl. diss., Harvard Business School, 1970.

Frederic D. Randall, "Corporate Strategies in the Drug Industry: A Study of Strategic Response to Social and Political Pressures," unpubl. diss., Harvard Business School, 1972.

3. Raymond A. Bauer and Dan H. Fenn, Jr., *The Corporate Social Audit,* Series in Social Science Frontiers no. 5 (New York, The Russell Sage Foundation, 1972).

Neil C. Churchill and John K. Shank, "Toward a Theory for Social Accounting," Working Paper, Harvard Business School, Division of Research, 1973.

Edwin A. Murray, "The Implementation of Social Policies in Commercial Banks," unpubl. diss., Harvard Business School, 1974.

Alden G. Lank, "The Implementation of Corporate Social Policies," unpubl. diss., Harvard Business School, 1974.

Frederick A. Cardin, "A Framework for Assessing the Impact of Selected Incentives for Recycling in the Paper Industry," unpubl. diss., Harvard Business School, 1974.

David B. Kiser, "Allocating Resources for Consumer Projects: The Corporate Dilemma," unpubl. diss., Harvard Business School, 1975.

4. Warren Bennis, "The Case Study," *Journal of Applied Behavioral Sciences,* vol. 4, no. 2, 1968.

Barney Glaser and Anselm Strauss, *The Discovery of Grounded Theory,* (Chicago, Alden Publishing Company, 1967).

George F. F. Lombard, "From Clinical Research and Research

Reports in Human Relations," *Journal of Behavioral Sciences,* vol. 4, no. 2, 1968.

Chapter I: Introduction

1. George Cabot Lodge, "Why an Outmoded Ideology Thwarts the New Business Conscience," *Fortune,* October 1970.

2. Neil W. Chamberlain, *The Limits to Corporate Responsibility* (New York, Basic Books, 1973).

3. For a concise review of the literature, see Robert W. Ackerman, "Public Responsibility and the Businessman," in *Top Management: Business Strategy and Planning,* ed. Bernard Taylor and Keith Macmillan (London, Longman Group, 1973).

4. Kenneth R. Andrews, *The Concept of Corporate Strategy* (Homewood, Ill., Dow-Jones Irwin, 1971), chap. 5.

5. Raymond A. Bauer and Dan H. Fenn, Jr., *The Corporate Social Audit* (New York, The Russell Sage Foundation, 1972).

6. Clarence Randall, *The Executive in Transition* (New York, McGraw-Hill, 1967).

7. Theodore Levitt, "The Dangers of Social Responsibility," *Harvard Business Review,* September-October 1958.

8. John Kenneth Galbraith, *American Capitalism: The Concept of Countervailing Power* (Boston, Houghton Mifflin, 1956); Edward S. Mason, "The Apologetics of Managerialism," *Journal of Business of the University of Chicago,* 21:1 (January 1958), 19; Carl Kaysen, "The Corporation: How Much Power? What Scope?" in *The Corporation in Modern Society* (Cambridge, Mass., Harvard University Press, 1959).

9. John Gardner, speech, October 29, 1969.

10. "The War That Business Must Win," *Business Week,* November 1, 1969.

11. Kenneth R. Andrews, "Can the Best Corporations Be Made Moral?" *Harvard Business Review,* May-June 1973.

12. Committee for Economic Development, "Social Responsibilities of Business," Statement of the Research and Policy Committee, June 1971.

13. D. Yankelovich, *Corporate Priorities,* 1972.

14. *ORC Public Opinion Index,* vol. 29, no. 21, mid-November 1971.

15. "The Social Impact of the United Church of Christ Invested Funds 1971-1973," Report of the Four National Instrumentalities with Invested Funds, New York, United Church of Christ, 1973.

Chapter II: Social Demands from the Corporate Perspective

1. John J. Carson and George Steiner, *Managing Business's Social Per-*

formance: The Corporate Social Audit (New York, Committee for Economic Development, 1974).

2. Meinoff Dierkes et al., "Social Pressure and Business Decisions," in *Corporate Social Accounting,* ed. Meinoff Dierkes and Raymond Bauer (New York, Praeger, 1973), pp. 57ff.

3. Ralph Nader *Unsafe at Any Speed* (New York, Grossman, 1965).

4. The initial phases of this work have been reported in Earl B. Dunckel, William K. Reed, and Ian H. Wilson, *The Business Environment of the Seventies* (New York, McGraw-Hill, 1970).

5. "Prometheus Bound: Blind Opposition is Hobbling the Development of Nuclear Energy," *Barrons,* March 8, 1971.

6. *Business Week,* April 27, 1972, p. 35, and May 19, 1973, p. 78. Roughly comparable figures were estimated in the July 1974 *Survey of Current Business* (U.S. Government Printing Office, pp. 58-64) of $4.9 billion for 1973 and $6.5 billion forecasted for 1974.

7. "Company Environmental Commitment Costs — 1971," *The Conference Board Report,* April 1972, p. 61.

8. *The Economic Impact of Pollution Control, A Summary of Recent Studies,* Prepared for Council on Environmental Quality, Department of Commerce and Environmental Protection Agency, Washington, D.C., March 1972.

9. "Impact of Pollution Control Costs Less than Had Been Feared," *New York Times,* February 17, 1973.

10. *Wall Street Journal,* October 3, 1973, p. 34.

11. "Steel Mills and Ecology," *New York Times,* May 5, 1973.

12. *A Study of the Ecological Impact on the Steel Industry of the Costs of Meeting Federal Air and Water Pollution Abatement Requirements,* prepared by Booz Allen and Hamilton, Inc., for the Environmental Protection Agency, 1972. *Environmental Steel — Pollution in the Iron and Steel Industry,* Council for Economic Priorities, May 1973. *Steel and The Environment, A Cost Impact Analysis,* Arthur D. Little. Inc, March. 1975.

13. "Bethlehem Steel to Cut Capacity Sharply at One Plant, Partly Due to Pollution Costs," *Wall Street Journal,* June 14, 1973. "Steel: Clean up or Close Up?" *Business Week,* April 6, 1974, pp. 72-73.

14. "Settling for Less on Health and Safety," *Business Week,* May 26, 1973.

15. "The High Price of Job Safety," *Business Week,* May 23, 1973, p. 27.

16. "The Big Rush to Enforce Health Standards," *Business Week,* January 15, 1972, and "Future Shock: OSHA Will Change the Way U.S. Industry Does Business," *Barrons,* August 14, 1972, p. 9.

17. "The Black Message: Business Must Do More," *Business Week,* January 22, 1972, pp. 79-80.

18. "How 'Equal Opportunity' Turned Into Employment Quotas," *Fortune,* March 1972.

19. *A Study of Black Male Professionals in Industry,* Manpower Research Monograph No. 26, Manpower Administration (Washington, D.C., U.S. Department of Labor, 1973).

20. "Discrimination Suits Hit More Companies," *Business Week,* July 8, 1972.

21. "Jesse Jackson's 13 New Targets," *Business Week,* October 7, 1972, p. 32.

22. The classic theoretical statement of the problem was written by Gary S. Becker in *The Economics of Discrimination* (University of Chicago Press, 1957).

23. Anthony Athos, "Is the Corporation the Next to Fall", *Harvard Business Review,* January-February 1970; *Work in America,* prepared for the Department of Health, Education and Welfare by the Upjohn Institute for Employment Research, 1973; Richard E. Walton, "How to Counter Alienation in the Plant," *Harvard Business Review,* November-December 1972.

24. "Consumer Proposals Bring about Changes in American Business," *Wall Street Journal,* June 12, 1971.

25. Mark V. Nadel, *The Politics of Consumer Protection* (New York, Bobbs-Merrill, 1971).

26. "Dictating Product Safety," *Business Week,* May 18, 1974, p. 56.

27. Walter E. Schirmer, "Product Liability and Reliability: The View from the President's Office," in *Consumerism: Search for the Consumer Interest,* ed. David A. Aaker and George S. Day (New York, The Free Press, 1971), pp. 328ff.

28. "The Packaging Problem Is a Can of Worms," *Fortune,* June 1972.

29. A thorough evaluation of the prospects for recycling in the paper industry has been done by Frederick A. Cardin, "A Framework for Assessing the Impact of Selected Incentives for Recycling in the Paper Industry," unpubl. thesis, Harvard Business School, Boston, Mass., 1974.

30. Jentz Gaylord, "Federal Regulation of Advertising," *American Business Law Journal,* 6:427 (January 1969).

31. "The Advertising Industry Gets a Controversial Watchdog," *Business Week,* May 12, 1973, p. 130.

32. Warren G. Magnuson and Jean Carper, *The Dark Side of Enterprise* (Englewood Cliffs, N.J., Prentice-Hall, 1972).

33. "More Talk than Action on Consumer Complaints," *Business Week,* May 19, 1973, p. 66.

Chapter III: Social Change and Corporate Choice

1. Anthony Downs suggests that such a maturation sequence may be observed in the public attention devoted to a social issue. "Up and Down with Ecology: The Issue Attention Cycle," *The Public Interest,* Summer 1972, pp. 38ff.

2. This episode is described in an unpublished paper by George Hoguet, "United States Steel and the Acceptance of Unionism," written at the Harvard Business School, Boston, Mass., April 1973.

3. K. William Kapp, *The Social Costs of Private Enterprise* (New York, Schocken Books, 1971), p. 77.

4. "Budget Ax Spares Minority Programs," *Business Week,* March 24, 1973.

5. Adolf A. Berle and Gardiner C. Means, *The Modern Corporation and Private Property,* rev. ed. (New York, Harcourt, Brace & World, 1967).

6. According to one estimate, the proportion of trading on the New York Stock Exchange accounted for by financial institutions approximated 70 percent in 1973.

7. Shareholder surveys such as that conducted in 1971 by the Wellington Management Company (a mutual fund management company) indicated either disinterest or support of management in questions related to social responsibility.

8. *Wall Street Journal,* April 17, 1972, p. 39.

9. John Kenneth Galbraith, *The New Industrial State* (Boston, Mass., Houghton Mifflin, 1967).

10. *Paper Profits* (New York, Council on Economic Priorities, 1970).

11. Joseph H. Bragdon and John Tepper Martin, "Is Pollution Profitable?" *Risk Management,* April 1972, pp. 9-18.

12. *Environmental Steel-Pollution in the Iron and Steel Industry* (New York, Council on Economic Priorities, 1972).

13. *The Price of Power* (New York, Council on Economic Priorities, 1972).

14. *Wall Street Journal,* January 18, 1973, p. 1.

15. Frederick Randall, "Corporate Strategies in the Drug Industry: A Study of Specific Response to Social and Political Pressures," unpubl. diss., Harvard Business School, Boston, Mass., 1972.

Chapter IV: Organizational Barriers to Social Responsiveness

1. Union Carbide's Marietta Plant, Intercollegiate Clearing House,

Harvard Business School, Boston, Mass., 1972, 9-372-294. This case was prepared from public sources.

2. Graham Allison, *The Essence of Decision: Explaining the Cuban Missile Crisis* (Boston, Little, Brown, 1972).

3. Alfred D. Chandler, *Strategy and Structure* (Cambridge, Mass., MIT Press, 1972).

4. The critical role of the middle-level general manager has been described in Joseph L. Bower, *Managing the Resource Allocation Process,* Division of Research, Harvard Business School, Boston, Mass., 1971, and Hugo Uyterhoeven, "General Managers in the Middle," *Harvard Business Review,* March-April 1972.

5. We include among corporate-level general managers those with such titles as "group vice president," who in many companies oversee a number of related divisions.

6. Some large diversified European companies continue to be managed by a functional organization with a management committee. Scott argues that this may be a function of an historically less competitive climate, a condition that may now be changing as a result of government action and the intrusion of the multinational corporation. See Bruce R. Scott, "The Industrial State: Old Myths and New Realities," *Harvard Business Review,* March-April 1973.

7. Norman A. Berg, "Corporate Role in Diversified Companies," Division of Research, Working Paper, Harvard Business School, Boston, Mass., 1971.

8. Alfred A. Sloan, *My Years With General Motors* (New York, Doubleday, 1963), p. 140.

9. Malcolm S. Salter, "Tailor Incentive Compensation to Strategy," *Harvard Business Review,* March-April 1973.

10. Chandler, *Strategy and Structure.*

11. Bruce R. Scott, "Stages of Corporate Development," Case Clearing House, Harvard Business School, Boston, Mass., 1971 (9-313-372).

12. Leonard Wrigley, "Divisonal Autonomy and Diversification," unpubl. diss., Harvard Business School, Boston, Mass., 1970.

13. Richard Rumelt, "Strategy, Structure and Economic Performance," unpubl. diss., Harvard Business School, Boston, Mass., 1972.

14. Scott has summarized four research projects surveying strategy and structure in the United Kingdom, Germany, France, and Italy in "The Industrial State: Old Myths and New Realities," *Harvard Business Review,* January-February 1973.

15. Ibid., p. 141.

16. Robert W. Ackerman, "The Impact of Integration and Diversity on

the Investment Process," *The Administrative Science Quarterly,* September 1970.

17. "We're Going for Companies' Throats," *Dun's Review,* January 1974, p. 37.

18. Raymond A. Bauer and Dan H. Fenn, Jr., *The Corporate Social Audit* (New York, The Russell Sage Foundation, 1972), p. 67.

19. Joseph L. Bower, *Managing the Resource Allocation Process,* Division of Research, Harvard Business School, Boston, Mass., 1970.

20. Kenneth R. Andrews, "Can the Best Corporations be Made Moral?" *Harvard Business Review,* May-June 1973.

Phillip T. Drotning, "Why Nobody Takes Corporate Social Responsibility Seriously," *Business and Society Review,* Autumn 1972.

21. Robert L. Heilbroner et al., *In the Name of Profit, Profiles in Corporate Irresponsibility* (Garden City, N.Y., Doubleday, 1972).

22. In a provocative paper, Bower argues that the management practices in the large corporations result in social immoralities. See Joseph L. Bower, "The Amoral Organization," in *Technology, the Corporation and the State,* ed. R. Morris and E. J. Mesthene, Harvard University, Cambridge, Mass., 1973.

Chapter V: The Process of Corporate Responsiveness

1. Henry Eilbert and Robert I. Parker, "The Corporate Responsibility Officer," *Business Horizons,* February 1973, pp. 45-51; *A Nationwide Survey of Environmental Protection,* conducted by Erdos and Morgan, Inc., for the *Wall Street Journal,* 1971; Jules Cohen, "Is Business Meeting the Challenge of Urban Affairs?" *Harvard Business Review,* March-April 1970.

2. Several case studies have been prepared on the initial phases of a social audit, including Parker-Perry systems (4-373-176), Illinois Investors Insurance Company (A) (B) (9-375-177, -178), and Eastern Gas and Fuel Associates (A), (B), (C) and (D) (4-374-070, -071, -072, -073).

3. Bauer and Fenn, *The Corporate Social Audit,* pp. 29-31.

4. Edwin A. Murray, Jr.,"The Implementation of Social Policies in Commercial Banks," unpubl. diss., Harvard Business School, Boston, Mass., 1974.

Chapter VI: The Response to Ecological Demands: Weston Industries

1. This form of analysis is not unique. In particular, I note its use by

Erik Erikson in his stages of the life cycle (for a summary see David Elkind's "Erik Erikson's Eight Ages of Man," *New York Times Magazine,* April 5, 1970, pp. 25ff); Charles H. Savage, in his study of economic development (*Sons of the Machine,* in press), and Lawrence E. Griener in his study of organizational development ("Evolution and Revolution as Organizations Grow," *Harvard Business Review,* July-August 1972).

Chapter X: Managing the Response Process

1. Joseph Bower, *Managing the Resource Allocation Process,* Division of Research, Harvard Business School, Boston, Mass., 1970, pp. 15-17.

2. Allen T. Demasee, "G.E.'s Costly Ventures into the Future," *Fortune,* October 1970.

3. "G.E.'s New Strategy for Faster Growth," *Business Week,* July 8, 1972, pp. 52ff.

4. T. A. Wise, "IBM's $5,000,000,000 Gamble," *Fortune,* September 1966, and "The Rocky Road to the Marketplace," *Fortune,* October 1966.

5. One interesting example of research on strategic issues of corporatewide significance is contained in Clark Gilmore, "The Divestment Decision Process," unpubl. diss., Harvard Business School, Boston, Mass., 1973.

6. There may be analogies to the phases in the social issue response process in the corporate adaptation to new administrative systems. A close parallel is described in Cyrus F. Gibson and Richard L. Nolan, "Organizational Issues in the Stages of EDP Growth," paper presented at the First Conference on Research on Computers in Organizations, August 1973.

7. Philip Selznick, *Leadership in Administration* (New York, Harper & Row, 1957), pp. 16-17. "Infusion with Value" is a concept developed earlier by Chester I. Barnard in his classic book, *The Functions of the Executive* (Boston, Mass., Harvard Business School, 1938), chap. 11.

8. Arthur B. Toan, Jr., "The Social Audit — a Progress Report on the Activities of the AICPA Committee," paper delivered to the Public Affairs Council, June 13, 1974; Raymond Bauer, "The State of the Art of Social Auditing," in *Corporate Social Accounting,* ed. Meinoff Dierkes and Raymond Bauer (New York, Praeger, 1963). Among those few who advocate social audits in financial statement terms are Clark C. Abt, "Social Audits: The State of the Art," address presented at Conference on Corporate Social Responsibility, sponsored by *Business and Society* and *Business and Society Review,* October 1972, and David S. Linowes, "Lets Get on with the Social Audit: A Specific Proposal," *Business and Society Review,* Winter 1972-73.

9. Edwin A. Murray, "The Implementation of Social Policies in Com-

mercial Banks," unpubl. diss., Harvard Business School, Boston, Mass., 1974.

10. Michael L. Lovedal, "The Hudson Institute," Intercollegiate Case Clearing House, 2-373-329, Harvard Business School, Boston, Mass., 1973.

11. Roy Amara, "The Institute for the Future: Its Evolving Role," *The Futurist,* June 1973, p. 125.

12. Robert W. Ackerman, "The Role of the Corporate Planning Executive," paper prepared for the Fifth Annual Conference of Planning Executives, Harvard Business School, Boston, Mass., 1972.

13. Using concepts developed by Lawrence and Lorsch, the specialist may find that his task is highly differentiated from others in the corporation yet requires a high degree of integration to be conducted effectively. Paul R. Lawrence and Jay W. Lorsch, *Organization and Environment,* Division of Research, Harvard Business School, Boston, Mass., 1967.

Chapter XI: Toward a Strategy for Social Responsiveness

1. Raymond A. Bauer and Dan H. Fenn, Jr., *The Corporate Social Audit* (New York, The Russell Sage Foundation, 1972), p. 85.

2. "The Chief Executive Office," *Business Week,* May 4, 1974, pp. 37ff.

3. "The 'Legal Explosion' Has Left Business Shell-Shocked," *Fortune,* April 1973, pp. 65ff.

4. In this respect the chief executive bears similarity to the President of the United States as described in Richard Neustadt, *The Power of the President* (New York, John Wiley, 1960).

5. The discussion here relates closely to the "Economy of Incentives" in Chester I. Barnard, *The Functions of the Executive* (Cambridge, Mass., Harvard University Press, 1938), chap. 11.

6. Hugo Uyterhoeven et al., *Strategy and Organization, Text and Cases in General Management* (Homewood, Ill., Irwin, 1973); C. Roland Christenson et al., *Business Policy, Text and Cases* (Homewood, Ill., Irwin, 1973).

David Baybrooke and Charles E. Lindblom, *A Strategy of Decision* (New York, The Free Press, 1963).

Herbert A. Simon, *Administrative Behavior* (New York, The Free Press, 1957).

7. Edward H. Wrapp, "Good Managers Don't Make Policy Decisions," *Harvard Business Review,* September-October 1957.

8. "Exit, Voice or Loyalty," in Ralph Nader et al., eds., *Whistle Blow-*

ing (New York, Bantam Books, 1972).

9. David Jenkins, *Job Power, Blue and White Collar Democracy* (Garden City, New York, Doubleday, 1973).

10. Raymond Vernon, *Sovereignty at Bay* (New York, Basic Books, 1971).

11. Louis T. Wells, Jr., "The Multinational Business Enterprise: What Kind of Organization?" *International Organization,* vol. 25, no. 3 (1971), p. 450.

12. Raymond Vernon, *Social Responsibility in Foreign Operations* (Harvard Business School, Boston, Mass., March 1973).

13. Peter C. Hobbias, "Moving Towards the Systems Oriented Organization," *European Business,* January 1970. Also John Stopford and Louis T. Wells, *Managing The Multinational Enterprise* (New York, Basic Books, 1972).

14. Although there may be some conspicuous exceptions, such as Leon Sullivan at General Motors, Myles Mace in *Directors, Myth and Reality* (Division of Research, Harvard Business School, Boston, Mass., 1971) argues that directors are not now performing this role.

Index